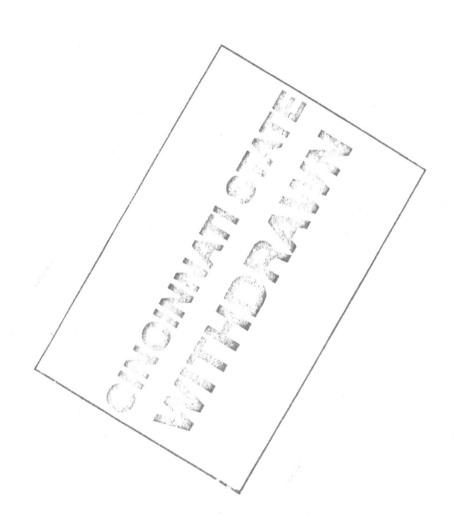

D0931525

A
&RESTAURANTS
INSTITUTIONS
BOOK

# Restaurant Basics

## Why Guests Don't Come Back . . . and What You Can Do About It

Bill Marvin

**THE RESTAURANT DOCTOR™**

**JOHN WILEY & SONS, INC.**

New York • Chichester • Brisbane • Toronto • Singapore

Restaurants & Institutions books—co-sponsored by John Wiley & Sons, Inc., and Restaurants & Institutions magazine—are designed to help foodservice professionals build stronger operations.

The Restaurant Doctor is a registered trademark of William R. Marvin.

**Library of Congress Cataloging-in-Publication Data**

Marvin, Bill.
    Restaurant basics: why guests don't come back . . . and what you can do about it/Bill Marvin.
      p.    cm.
    Includes bibliographical references.
    ISBN 0-471-55174-0
    1. Restaurants, lunch rooms, etc.  2. Customer relations.
    I. Title.
    TX911.3.C8M38  1991
    647.95'068'8—dc20               91-29481

Printed in the United States of America

10 9 8 7 6

# Contents

Why don't guests come back and what can you do about it? What does your point total have to do with your success?

How can your outward appearance present a stronger image than your advertising? What causes guests to draw conclusions about your restaurant before they ever enter the building? Why are you always the last one to know?

How can you drive your guests away before they even arrive? What makes people decide they will have a good time or a bad time in your restaurant before they get to the table? How does your seating style set the mood for the evening?

What are the silent messages waiting at the table? How can your bussers play a major role in determining if your guests will be ecstatic or enraged?

What is the environment in your restaurant and what can you do to save it? What are the sights, sounds, smells, and feels that set the stage for the dining experience?

How effective is your menu as a merchandising tool? Does it make your guests want to buy . . . or want to leave? How could your wine list make your guests want to stay with ice water?

# Foreword

In all my years as a hotel and restaurant professional, I associated with thousands of staff people. I don't think I've known more than two or three who were possessed of an innate sense sufficient to qualify them as having a complete understanding of that extraordinary world of "MONUMENTALLY MAGNIFICENT TRIVIALITIES." This book is not for them!

The doors of this world opened for me at the earliest stages of my career while in school in Lausanne, Switzerland. It was during this time I experienced my first of the great restaurants of France: Maxim's of Paris and La Pyramide in Vienne. Both were legendary, and the latter was owned by one of the few really creative restaurant geniuses who ever lived . . . Fernand Point. I was struck by the credo by which he lived and which became indelible in my mind for all the years which I would face in the exercise of my profession. He said, "Success is the sum of a lot of little things correctly done."

Among those truths which never change is that man is a gregarious animal who needs to belong. The individual counts most and all must be designed to fit the individual's scale . . . human scale. Human needs, human emotions and human sensitivities remain basically unchanged. It was Ellsworth M. Statler who said, "The majority of the complaints in a restaurant or hotel are due more to the guest's state of mind than to the importance of the things about which he complains." Otherwise stated, more often than not, the reason for the complaint is trivial. However, this triviality achieves a level of such monumental importance to the one who comes forth with the need to complain that we suddenly and unwittingly become confronted with a phenomen which has never ceased to fascinate me . . . that of monumentally magnificent trivialities.

These trivialities abound in our restaurant business and they surround us like millions of molecules. Most are so obscure and so taken for granted that the restaurant owner-operator pays little heed to how critically important they are or is even unaware that they must be accommodated in context, with consequences of failure or success.

This is what this book is about. It is an assemblage, a compendium of a whole wide range of MONUMENTALLY MAGNIFICENT TRIVIALITIES. Surprisingly this book is not yet finished and it never will be. The list of "trivialities" is infinite and never ending.

As a source-book and reference guide, the listings which follow are of inestimable value in the successful carry through of one's restaurant business. Success will come to those who develop the disciplines and motivate others to recognize the tiny little details and to bring them to some form of order so that the results really are the sum of a lot of little things correctly done!

> ... the ever present menace of mediocrity
> calls for untiring vigilance.
>
> James A. Nassikas

# Preface

## You Wonder How These Things Begin

Eight years ago I was doing a consulting project for a hotel in California. The property's food and beverage director shared a little card with me. It was a wallet-sized list of 25 details the hotel had learned were important to their guests. All their managers carried one as a reminder to take care of the little things. I added the card to my library and didn't think much more about it at the time.

Five years later, on a visit to Cape Cod, I went out for dinner with my father. The restaurant was one of his favorites, but it was not having a good night. As the evening got worse, we started discussing what was happening and why. We noticed the details the restaurant staff were missing and the opportunities to salvage the evening that were being lost. The staff was trying hard, perhaps *too* hard. They just didn't realize how they were alienating their guests. As the evening unfolded, we agreed that if the restaurant had handled the small points better, the entire experience would have been much different. "You should write a book about this," my father said. "Someday I might," said I and went on to other projects. By the way, he never went back to that restaurant!

While assembling material for a seminar last year, I thought of the little card I had received from the California hotel. I added a few thoughts and used it in my program. I received an enthusiastic response from this list of 75 points, the sheer length of which looked staggering to me at the time! Later I thought more about it and added another 75 points to the list. When I got to 200, I was certain I must have covered nearly all the potential problems! As the list continued to grow, I found I had a tiger by the tail. Having become more sensitive to what some might consider minutiae, I started to notice nuances I had overlooked before. The list turned into a project.

As I talked about what I was doing, people both inside and outside the industry added more observations. Everybody, it seems, had a few pet peeves about restaurants. It also became obvious there were many more reasons why people *don't* go back to restaurants than reasons why they *do!* As the list nears 1,000 entries, it has become the book we joked about at dinner three years ago.

This book is about common, ordinary, simple things that can trip up even the best operation. We are not talking about rocket science. This is not about the complexities of food chemistry or the nuances of French Burgundies. I hope most of the items in the book are details you already have under control. With luck, there will be a few you haven't thought about that will give you a way to be even better at what you do.

# Terminology Traps

In reading this book, you will notice that I don't use some of the words you may expect to see. I also use some terms that may sound different to you. My reasoning is that if you want to change your results, change your language. The words we use unthinkingly may contribute to many of our problems in these areas. Here are some examples of what I mean:

**Customer**   The word customer suggests a relationship based on the transfer of money and is less gratification-oriented than using the word "guest." Customers are just people who walk in the door. Guests, on the other hand, are special people to whom you extend courtesy and hospitality.

**Employee**   Employee is another word based on the transfer of money. I prefer "staff" although many companies use "crew member" or "associate" with good results. Team-oriented words help create a more empowering work climate.

**Service**   The word service is dangerous because it can be too easily defined just from the perspective of the provider. ("I can't understand why Table 6 is complaining. I gave them good service!") The fact is that good service can only be described and understood from the guest's point of view. Even "satisfaction" isn't powerful enough—it only means the guests got what they expected. Simply meeting expectations is not enough to make you a legend in today's market. Doubletree Hotels, for example, wants to provide service that "astounds" you. Play the game of semantics. Focus on "gratifying" or "delighting" your guests and see what happens!

**Manager**   If you call people managers, they may just think their job is to manage the staff. This attitude can easily lead to control, manipulation, and destruction of incentive. I prefer the word "coach." I think it better represents the model for effective leadership in a restaurant. A manager looks for problems, a coach looks for strengths. Think about it.

**Waiter; Waitress; Server**   Using these job titles may cause your crew to think their job is to wait or to serve. This can be a very costly misunderstanding for your restaurant. Consider the possibilities if you described the position as "service manager" or "sales manager." Their role truly is to manage the process of making sales and merchandising your products to your guests. Maybe if you hired people to sell instead of to wait tables, you would get fewer order takers and have higher sales.

# How This Book Is Organized

For ease of reference, I have divided the material into chapters by general subject matter. This allows the kitchen staff, for example, to identify items of interest to them without wading through 150 points that mainly concern the service staff. Because restaurant positions are so interdependent, there was often not a clear choice about where a particular point belonged. For this reason, I chose to mention some points in more than one place. I don't want anyone to miss an important detail by looking in the wrong chapter!

Although the emphasis of this material may be toward full service restaurants, there are specific suggestions for cafeterias, fast feeders, caterers, and most other types of foodservice operators. Conscientious restaurateurs committed to delighting their guests can extract numerous insights and opportunities from this material, regardless of its focus.

My problem has been in being able to stop adding to the list. For as much as it contains, it is still a work in progress. I'm sure you will notice points that I missed. When you do, I encourage you to jot them down and send them along. Why share some of your best secrets? First, your direct competitors already know what you are doing. More important, it is in our collective interest to make dining out a universally positive experience. Inept operators only educate the public to stay home. The better the dining experience is, the more people will dine out. The more firmly ingrained the dining out habit becomes in the public, the more we all will benefit.

I hope this book helps you better understand the process of guest gratification in restaurants. Regrettably, I must also warn you that the list is incomplete. I suspect the minutiae that affect human beings are endless, but the quest is rewarding. While you are busy solving the problems in this book, I will be getting the next list ready for you!

# Acknowledgments

So many people have contributed to this effort that it's hard to know where to start. My wife Margene has been steadfast through the months of self-imposed exile to my computer. Of course, she went out to dinner a lot in the cause of research, so there were *some* consolations! My father and stepmother, Ed and Jeanne Marvin, gave me the idea for the book and even paid for dinner that night! My deepest thanks to Toni Lydecker, Lisa Bertagnoli, and Mike Bartlett at Restaurants and Institutions and Claire Thompson at John Wiley & Sons for believing in the project and making it happen. My agent, Carol Cartaino, has been a valuable counselor and resource from the beginning.

I am indebted to Sandy Spivey, Carroll Arnold, and George and Kristi Blincoe for their many suggestions. Bill Main and his class at the University of San Francisco provided at least a chapter's worth of good ideas. I am grateful to Rich Keller, George and Mary Atwell, and Robin Cyr for their technical advice. Bob Wade and his staff at Wade's Westside helped more than they realize. Thanks to Brad Moss, Lee and Lynn Sterling, and the staff of the Colorado School for the Deaf and Blind. I appreciate the advice of the staff at Silver Key Senior Services and to Michael and Chrissie Nemeth and their friends. Jim Sullivan, Dru Scott, and Gary Penn, among many others, have some wonderful ideas that are reflected in my thinking. And finally, I cannot say enough about Ken Burley, Mike Hurst, Don Smith, Robert Kausen, George Pransky, and the many others who have been my teachers over the years. Their attitudes and ideas have shaped my understanding of how our wonderful business works. I am profoundly grateful for their support and patience.

Bill Marvin
The Restaurant Doctor™
Colorado Springs, Colorado
December 1991

# 1
# Momentous Minutiae

Hotelier James Nassikas coined the term *monumentally magnificent trivialities* to reflect his obsession with details. He built one of the most respected hotels in the world, the Stanford Court in San Francisco, on his passion for attending to the little points that he knew were important to his guests.

Industry observers note that the distinguishing feature between legendary operators and mediocre managers lies in their absolute belief in mastering the details. Many failed restaurateurs have learned this lesson the hard way. What they thought was trivial turned out to be monumental in the minds of guests who didn't come back.

## What Makes Minutiae Momentous?

To understand how minutiae can destroy your business, you must understand why people have a good time and why they don't. The answer is not as obvious as it may appear. It is, however, surprisingly simple.

You know from personal experience that when you are having a bad day, *everything* is a disaster! Conversely, when you feel wonderful, the whole world just works more easily for you. The events of the day don't change, but their impact changes significantly!

It works the same way for businesses. If you enter a business that has a depressing environment, it affects your mood and starts to bring you down. In your lower mood, minor events take on more significance. You are less trusting of people. You are more likely to find fault and complain. You are harder to please. Because they are unaware of the importance of the atmosphere they create, many businesses foster an environment that almost guarantees their customers cannot have a pleasant experience. Just think of the mood you were in the last time you had to go to a typical post office or bank! These are operations that have traditionally focussed on their own needs rather than on the needs of their customers. In so doing, they create an expectation of general inefficiency and lack of concern that places their clientele in a state of mind where they are less likely to experience being well-served.

Fortunately, restaurants have a natural advantage over many other businesses. Because people go to restaurants *expecting* to have a good time, they usually arrive in a pleasant mood. A higher state of mind predisposes them to enjoy themselves, and people will have a good time *anytime* they are in a high state of mind, anytime they feel good. For example, just *try* to have a bad day when you're in love! When guests are in good moods, they are more forgiving and more generous. They spend more. The food

1

tastes better. They are more open to your recommendations. They tip better. They are more likely to tell their friends what an exciting restaurant you have! All we have to do is create and maintain an atmosphere where people are drawn into a good mood, and they will always have an enjoyable experience. It seems almost too simple!

Here is where minutiae become momentous.

People enter your restaurant focused on having a good time. Anything that catches your guests' minds can divert their attention from a good time and be a distraction. Distractions change a person's mood. Every distraction, every minor irritant that affects your guests, is like tying a small weight onto the helium balloon of their higher states of mind. As these little annoyances add up, they create more weight pulling your guest's mood down. As your guests' mood drops, their thoughts become more negative. Their level of security goes down. They are more critical and abrupt with your staff. They become more difficult to please. Your staff, in turn, can easily become defensive and less responsive to these suddenly impolite people. The experience can spiral down quickly for everyone. When a guest is in a lower mood, even the finest food and service will draw complaints. You can't fix it. It is just the way people view the world when they are in a low state of mind.

It is as simple as this: Your guests will inevitably have an increasingly worse time as the accumulation of distractions drops them into increasingly lower states of mind. Things they wouldn't even notice at a higher level become intimidating at lower levels. Yet, without the weight of these distractions, people are likely to remain in good moods and enjoy themselves. This is how minutiae destroy your business.

Throughout this book, you will find seemingly insignificant items, momentous minutiae, that can distract your guests and affect their moods. Is this list picky? You bet it is! No one who has ever been in the business would deny that foodservice is a game of details. The size and content of the list can be overwhelming. Still, the price of success in our industry is attention to the small points. The first step in solving a problem is always to realize the nature of the problem.

A few of these details are obviously sudden death. For example, if you send guests to the hospital with food poisoning, don't expect to see them back as patrons. If your staff embarrasses a businessperson in front of his or her clients during an important luncheon, that guest is history. Most of the points are not as terminal as that. They are just distractions and petty annoyances. But remember the idea of weights on the balloon or the straw that breaks the camel's back. If you want to be a legend, you can't afford to dismiss anything as too trivial.

## Why Guests Don't Come Back

It may help to think of the quality of your guests' dining experience as a game. Because people want to have a good time in restaurants, you start this game with a perfect score, say 100 points. As guests approach the restaurant and progress through their meals, you gain or lose points.

This book deals with the details that can raise or lower your score in the guest's mind. Most are things for which you will *lose* points when they happen, but you won't necessarily *gain* points if they don't. On the plus side, there are a few unexpected touches for which you can gain points and improve your score. It's not fair, but it's the way human nature works.

There is no particular point value to anything other than the value arbitrarily given by the guest. For example, something one person might not even notice could cause someone else to walk out in a rage! As we have already discussed, people's perceptions are a function of their states of mind. The lower they get, the more serious and threatening life appears to them. The more threatening something appears, the more points it costs you.

Your guests are not aware of it, but they keep a mental score. As they leave the restaurant, they assign a subconscious point total to their experience. The more positive the experience, the higher your score. Your point total also has relevance in comparison to your competition. If, for example, you receive 75 points and your competitors are scoring 70, you will be the restaurant of choice. Let a competitor get 80 points and *you* will be in trouble.

One other thing: The higher the check average, the higher the necessary point total to satisfy your guests. People have higher expectations of a $50 dinner than they do of a fast food lunch . . . and they should!

Exceeding expectations creates delighted guests. If you score higher than people expected, they will love you, at least for now. If you score less than they expected, no matter how good a job you do, you won't be on their "A" list. Worse yet, if you are inconsistent—up one time and down the next—your guests will not trust you. When people mistrust your restaurant, you must score higher to reach the same level of guest satisfaction. For every person (in relation to every individual restaurant), there is a score so low it will cause the person never to patronize the place again.

## What You Can Do About It

It is hardly reasonable to expect that none of these errors will ever happen in your restaurant. Nonetheless, you can significantly reduce minor irritations through awareness, careful staff selection, continual training, and passionate attention to detail. It is important that your guests sense how important the details are to you and your staff. It is critical that your guests see that your entire operation focuses on their satisfaction and that you are making a sincere effort to correct any lapses. This level of focus and caring creates and maintains an environment where a guest will have a high sense of well-being.

Personally, I appreciate when an error is swiftly and skillfully corrected. It often shows me more than if the mistake never happened in the first place. Perhaps it is the humility and personal concern shown. If your heart is in the right place, you usually will not lose points for occasional oversights. Don't get me wrong—I'm not advocating making errors just so you can correct them. As you will see, there are plenty of opportunities to lose points without doing anything intentional!

Throughout this book I deal with minutiae from your guests' point of view. I have stated points in the negative if they are likely to weigh down people's moods; I have stated items likely to delight your guests in a Bonus Points section at the end of each chapter. This is consistent with the idea that our primary job in the restaurant industry is to give our guests a wonderful experience. If our guests do not enjoy themselves, nothing else really matters.

As strange as some items may appear, everything in this book has actually happened, either to me or someone I know. Not all details are issues to every one of your guests. Many of them do not even apply to your restaurant. Still, each of them has the potential to weigh down someone's experience of your restaurant and you will pay a huge price every time that happens. Every bit of minutiae I discuss is a distraction for someone.

You will find yourself at odds with some of the ideas in this book. When that happens, be careful. I do not suggest this material is any sort of gospel. However, it is consistently oriented from the guest's perspective of the dining experience. Anytime you run your business for the convenience of the staff or owners rather than for the enjoyment and pleasure of your guests, you are working against yourself. Consider these ideas with an open mind, because we all have our blind spots. Items that look like they will take too much work, too much money, or too much training to correct are the ones most likely to be your undoing.

You cannot avoid every potential problem, but you can work toward continual improvement. There are items on this list you won't do anything to correct, but you could. There are even items that will annoy you just by being on the list at all. (Those are usually the ones that hit too close to home!) Think about the risk to your business before you decide a particular point is unreasonable or that you can't afford to solve it.

If you start to think of your operation differently, if your priorities shift a bit, if you see a few new ways to become more responsive to the needs of your guests, then this book will have served its purpose—and you.

Now let's get to work!

# 2
# Outside
# Oversights

Your building and your outward appearance present a clearer image than your advertising. Your point total starts changing as soon as your guests start traveling toward your restaurant. Do you get a head start on a great score or start at a disadvantage? In a business where creating and exceeding people's expectations is essential, does your exterior make potential guests excited or apprehensive? Does it make them feel good about their decision to dine with you or make them question their judgment? Does it honestly reflect the care and attention they can expect inside?

The difficulty with outward appearances is that the focus of the management and staff is typically inside the restaurant. The staff often enters and leaves through a back door and seldom sees the operation from the perspective of their guests. Compared to the dynamic environment inside, it is easy to think of the exterior of the restaurant as relatively unchanging. Although some aspects of the outside do not need daily attention, many do. Assign responsibility for monitoring the outside appearance of the property in the same way as any other job.

# Design Deficiencies

These are problems created by the physical design of the building and grounds as well as the realities of land area and access. You cannot correct all design deficiencies, but you can work around many of them.

**Poorly lit parking areas**  If guests are uncertain about their safety, they will go elsewhere. Dim shadows in the parking lot make perfect hiding places for muggers and create anxiety in your guests. I doubt this is the sort of first or last impression you want guests to have of your restaurant, so install bright lighting in your parking lot. Go one step further and install accent lighting for your landscaping. It will provide more light on the grounds and gives a more attractive look to the restaurant at night.

**Difficult or inconvenient access to the property**  If your establishment is too hard to get to, the public will find somewhere else to go. An interesting exercise is to have an out-of-town friend drive you to your restaurant. See how easily they can find the way into the parking lot. Remember that you are not an impartial judge of how easy it is to find your restaurant.

**Inadequate or inconvenient parking**  How often are you in your parking lot in the midst of the rush? Do you really know if your guests have trouble finding parking space? If your guests can't park easily, eventually they won't try to park at all. After business hours, is there available parking space in the lots of nearby businesses? If so, make a deal with them to use the space. Don't just commandeer it! Often a trade for meals is enough of a gesture to maintain good neighborhood relations.

If your parking lot is a long way from the restaurant entrance, you also have a problem, particularly in cold climates. Inconvenient parking can discourage patrons and cause them to get in the habit of going elsewhere. To make it as easy as possible for your guests, you may want to consider valet parking. Let the valet run down the block. Don't ask your guests to do it. Consider making the valet service complimentary; after all, you don't make a cent unless guests come in to dine in the first place!

**Improper parking lot drainage**   Poor drainage creates puddles for your guests to walk through. In wet weather, portions of your lot could turn into small lakes and become unusable. Worse yet, guests could arrive when the lot was dry and later find their cars marooned due to a sudden rainstorm. Standing water in the lot also leads to major maintenance problems. The next time the weather reporter predicts a thunderstorm, bring your umbrella and boots to work and take a walk in your parking lot.

# Quarterly Questions

Quarterly questions require some level of action several times a year. In most cases, seasonal attention is sufficient. In harsh climates, the the following details may need attention more frequently.

**Poorly marked parking spaces**   Maintaining proper spacing in the parking lot reduces the chance of damage to guest vehicles. It also helps assure you get the full number of cars into the lot. Your climate will determine how often you need to blacken and restripe the pavement.

**Potholes in the parking lot**   This includes any hazard that could damage a guest's car. Watch limbs and branches that could scratch a car's paint. If potholes develop, fill them with gravel until you can make permanent repairs. Remember, potholes never get smaller and never go away by themselves. Be aware of any sharp grade changes between the parking lot and the street that could cause a guest's car to bottom out. If you can't fix these grades, your guests will appreciate a sign warning them of the hazard. Guests will remember a repair bill long after they have forgotten your restaurant.

**Broken sidewalks**   You do not want to create personal injury or discomfort for your guests. If you are in a part of the country where you experience continued freezing and thawing, your walks take a particular beating. Ice-melt products can pit and scar the surface. Concrete needs maintenance and attention, so keep an eye on it and plan for periodic repair or replacement.

**Faded exterior paint**   Particularly in climates that enjoy intense sunlight, paint fading can sneak up on you. Fading happens gradually and our sense of time gets distorted. For example, we had an addition put on the family homestead in 1960 that we still call "the new room"! Take a critical look at the building at least once a quarter. Pick a sunny day, look from several different angles to see if the building looks fresh.

**Handrails that give guests splinters**   With continual exposure to the elements, the grain on wooden handrails opens and becomes a hazard. Make it a habit to slide your hand up and down the railings to test their condition. Reapply a good sealer regularly. Do not wait until you have a problem.

**Old, dirty, or stained menu in the window**   Your menu is a sales tool. Be sure your posted menu looks as fresh and appetizing as the ones in your dining room. Remember that the sun will take a toll on a posted menu. Does the menu display cabinet have any leaks and is it lighted at night? Pay as much attention to the decor of the menu display case as you do the decor of the restaurant. It's a "sneak preview" of what people can expect inside. If your restaurant is up a flight of stairs, consider displaying some professional color photographs to show potential guests what to expect.

**Grass or weeds growing through the pavement**   If you have grass or weeds growing through your sidewalks or in the parking lot, people might think you don't do any business! Fortunately, a few well-placed shots of a grass or weed killer can keep this problem under control.

**Jumble of newspaper racks**   I have had newspaper vendors place racks on my property without even asking permission! Look at this area with fresh eyes every so often. Make vendors replace dented or faded racks. Have unwanted racks removed. Consider combining newspaper racks into an integrated unit.

**Water dripping off the roof onto guests**   Of course this only happens on rainy days or when snow is melting. Neither is a time when you really want to be wandering around outside! If the cause is not a design problem, it may be a maintenance issue. Gutters and downspouts must be in place and free-flowing.

**No (or inaccurate) hours posted**   To make it easy for guests to patronize you, they have to know when you are open. This is particularly true if you are closed when they pull up! Posted hours also enable guests to arrive when they can avoid the rush (and give you business when you are most able to take it). If you usually enter the restaurant through the back door, change your pattern now and then. You may notice that the hours posted on the front door do not reflect the changes you made last month. You won't make any friends if guests arrive during posted hours only to find you are not open. Also, make it a habit to open 10 minutes early and close 10 minutes late. Who needs an argument over whose watch has the correct time?

**Disorderly cluster of decals on the front door**  Decals and stickers on the doors accumulate over time and become almost invisible to operators. They are not, however, invisible to your guests. A neat display of current decals from the Restaurant Association, Chamber of Commerce, and so on can be a plus. Replace any torn or faded decals, and if any have expired, remove them. If you are no longer a member of an organization, remove its sticker from your door.

**Faded or broken sign**  Wind, weather, vandals, and the forces of nature will have their way with your sign. Take a close look every few months and see if it projects the image you want. Often, just washing it can make a big difference.

# Daily Duties

To stay on top of potential problems, there are actions you must take every day. In some cases, you may want to check on some of these points more frequently.

**Trash in the landscaping**  The wind is your worst enemy and the wind will not go away. It is critical to pull papers and other debris from the plantings every morning. Be sure to get it all, not just the pieces that are easy to reach.

**Bottles, cans, or broken glass in the parking lot**  You do not have control over what happens in your parking lot after the restaurant closes. Nonetheless, whatever happens during the night becomes your re-sponsibility at sunrise. The cleanliness of your parking lot clearly tells your guests about the care they can expect inside. Clean all glass, cans, and cigarette butts from the parking lot every morning.

**Missing lights in the sign**  This condition presents an uncaring image to the passing public. Of course, you never look at the signs in the daytime. When the signs are on at night, everybody is going crazy inside the restaurant! You may not be able to do much on a Saturday night, but Monday evening might be a perfect time to assure the integrity of the lights in the signs. Keep spare bulbs on hand, particularly if they are a special size. Also be sure to have a long ladder or bulb-changer to make the job faster and safer.

**Doors that are hard to open**    Even doors that work easily most of the time can be a real struggle in damp weather. Be aware of how easily the door swings when you open it. Watch your elderly guests to see if they have problems. Ask them if it's a problem! Better yet, have someone on your staff open the door for guests.

**Dirt or debris on the walkways**    Keeping your walkways clear and inviting is as important as vacuuming your carpets. Besides the liability and public safety issues, a spotless exterior delivers a strong message about your caring. Sweep away dirt, leaves and cigarette butts every morning. Do people notice outdoor cleanliness? Ask Walt Disney World!

**People loitering on the property**    Groups loitering in the parking lot or in front of the restaurant can intimidate your guests. How can you discourage the congregation without causing a confrontation? Often just increasing the lighting will make another location more attractive to them. Encourage local police to drop by your restaurant for coffee. If the neighborhood is marginal, a security guard can make your guests more comfortable and discourage the flock on the street.

**Overflowing trash cans or dumpsters**    This is particularly annoying when it can be seen from the parking lot. Trying to save money with fewer trash pickups is false economy. Remember that lost business has a far higher cost. To reduce the bulk of your trash, use a garbage disposal for food waste, bale your cardboard, and recycle glass and plastic. Have trash removed before it accumulates enough to detract from your image.

**Loose door hardware**    The heavier the door is, the more the strain on the hardware. Check the integrity of latches, locks, and hinges every time you open the door. Tighten them regularly, not just when they become noticeably loose.

**Cluttered entry**    Many restaurants are a central point for information on what's happening in town. Your operation may serve this purpose, but it does not mean you can abandon control of your entryway to flyers, posters, and free newspapers. Approve all materials before anyone places them in your restaurant. Remove dated flyers and posters promptly after the event and assure the display is neat and tasteful. If necessary, build a rack for free newspapers and put up a bulletin board for notices. Look at it critically every day to see that it reflects well on your restaurant.

**Unkempt landscaping**    You can't afford to spend good money for quality landscaping and let it deteriorate. Particularly during the growing season, the look of your shrubbery can change quickly. Assign responsibility for keeping your landscaping neat, either to a member of your staff or a landscape service. When planning new landscaping, it is better to have low-maintenance rather than high-maintenance plants.

**Lobby full of leaves, dirt, or debris**   Every time a guest opens the front door, anything that is blowing around outside could blow inside your restaurant. Assign someone to keep an eye on this and stay ahead of it, particularly on stormy or windy days.

**Flies in the trash containers**   A mass of insects is incompatible with creating guest comfort and enthusiasm. Reduce the amount of wet garbage in the trash and always keep containers tightly covered. Clean the trash containers regularly, remove refuse frequently, and spray as necessary to keep this problem under control.

**Dirty glass on entry doors**   You must clean the glass on your front doors several times a day, particularly if you serve children. If you clean the glass thoroughly and apply a clear silicone car polish, you can just wipe away many fingerprints!

**Reader board without the proper letters**   Reader boards can gain points for your restaurant. They also can work against you if you try to use a "5" where you need an "S" or hope an inverted "3" will substitute for an "E." Be sure your reader board advertises your concern with details, not just your daily special.

**Reader board with old or incomplete messages**   A reader board is a constant caretaking job. Always have a message on your reader board. You must be sure to remove your St. Patrick's day message on March 18. Every day, you have to check it for uneven or missing letters. The appearance of your reader board delivers a message about your restaurant, good or bad. It can be a real asset if you are willing to invest the time to use it properly. It will help sink you if you don't stay on top of it.

# Policy Perils

Some problems exist only because you have chosen to have (or not have) a policy about something. If you choose to change the policy, you can eliminate the potential irritant.

**Staff autos in parking spots by the front door**   The restaurant is in operation for the enjoyment of guests, not the convenience of the staff. Make it as easy as possible for guests to patronize your restaurant. As part of your orientation, tell your staff where to park their cars and why. Follow up with violators until they get the message. Make an escort available for staff concerned about walking alone to their cars in the evening.

**Charging guests to park their cars**    In some cities, valet parking fees are the norm. In other areas, it's an annoyance for your guests. If a charge is needed to maintain the legal separation between yourself and the valet service, credit the cost against the guest's bill. The goodwill and repeat patronage will more than pay for any additional costs.

**Damage to guests' cars while dining**    In a strict sense, you may not have control of what happens in your parking lot. Still, you can reduce the potential for damage and have a plan to deal with a problem if it arises. Check with your insurance carrier to see if your liability coverage extends to cars in your lot. If not, see if they could provide coverage. "It's not my responsibility" is not the answer you want to give a guest whose car window has just been broken while parked in your lot!

**No menu in the window**    It won't make a difference to guests who have been there before, but it can be the deciding factor for first-timers or people who are just strolling past.

# Bonus Points

Everyone likes pleasant surprises. These little unexpected touches are opportunities to improve your score and put your guests in a better mood. They help make up for any lapses in the operation and give people something to talk about to their friends.

**Complimentary valet parking**    One operator I spoke with figured that each car in his lot was worth $45 in sales to him. Could you put more of those cars in the lot if you offered complimentary valet parking? If people in those cars would otherwise be dining with your competition, the numbers have to work out in your favor.

**Guests' names on the reader board**    People love to see their names up in lights, and you could give them their 15 minutes of fame. You have as much to gain by using your reader board to make your guests feel special as you do by using it to advertise your specials. When guests make a reservation, ask if they are celebrating a special occasion. If so, see if they would mind if you put it on the reader board. You could easily become *the* place in town to celebrate!

**Complimentary umbrellas in inclement weather**    Use large golf umbrellas with your restaurant's name prominently silk-screened. The gesture will be so impressive that you will probably have little problem with people returning the umbrellas. If you are concerned about losing umbrellas, offer an incentive for their return, perhaps a coupon for a complimentary glass of wine with their next meal. You could do your guests a favor and build repeat business simultaneously.

Ask guests to drive past the front door on their way out and have a staff person there to retrieve the umbrella from their car. Even if a guest keeps the umbrella, you get free promotional exposure every time it rains! Schedule an extra person when the weather is stormy to walk people to their cars with an umbrella. Bad weather makes many people reluctant to go out. A service like this (or the free valet) can bring you business you would otherwise not get.

**Pleasant surprises**   The staff at McGuffey's Restaurant in Asheville, North Carolina, noticed their guests' cars were getting covered with dust blowing from a construction site adjacent to their property. Their solution was to wash the cars in their lot while their diners were having lunch! The response was so enthusiastic, that they still wash patrons' cars during every Monday lunch! Can you imagine how much goodwill you would create by an unexpected gesture like this at your restaurant? What is the potential for taking the sting out of waiting in line at a quick service drive-up window by washing guests' cars? You could have a school group do the work as a fund raiser except that *you*, not the guest, pay them for the service. You could even get a few points just by cleaning windshields!

# 3

# Annoying Impressions

Your point total starts changing again when your guests enter the restaurant. What they see, what they hear, and what they feel will affect how they think. Their first and last contact with your staff is usually in the lobby area. This presents incredible opportunities to create goodwill. How you capitalize on those opportunities is up to you.

Annoying impressions arise from actual contact with your staff, making these encounters more important than opinions garnered from the outside of your establishment. The good news is that all these shortcomings can be eliminated through conscientious staff selection, thorough training, and regular coaching. The bad news is that, to the extent they exist in your operation, they indicate lack of management attention. If awareness is the first step toward solving a problem, here is an opportunity to improve your point total in the area of initial guest contact.

## Telephone Trauma

For many guests, the telephone is the first contact they have with your restaurant. Your advertising urges them to call. What happens when they take you up on your offer may determine if they arrive in a good mood, a cautious mood, or don't arrive at all.

**Poor telephone etiquette**   This is particularly important when the telephone is answered in the kitchen. Train everyone in the restaurant on why telephone manners are so important. Coach your staff on what to say, how to say it, and what to do with questions they can't answer. Everyone on the staff ought to know the procedure for taking reservations. Be sure to have the staff take complete and accurate messages.

**Talking on the phone while dealing with guests**   Only undistracted, focused attention will cause your guests to feel served. By trying to do two things at once, you tell your guests that their arrival is not the most important event of the moment. I have seen more than one party walk out when faced with this thoughtless behavior. If you are involved in something else when guests arrive, at least acknowledge their presence with eye contact and a smile. Let them know you know they are there and that you will be right with them. Complete your call within 1 minute and welcome your new guests properly.

**Treating telephone calls from guests as an intrusion**
Everyone gets in a routine and resents breaks in that pattern. Continually

remind your staff that guest service is the only reason the restaurant exists. Pay particular attention to the tone of voice your staff uses on the phone. Remember, your guests have many other dining options.

**Wrong or unclear directions**    Develop concise descriptions of how to get to the restaurant. Work up a set for all major directions of approach and test them. Post them by the phone and coach all your staff in delivering the instructions cheerfully. An interesting exercise is to sit (silently) in the car while an out-of-town friend drives you to your restaurant. Make sure they have no other directions besides what your staff told them on the telephone.

**Putting guests on hold for more than 30 seconds**    If you can't get back to a caller promptly, take a number and call back within 3 minutes. It pays to be organized when you do this. Make notes of the name, telephone number, and the time the person called. You can pick up points for handling the situation smoothly. You will lose points if you promise to call and don't.

**Answering the phone and saying nothing but "hold, please"**    No matter how busy you are, it takes only a few seconds to be polite. Take a second to thank people for calling. Explain that you are on the other line and will be back to them within 30 seconds. If you can't meet that schedule, take a number and call right back. If you are abrupt on the phone, you tell guests that they are not important to you.

**Letting the phone ring more than four times**    When guests call, they are trying to do business with you. Why make that difficult? Give some thought to how easy it is for your staff to answer your telephone, particularly before the restaurant opens for the day. If you can't guarantee responsive coverage, consider forwarding your main number to another phone during those periods. Perhaps there is someone at a central office who can provide the level of service you need.

**Not knowing operating hours, daily specials, and so on.**    Guests who call don't know who is answering the phone. All they know is whether they were treated respectfully and whether their questions were answered courteously. Every staff member ought to be able to answer basic questions about the restaurant to avoid inconvenience to callers.

# Lobby Lapses

As guests walk into the restaurant, their opinions (and moods) take shape rapidly. Their first and last contact with your staff is usually in the lobby area. This first impression sets the stage for the evening . . . one way or the other.

## Opening late or closing early contrary to posted hours

You can never win arguments with guests, particularly about whose watch is right! Play it safe. Open at least 10 minutes ahead of schedule and stay open at least 10 minutes past posted closing. Have guidelines for your staff about how you will handle guests who want service outside regular hours. Also be sure you provide full service during all posted hours. Your scheduled closing time is not the hour your staff should expect to go home! If this is not clear, guests who arrive just before closing will feel the hostility.

## Banquets, receptions, or coffee breaks that start late
You can be early but never late. Have functions ready to go at least 15 minutes before the scheduled start. It keeps the client from getting nervous. Besides, someone will always be early and it is unprofessional if they "see you in your underwear" as you scramble to set up at the last minute!

## Inconsistencies between the exterior appearance and the style of the restaurant
If what you see is not what you get, you have a problem. There are many examples of good restaurants that failed because the exterior of the building and the operation inside were at odds. I remember a restaurant in San Diego that looked like an elegant supper club from the 1930s. The building was painted a pale pastel and featured a sweeping porte cochere for arriving cars. The only problem was that it was a coffee shop! People looking for a formal meal were disappointed when they got inside. People looking for a casual meal never stopped.

## Unclear entry into the building
I was at a restaurant in Pennsylvania, an interesting building with several porches. I tried four different doors before I found the entrance to the restaurant! It didn't even look like a likely entry. I'm not sure I would even have seen it if some others hadn't been leaving. When I got inside, I was *not* in the best of moods! A simple sign could have avoided the problem.

## Clutter and junk at the greeter or cashier stand
This first impression can set the tone for the evening. Make it a point to enter your restaurant by the front door and look around from the perspective of a first-time guest. What catches your eye? What degree of caring does the look of your reception area create?

## Poorly located pay phones
Telephone calls are personal events. When a guest must make a call, the degree of comfort they feel may determine how they feel about being in your restaurant. If your pay phones are located in an area without privacy or where it is too loud to talk, your guests will not be happy. As with everything else in your operation, consider placement and use of pay phones from your guests' perspective.

## Decor that doesn't fit
This challenge always presents itself when converting an existing operation to a new concept. You must make the look

and feel of the new restaurant completely fresh and consistent. If not, you will only remind your guests that you do not pay much attention to detail. Inconsistent elements affect your patrons, even if they don't know why. They will leave with a slightly uncomfortable feeling that something was wrong, not exactly the sort of lasting impression you want to encourage. Recycling restaurants can be a profitable venture but do yourself a favor— spend the money to do it right.

**No hallway between the restrooms and the dining room or bar**   Most building codes now require that restrooms do not open directly into either dining rooms or kitchens. In older restaurants and in many bars, this is not so. Despite what the law says, do your guests a favor. Be sure there is not a direct sight line into the restrooms from the occupied areas of the restaurant.

**Holiday decorations still up weeks after the event**   You know how tacky it looks when campaign signs are still in place weeks after an election? Your restaurant is no different. Unless out-of-season decorations are part of your concept, the holiday celebration is not over until you have packed the decorations and safely stored them for next year. Remove the decorations the morning following the main holiday celebration. This is when your staff is least likely to want to take them down, but life is like that. Be sure your planning includes scheduling the timely removal of seasonal items.

**Being greeted with a number—"Two?"**   This greeting does nothing to reinforce people's confidence in choosing your restaurant. Your first words should thank the guests for coming and welcome them to the establishment. After that, you can deal with the details of how many in the party. Perhaps asking if there is anyone else joining them might be a less impersonal way to find the size of the party.

**A greeting that focuses only on the greeter**   Welcoming guests to your restaurant by asking "Smoking or nonsmoking?" is as bad as greeting them with a number. The preceding comments apply. First thank them for coming, then get other necessary information.

**Cigarette vending machine a focal point**   Whose restaurant is it anyway? If you are going to advertise inside the restaurant, promote your operation, not cigarettes! Cigarette vending machines catch the eye and are a distraction, particularly for nonsmokers. If you have such a machine on the premises, it belongs out of the major traffic flows. For example, consider placing it in the hallway to the restrooms. Don't create a diversion in your prime revenue-producing space.

**Unclear or absent signs at the entry**   People do not like to feel incompetent or not in control. For maximum peace of mind, they want to know where to go and what to do. Should they wait for a greeter or seat themselves? Is there a nonsmoking section and where is it? Ideally, the greeter will be at the door when guests arrive, but cover yourself by displaying clear directional signs for those times when the staff is elsewhere.

**Interiors and staff that don't look like your advertisements** Foodservice is a business of creating and exceeding expectations. If you have created an expectation through your advertising that you are unable to deliver in your restaurant, you are working against yourself. If your television commercials picture smiling staff in crisp uniforms, be sure that is the way your restaurant runs. Creating a misleading image will disappoint your guests, even with an otherwise pleasant experience.

**No indication of form of payment accepted** Do you honor credit cards? If so, which ones? Do you accept personal checks? Is your operation cash only? How are your guests going to know this? If they only get the answer when the check is presented, you are setting up another potential irritant. Why create a problem that can be so easily avoided? Let your guests know the rules before they get too far into the meal. All credit cards provide decals you can place on the front door. A discrete sign in the lobby or on the menu outlining your policy on accepting checks will avoid embarrassment later in the evening.

**Being greeted with arm and hand signals** Many greeters could easily have a second job parking airplanes. They wave, they point, they make a variety of signals that have no meaning at all to the guest. I assume there is some element of imagined efficiency behind this, but it usually comes across as uncaring and impersonal.

# Attitude Atrocities

The way your staff interacts with the guest is critical. The quality of this interaction is determined by the staff's presence and compassion. This is a combination of their innate personal characteristics, their level of coaching, and the effectiveness of your operating systems.

**Not being acknowledged with eye contact and a smile within 30 seconds** Your initial contact sets the tone for the rest of the meal. Many people have a natural insecurity when entering a business for the first time. This first impression tells them whether they made a good decision or whether they may have made a mistake. Nobody is comfortable when they think they have blundered.

**Grossly inaccurate estimates of waiting time** You can't get it right every time, but you can make a game of seeing how close you can be. You also can keep guests informed of the status of their wait so they won't feel abandoned.

**Inattentive greeters**   Drop *all* routine sidework and welcome guests to the restaurant as soon as they walk in your door. Sorting guest checks is less important than creating a positive first impression for paying patrons. If your actions give people the impression that something routine is more important, they will become irritated. If they become irritated, you will be playing catch-up all night.

**Not keeping the guest informed on the status of their wait**
Delays happen and most people understand that the restaurant doesn't have total control on how long people stay at the table. Make it a policy to check back with waiting parties several times. Visit them about halfway through their quoted wait to let them know you remember they are there. Let them know if their wait is likely to be a few minutes longer than quoted. Advise them when their table is getting ready to leave. If you are going to *sell* the wait you have to *manage* the wait. Your guests will appreciate and remember your concern.

**Mumbled communications**   People can get uninspired attention lots of places. Look them in the eye, smile, and speak up. Be sure they know you are glad they came.

**Calling a guest by the wrong name**   Nothing is sweeter to someone than the sound of their name. At the same time, using the wrong name is rude and disturbing. Make it a game to get to know the regulars. Use their names often . . . and correctly.

**Insincere smiles**   A smile with no feeling behind it is probably worse than no smile at all. When you can create as positive an atmosphere for your staff as you do for your guests, smiles will become natural and spontaneous.

**Sitting down on the job**   We all get tired, but you can never take a break when you're onstage. Give some thought to where and how often your crew can get off their feet.

**Not thanking the guests as they leave**   How would you feel if you left a friend's home after a pleasant evening and they didn't say goodbye? It is no different in our industry except that we have a business reason for doing it! A positive final impression validates the guests' experience and makes them feel good about the money they have spent. Coach your greeters to thank guests for coming and invite them back. Do *not* ask, "How was everything?" The answer to that question is always, "It was fine." Be more creative and personal in forming your questions and you will receive more meaningful answers. The most important point is to make sure your thank-you is as warm and sincere as your hello.

**Unintelligible speaker at the drive-up window**   Few things are as frustrating as an inability to communicate. When your guests cannot understand what is being asked of them or if they cannot make themselves understood easily, they get angry. Periodically check your drive-up window equipment to be certain it allows communication. An angry guest cannot be a happy guest.

# Policy Perils

Some negative first impressions result from management policies. If you see a guest annoyance that can be eliminated by changing your position on something, do it. After all, there is enough that can go wrong without creating more problems for you and your guests.

**Not honoring an advertised policy**   For example, if you advertise that you accept reservations, it will annoy your guests if you refuse to do so. Whatever you include in your ads is a commitment. Your ad in the Yellow Pages commits you for a year. Once you have gone public with a policy, it's hard to modify it. If you have changed your policies, your staff needs permission to use their initiative when a problem arises.

**Not accepting reservations**   I know, I know. There are reasons why some restaurants don't take reservations and I respect that. Just understand that you will alienate some people if you don't. For example, a survey of American Express cardholders in southern Florida determined that the ability to get reservations was a prime reason for people to select a restaurant. Trying to reserve all your tables can easily backfire, so perhaps you could take limited reservations during the evening and seat everyone else as they arrive. Red Lobster, a national midscale seafood chain, allows guests to call the restaurant and place their names on the waiting list. This shortens the wait when they get to the restaurant. This is a good compromise reservations policy.

**No separate smoking and nonsmoking areas**   The need for separation goes beyond the requirements of any ordinances. It is just difficult for smokers and nonsmokers to coexist without proper separation. If local ordinance permits, you might consider declaring your entire restaurant to be nonsmoking. You will lose some smoking guests, but you may gain a unique market position with nonsmokers.

# Sticky Situations

There are several scenarios that get the evening off to a poor start. They may be created by policies of the house, lack of training, or just by chance. It's not as much what happens as how skillfully you handle it.

**Having to wait hours for a table**    In the industry, we look on a wait as a positive point. It is not a positive point for many of your guests even if it is a mark of your popularity. If you must make a guest wait for a table, sell the wait. Coach your greeter to be sensitive when they explain where guests can wait and what you can do for them until their tables are ready. If you have an appetizer menu in the bar, suggest two choices. If you have a drink special, point it out. Assure guests you will remember they are waiting. They must feel served, not processed.

**Waiting in line when empty tables are visible**    There is no reason you can give for this that will make any sense at all to your guests. Seat them at once and get on with the evening!

**Asking about reservations in an empty dining room**    You may want to know if the party was on your reservation list, but don't make it your first question. Obviously, with an empty dining room, whether guests have a reservation is really irrelevant. Asking them if they called earlier can be a smooth way to find out if they made an earlier reservation.

**Lost reservations**    It is not worth a confrontation with a guest. Even if you suspect the person is not being truthful, smile and make it right with them. The distraction of an argument can bring down the tone of the entire restaurant, staff and guests alike. Better yet, design a reservation system with enough slack to accommodate the unexpected.

**Accepting a reservation, then making guests wait**    Your guests may tolerate a short wait, but anything more than 5 minutes defeats the purpose of a reservation. This situation suggests a system problem to be addressed. Monitor guest dining time to be sure you are accurate in estimating how quickly tables will turn. If you have walk-in clientele, do not take reservations for every one of your tables. Accept reservations for, say, 75% of the dining room. In this way, if a table stays longer than expected, you will have more seating possibilities for parties with reservations. The walk-in guests will keep your tables full and be more accepting if they have to wait a little longer to be seated. If a reserved party has an unexpected wait, be sure to do something to make it right with them.

**No place to hang a coat**    It is not terminal, but it *is* an inconvenience. Invest in a few coat trees, put some hooks in the walls, or even convert a closet for this purpose. If there is no space in the lobby area, carry the coats to the manager's office. Bring them back when the guests are ready to leave.

**No place for people to wait**    If you provide take-out service, where do people wait for their orders? Is there a place for nonsmokers to wait other than in a smoke-filled lounge? Can families or elderly guests sit somewhere comfortable until their tables are ready? Remember that serving the guest also applies to those who are not yet dining.

# Seating Snafus

Just when you thought it was safe to go into the dining room, I have to warn you about losing points in the seating process.

### Racing off to the table and leaving the guests in the dust
This is probably the fault of a job description that focuses on activities instead of results. If you tell people their job is to seat people, you can get mechanical actions. If you define the job by what you want to accomplish, you get something different. What if you told the greeter to create a positive first and last impression? What if the greeter had the responsibility to assure that guests feel cared for and welcome? What if part of the job was to find out something about the guest on the way to the table? What if you coached the greeter to tell guests something about the restaurant while escorting them to the table? What if you defined an appropriate table as one the guests would enjoy? It changes everything and involves the greeter in the process of guest gratification.

### Dropping the menus and leaving before guests are seated
The greeter's job is to create a positive first impression, not to deliver menus to the table. Coach your staff on the human aspects of the position as well as the mechanical ones.

### Seating smokers beside nonsmokers
If you do not have separate dining areas, expect complaints any time you have to put smokers and nonsmokers next to each other. It is an immutable law of nature that smoke will always move toward those who cannot tolerate it, despite your ventilation system! The smokers will feel attacked while the nonsmokers will feel violated. When a dispute arises (and you can count on it), both groups will get angry and have an unpleasant evening.

### Accepting a bribe for preferential seating
This is extortion that only serves the ego of the person asking for the spiff. Have a clear policy against this and fire the staff member involved if it happens. Be sensitive enough to make it right with any other guests inconvenienced by the incident.

### Giving smokers (or nonsmokers) the better tables
The problem with creating two classes of guests is that both must have equally attractive seating. In the 1990s, any sort of favoritism or discrimination will cost you business.

### Seating a guest at a dirty or unset table
There is no excuse for seating a guest before the table is ready, no matter how busy you are.

You have to clean and set the table before you can start the meal service anyway, so you will not speed service to the guest by seating them too quickly. Monitor the lines of communication between the greeter and the dining room staff. The person responsible for seating guests must receive timely and accurate information on table status. This will allow them to keep the dining room turning without the danger of seating a guest at a table that is not fully ready.

You have less control in a cafeteria or a restaurant where guests seat themselves. If you are responsible for an operation like this, keep an eye on your tables during the rush and assign enough staff to keep them clean. Even if your clientele is trained to bus their own trays, there is still debris left on the tables. A breakdown in prompt table clearing will *force* your guest to sit at unclean tables and interfere with their enjoyment of the meal.

**Seating a guest in a "black hole"—a table not on anyone's station**    The problem here is that nobody knows it has happened until it happens. Take extra care at preshift meetings to be sure to assign all tables. Assure that everyone knows the tables on their station. Have a brief walk-through if necessary. Watch carefully during shift changes. Pay attention to shifting stations as additional staff come on the floor.

**Seating guests at a table with a tip on it**    It is unprofessional to seat your guests at a table that is not completely theirs. With children, it can even be dangerous because they will put the money in their mouths! Give bussers permission to pick up tips and give them to the sales people. If a sales person has a problem with this, handle it individually.

**Having to walk through the smoking section to get to the nonsmoking section**    The layout of your restaurant may determine how effectively you can separate smokers from nonsmokers. Nonsmokers are usually sensitive to the smell of smoke. If you can avoid this potential irritant for them, they will appreciate it.

**Not allowing guests to change tables**    To be successful, the restaurant has to exist for the enjoyment of the guests, not the convenience of the staff or management. There is seldom a justifiable reason not to accommodate so simple a request, particularly in a half-empty dining room.

**Handing guests the wrong menus**    If you have separate menus for each meal period, be sure your staff can distinguish between them. Although having to exchange menus is not a "hanging offense," it does show a lack of attention to detail. It is a distraction you can easily avoid.

# Buffet Boo-Boos

There are a few important elements that influence guests' first impressions of your cafeteria or buffet before they even experience your wonderful food.

Take another look at your operation and see if you are creating any of these problems for yourself.

**Confusing traffic flow**   Your guests' experience is more pleasant when they have a clear idea of how the line is arranged. If you cannot change the layout, consider signs that identify where guests can find specific types of foods.

**Serving lines that look the same every day**   You can become the destination of choice even if people don't have a choice! The danger of a built-in clientele is that you continually need to show a new face to prevent boredom. An unchanging routine is also boring for your staff. The only sure way to sustain this variety over time is to get your staff involved in finding new and different ways to present your fare. Their good ideas will surprise you!

**Not being able to bypass portions of the line**   It is frustrating to wait in a line, particularly behind people who are taking something you don't want. Give some thought to how you can help people get served more promptly. Your guests will be appreciative.

**Long delays at the cashier station**   While guests are waiting their food is getting cold. Even the most skillfully prepared and attractively presented dishes will not make people happy when the food is lukewarm. Plan your schedule to have enough cashiers on duty. Delayed guests are unhappy guests. Unhappy guests either don't come back or start bringing their own lunches.

# Bonus Points

Everybody likes pleasant surprises. These little unexpected touches are opportunities to improve your score and put your guests in a better mood. They help make up for any lapses in the operation and give people something to talk about to their friends.

**Using the guests' names respectfully**   No matter how casual your restaurant is, it is impolite to address guests by their first names until and unless they ask you to do it. You will never lose points by being too polite. The more often you use the guest's name, the more often you will see the guest.

**Remembering guests' likes and dislikes**   The Rattlesnake Club in Detroit makes a biography card on their regular guests. The cards include all the information the restaurant knows about each guest's needs, inclinations, patterns, and desires. After checking the night's reservations, the staff reviews the cards. How much do *you* know about your regulars?

**Opening the front door for guests**   The Olive Garden, an Italian dinner-house chain, has a staff person whose sole job is to greet guests enthusiastically and open the door for them. Christopher's in Phoenix goes one step further. The restuarant captains are required to walk guests to their cars. They report it is an excellent way to provide personal service and find out what guests *really* thought of the evening.

**Finding a seat for guests who have to wait**   When guests have to wait, too often we just point them in the direction of the lounge and let them go. Consider having one of your staff escort them to a place where they can wait comfortably. It may be in the bar or just a spot in your waiting area. This offers one more chance to sell the wait, offer drinks or appetizers, and reinforce your commitment to guest service.

**Free beverages during the wait**   I remember when the Pacific Cafe opened in San Francisco. It was out toward the beach, not a particularly prime location, and the weather was often cold and foggy. It was a small restaurant and had no place inside for guests to wait. One night shortly after it opened, the manager saw a waiting line extending down the side-walk. Feeling sorry that his guests had to wait in the cold, he offered free wine to everyone until they could be seated. Needless to say, the waiting patrons loved it and didn't mind the wait anymore. The word spread quickly around the City. The next night there was another line and the manager gave away more wine. A tradition had been established. Pacific Cafe's popularity (and the complimentary wine) continues nearly 15 years later. The restaurant has given away a lot of wine but it has also sold a lot of dinners!

# 4
# Table Transgressions

When guests reach the table, what they see and feel is an important part of their impression of your restaurant. If you don't stop and read the silent messages delivered by the table and the items on it, you are leaving yourself open for problems.

We can trace much of the blame for tabletop problems to inadequate training of the bussers. Particularly since bussers are typically entry-level positions filled by workers in their first jobs, you can't assume anything. Bussers need to understand *what* you want done. They also need to know *how* you want it done and *why* it is important. The more they understand about their role in guest gratification, the better they will do.

## Setup Shortcomings

When guests arrive at the table, the condition of the table settings is their first clue about your professionalism and how seriously you address the details.

**Silverware set askew on the tables**  The ability to quickly reset a table is an important skill for a busser to master. Still, if the settings are not neatly and accurately placed, all the speed in the world is useless. Be sure they know how you want the place setting put down and that they do it that way consistently. Since bussers reset tables in view of your guests, watch their moves and do a little choreography if necessary. Train your bussers to handle silverware only by the handles and to handle glassware only by the stem or the lower third. Never let them put their fingers in the glasses!

**Tabletop that is not picture perfect**  If service is slow, guests may find themselves with nothing much to do but study and critique the tabletop. When setting the table, it is not enough to get it done, it must be done accurately.

**Forks with bent tines**  Think of how many people handle silverware from the time you clear the table until you reset it. It is discouraging that this problem exists at all. Train your dish crew to be aware of the condition of the silver as they load and unload the dish machine. Coach your bussers to check each piece of silverware before they place it.

**Tables set with napkins in the glasses**  I appreciate the look this can bring to the dining room. The problem arises if the glasses are later used for water or wine. Remember that the napkins have been well handled before they are placed into the glassware. In effect, this transfers that handling to inside the glass. If the glass is later used for a beverage, guests can question its sanitary condition. If napkins in the glassware are part of your tabletop, don't stop the practice. Just be sure to remove the glasses when your guests have unfolded the napkins.

**Unevenly folded napkins**   If you are going to the expense of a linen napkin, be sure it is neatly and evenly folded. I know that many napkins are far from rectangular when they return from the laundry. If this is an issue for you, use a different napkin fold that lessens the problem.

**Wrinkled paper napkins or placemats**   Paper is more delicate than linen. Once paper has been crumpled, you cannot smooth it out again. Be sure to store and protect your paper supplies. You don't gain any points if your napkins look like they have already been used!

**Boring, worn, or chipped glassware**   Sparkling glassware accents the excitement of the tabletop. If glassware has been scratched or chipped, it not only looks terrible but is a safety and sanitation problem as well. Glassware styles change over the years. When it is time to order more glasses, look at what you are using and decide if it still reflects well on your restaurant. If not, change your line of glassware. It's a simple way to inject some new life into a tired dining room.

**Flimsy flatware**   Lightweight silverware feels cheap in the hand. It may be less expensive to purchase initially, but it conveys a second-class image. Besides, it bends more easily and has a shorter life than more substantial stock. Be sure your flatware is at least as heavy as what your guests are likely to be using at home.

**Stained paper napkins**   It is common practice to store paper napkins in the service stands with the coffee and condiments. One spill on a stack of napkins sends the whole pile into the trash. Rearrange your service stands to store napkins away from anything that could spill. Alert your bussers to watch for stained paper napkins and never to set a table with them. Be sure there is enough light in the service stands to identify stained napkins before they get taken to the table.

**Tables not completely set when guests are seated**   No matter how busy you are, you don't save any time by seating a party before the table is ready. First, you can't serve the table before everything is in place. Second, it delivers a message to your guests that they are not very important to you. Were you ever checked into a hotel room where the beds had not been made or the bathroom was still dirty?

**Mismatched china or silverware (unless it is part of the concept)** If people don't know you're doing it on purpose, they'll think you don't know the difference! Be sure you have a record of your china pattern number to avoid mismatches on future orders. Every few years, you might consider upgrading your china to a new look, just to break the monotony for your guests and staff.

**Flimsy disposable serviceware** Use high quality serviceware that feels substantial. If you use single-service plates or utensils, get the highest quality products you can afford. If you offer outdoor dining, make sure the wind can't blow your serviceware around. This may mean installing wind screens or abandoning the use of disposables entirely. Your guests will not have a pleasant experience if they are chasing their meals around your patio.

**Wet ashtrays** Clean ashtrays are essential but wet ashtrays are infuriating. When a guest places a cigarette in a wet ashtray, everybody loses. The guest has a soggy cigarette and you have an angry guest as well as a mess to clean up. It is good to get in the habit of wiping ashtrays out with a dry cloth, paper towel, or cocktail napkin just to be sure.

**No ashtrays on the tables in smoking sections** This annoyance also applies when ashtrays are on tables in non-smoking areas. For many people, the only way they can tell if they are seated in the proper area is by whether or not there are ashtrays on the tables.

**Paper napkins in an upscale restaurant** The key to success in our industry is to create and exceed people's expectations. If you accept this premise, do you think guests expect to find paper napkins when dining at a pricey restaurant? Perhaps you can make it work, but I don't like the odds.

**Wet or sticky tabletops** I know your mom taught you not to put your elbows on the table, but you know everybody does it. If a guest's arm (or wallet, notebook, purse, or newspaper) *sticks* to the table, watch out! How are guests going to clean themselves up? What are they thinking about you while they are doing it?

# Aggravating Accessories

When you are aware of the impact your table decor has on the dining experience, you must pay more attention to it in your training and coaching.

**Dead or wilted flowers on the tables** Fresh flowers require attention. At least every morning, inspect all the flowers to be sure they still enhance the table. If they are getting a little weak, replace them. Trying to stretch them a day too long will undo all the good they do you in the first place.

**Incomplete table appointments**  Have you ever been at a table that had a salt shaker but no pepper? How about two peppers and no salt? This can often happen after you have combined several tables to seat a large party. If the busser is not paying attention when resetting the tables, condiments can be switched around. This creates a real annoyance for your guests, who may watch their meals get cold while they try to flag down someone who can get them some salt!

**Poor-quality artificial flowers on the table**  Whatever you put on the table ought to reflect favorably on your restaurant and enhance the dining experience for your guests. Saving a few dollars with cheap plastic flowers tells your guests you really don't care too much about how the table looks. They may make some assumptions (right or wrong) about how much you care about the other aspects of your operation. If you are going to use artificial flowers on the table, shop around for some good-quality silk ones.

**Unadorned tables**  Have *something* decorative on the table in any restaurant or cafeteria. Remember that people don't go out to eat just because they are hungry. If they have a candy bar at their desks, they can take care of hunger! Dining out needs to have a more special feel. The decor doesn't have to be elaborate or expensive, just something that will remind them that they aren't eating at home!

**Centerpieces that obscure the view of other diners**  Be sure your decor doesn't interfere with conversation. Once you get the table looking just the way you want it, have your staff sit in all the chairs. See if it is possible to carry on a conversation. Often the table looks different from a seated position than it does when you are standing.

# Physical Follies

Physical follies are the design deficiencies of your seating. Like other design problems, you can avoid them by proper planning. If you have inherited someone else's design, take a good look for the presence of these irritants.

**Tabletops too small for the service**  Just because a table has four sides doesn't mean it can seat four people. Determining the proper tabletop size takes some planning. There must be room for the place settings, of course. Is there room for the guests to rest their arms? What else are you going to place on the table during the meal and where is it going to go? You need space for shared appetizers, wine bottles, side dishes, and so on. Pizzeria tables must be large enough for the pizza pan. Cafeterias need to allow for trays. The additional money you may make by trying to pick up a few extra seats with small tabletops is not worth the points you will lose by crowding your guests.

**Chipped or worn laminate on tables or countertops**   If your operation has exposed laminate tops, keep an eye on them. When the edges get chipped, repair them. Chipped laminate is a safety and cleaning problem. When the finish on the top gets worn, replace the top. Worn tops make your entire dining room look run-down. If you have a problem with this, just think of the money you're saving on linen. If you *still* have a problem, think of how annoyed your guests get when they have to eat off a shabby table.

**Tight booths**   The advantage of booths, of course, is that you can get more seating in a given area than you can with tables and chairs. Of course, if you can't get your guests *into* the booths, extra capacity doesn't do you much good. When planning booths, make sure the spacing between the back of the bench and the edge of the table is adequate for the typical adult. Having to eat in an unpleasantly tight booth makes for an unpleasant meal. It is better to have fewer seats and happier guests.

**No wide chairs for wide people**   A friend of mine is a former United States heavyweight judo champion. As you might expect, he is a *big* guy. One of his complaints is that restaurants often have no chairs that he can fit into. Standard armchairs are often too tight. If the restaurant has armless chairs, the situation is a little easier, but not much. Booths are nearly always out of the question. There are enough wide people out there that it is worth considering having a few wider chairs available. They will appreciate it and are likely to become regular patrons. Remember that wide people usually got that way by having larger-than-average appetites!

**Chairs that don't slide easily**   For your guests to be seated, chairs must be pulled out and pushed in. During the meal, guests may wish to change position. Be sure the legs of your chairs have casters or slides that make movement as easy as possible. It is annoying to wrestle with a heavy chair that refuses to move across a dining room carpet.

**Uncomfortable seating**   Sometimes the physical design of the chairs is just not comfortable. There is more risk of this with trendy designs, but even chairs that *look* comfortable can be unpleasant to sit in for long periods. Have your designer or supplier provide you with a sample for testing. Ask as many people as you can to try it out and give you their opinions. Is it the right height? Is it easy to get in and out of? Is it comfortable? If you are after a rapid turnover, you may not want to make the chairs *too* comfortable. If this is your choice, make sure the theme of your restaurant is compatible with rapid meal service. A rule of thumb is that the higher the average check, the longer guests expect to stay. The longer guests stay at the table, the more comfortable the seating must be.

**Tabletops that are not level**   There is a difference between wobbly tables and tabletops that are not level. Off-level tables are often very solid, and even the most out-of-level tabletop will still hold place settings. The problem is that an off-level surface causes people to feel like something is wrong. This minor annoyance will color their entire dining experience and it will be difficult for them to enjoy their meals.

**Booth seats that pitch forward**   This is usually a symptom of home-built booths. Improper pitch causes your guests to spend the entire evening pushing themselves away from the table. When the seat pitches forward, it takes constant muscle tension to maintain position. By the end of the evening, your guests may be exhausted from the struggle! Usually, we want the dining experience to be more relaxing than that. If you have the problem, either rebuild the seats or install new cushions that correct for the slope.

# Condiment Calamities

You fuss over the food that you prepare in the kitchen, but have you thought about the edibles that already are on the table—condiments, crackers, and such? Here are some aggravating points to watch for.

**Salt and pepper shakers that are sticky, greasy, or half-empty**   Make wiping the shakers a regular part of the table setup process. This is also the time to check to be sure the tops are on tight, particularly if you have playful younger guests!

**Pepper shakers so full they won't pour**   Make your staff aware of this phenomenon and train them to fill only to within a half inch of the top.

**Ketchup bottles coated at the neck**   This applies to almost every condiment container that you refill and is everybody's complaint. Make sure to wipe the necks clean every night and every time you refill the bottles. Better yet, find another way to serve ketchup, such as using small portion cups.

**Condiment containers that are nearly empty**   Condiment containers often get overlooked in the heat of the rush. Check *all* condiment containers as part of your regular sidework. Take those that are less than one-third full out of the dining room. Either use them in the kitchen or donate them to a shelter or food bank.

**Empty or partially used packets in with the full ones**   This comes up most often with crackers and sugar packets. Train your staff to check for this every time they reset a table or take a cracker basket to the table. It's also a good idea to clean the sugar bowl every night.

**Baskets filled with packets of crushed crackers** Train your bussers to watch for this. In addition, make it a practice to empty the cracker baskets at the end of the day and start fresh the next morning. Save the crushed packets for use in the kitchen.

**Salt or sugar crusted inside the shakers** You create this problem when you wash shakers and refill them before they are completely dry. If possible, wash shakers in the evening, then leave them inverted overnight before refilling. Be sure they are on a rack where water can easily drain and where there is free air circulation.

**Separated mustard** Get in the habit of giving the container a shake before taking it to the table. (Make sure the top is on tight!) Be alert for caked mustard on the rim of the jar. Wipe the neck clean every night as you do with the ketchup bottles.

**Stained labels on condiment bottles** Nothing detracts from the look of a table like a messy condiment bottle. If you must refill condiment containers (see Note on page 38), be sure to refill the bottle that with the cleanest label, not just the one that is most full.

**Salt or sugar too caked to pour** This can be a problem in areas of high humidity. A little uncooked rice in the salt shaker will help. Sugar is a little tougher. Either use a sugar shaker that seals tightly or switch to individual packets.

**Wet sugar packets** If a guest's hand is damp when they pick up a sugar packet or if they place a wet packet back in the sugar bowl, an unpleasant surprise lies waiting for the next diners. Check sugar bowls and packets as you reset the table.

**No sugar substitute on the tables** With the national obsession with weight, sugar substitute is as necessary a condiment as salt or pepper. Stay in touch with your guests to be sure you are offering the particular brands they prefer.

**Loose tops on the condiments** Be sure condiment tops are on tight when you bring the container to the table. If a guest shakes the bottle, you don't want them (or the dining room) sprayed with A-1 sauce!

**Crystallized honey** Honey dispensers can be an annoyance when the honey is starting to crystallize and turn to sugar. This happens when the honey comes in contact with water. When cleaning honey containers, allow them to dry overnight before refilling. Take any crystallized product to the kitchen for use in cooking.

**NOTE: Although refilling condiment containers is common practice, be aware that condiment bottles are single-use containers. Most health departments do not allow them to be refilled because they cannot be properly cleaned and sanitized. There is also the potential for cross-contamination when you pour product from one container into another.**

# Devilish Details

There are a variety of small points that arise at the table with the potential to distract your guests from having a good time.

**Napkins too small to cover the lap**    When a napkin is so small you need one on each knee to cover your lap, you have a potential irritant! Within limits, the larger the napkin, the more luxurious the experience for the guest. Napkins, whether paper or linen, should be large enough to cover the lap easily. They also should be of a material that won't slide onto the floor every time the guest changes position. Remember, you get what you pay for.

**Placing silverware or unwrapped straws on a bare tabletop**    Guests can assume the tabletop is clean, but is it sanitary? Place settings belong on a placemat, napkin, or tablecloth, not on the bare tabletop. If additional silverware is needed at the table, place a plate or napkin underneath it. This may appear minor but if it bothers a guest, they will spend the rest of the meal in a state of upset. Wrapped straws are not a problem . . . and I suggest you *only* serve wrapped straws.

**Ashtrays with more than two butts in them**    Train your staff to watch ashtrays and regularly replace them. Common practice is to cover the dirty ashtray with a clean one when you lift it off the table to keep ashes from flying about. Replacing an ashtray that contains a lighted cigarette requires the staff member to handle the cigarette, a practice you want to avoid. Either wait until the guest has the cigarette in their hand or until it is stubbed out. Make sure the ashtray is clean when the guests arrive.

**No clean or safe place for a woman to put down her purse** Picture a singles bar in the middle of the Friday night crush. People are everywhere and the floor is awash with overturned margaritas and spilled beer. What is a woman going to do with her $100 purse? If she has to keep it in her hand, under her arm, or in her lap, she will be uncomfortable. Consider screwing small hooks (like coat hooks) under the table and bartops to give her a safe place to hang up her valuables.

**Napkins put into the dispenser backward**    Filling napkin dispensers is a simple task. Yet, how often have you tried to take a napkin only to find there was nothing to grab? This is a symptom of inattention by the staff. Coach your staff on how to fill the napkin dispensers and the importance of making sure the napkins are placed in the proper position. Then make it a practice for them to remove one napkin after filling the dispenser. This way they will know immediately if they have put the napkins in correctly.

**Ashtrays that do not hold the cigarette firmly**   Some ashtray designs will not hold a cigarette off the bottom of the ashtray. This causes the cigarette to burn unevenly and is most annoying to smokers. It is your decision whether to permit smoking in your establishment or not. If you do, make sure that what you do works for smokers.

**Knives too dull to cut**   My father always impressed upon me the need to use the right tool for the right job. Restaurant knives are no different. Be sure the knives you provide will cut the foods for which they are intended. The coward's way out is to use only steak knives in the place setting. A steak knife will cut anything you have (I hope), but it is not very impressive for spreading butter.

**Placing items on the table carelessly**   Always *place* items on the table rather than *put* them on the table. Coach your staff to take the extra second required to place items carefully, quietly, and respectfully without interrupting a guest's conversation.

**Chewing gum under the table, counter, or seat**   This is like gravity in our business. Whether you enjoy gravity or not, you cannot fight it! At least twice a week you need to scrape the chewing gum off the tables and chairs.

**No provisions for wheelchairs**   The Americans with Disabilities Act (ADA) will mandate what you must do in this regard. Even without a requirement, consider the comfort and convenience of your guests in wheelchairs. Make sure that some tables near the door can accommodate a wheelchair without the wheelchair sitting in the middle of a traffic lane. Disabled guests deserve the same comfort and ambiance as the rest of your patrons. It is only common courtesy for people who deserve it.

# Bonus Points

Everybody likes pleasant surprises. These little unexpected touches are opportunities to improve your score and put your guests in a better mood. They help make up for any lapses in the operation and give people something to talk about to their friends.

**Interesting flower arrangements**   This may only be practical in upscale restaurants, but a professionally designed floral piece on the table is both unexpected and memorable. If it helps keep you prominently in the minds of your guests, it is worth your consideration.

**Attractively coordinated tabletops**   Often, tabletops are not the result of planning, they just happen. Take a clue from the better restaurants and hotels and consider your tabletop as a complete picture. Coordinate china, glassware, silver, table coverings, napkins, and accessories to create a real impact on your guests. The cost is not much different from the piece-meal approach and you will elevate yourself in the eyes of your guests.

**Chopsticks for Asian guests**   Asians are an increasing segment of the market in many areas. Many Asians, particularly the newly arrived, have little skill in handling knives and forks. If you have a true sense of guest gratification, you will have chopsticks on hand to make it easier for them. Be sure your staff also knows what items on your menu are most compatible with chopsticks.

# 5

# Environmental Apathy

There has been much talk about the condition of the environment and what must be done to save it. What about the environment in your restaurant? What condition is *it* in and what are you doing to save it? Atmosphere or ambiance is what we call the internal environment of a restaurant. It is a major decision factor when people go out to restaurants. The difficulty in managing atmosphere is that you become too familiar with it. After awhile, you just don't notice the details.

Your environment is a feast (or famine) for the senses. Sight, sound, smell, and touch all combine to create the stage setting for the dining experience.

## Unsightly Scenes

Most environmental irritants relate to what your guests see as they look around your restaurant. Fortunately, not all your guests will notice every one of these points. Still, how many potential annoyances will you allow to exist in your restaurant? Remember that cleaning problems are also a form of visual pollution. I discuss cleaning calamities in more detail in Chapter 12.

**Table linen with small holes, rips, or burns**   People dine at "white tablecloth" restaurants for an elegant experience. It makes no sense to spend large sums on the finest ingredients and the most skilled chefs only to have the diner distracted by holes in the linen. If you are not getting the quality of linen you need, make a fuss about it. You do not have to accept everything the linen company sends you. Tell suppliers what you expect and refuse product that doesn't meet your standards.

**Lighting too dim to easily read the menu**   Your guests cannot order what they cannot read. This is a particular annoyance for older diners who dislike reminders that their eyes are less sharp. The options are to either raise the lighting level or use larger type on the menu. Sometimes, changing the paper or ink colors on the menu will improve the contrast and make it more readable. Watch your guests as they read your menu. Be alert for signs of difficulty and take any necessary action.

**Sun in the diner's eyes**   Large windows can be a real attraction for your guests. However, sun in guests' eyes will always distract them, both from their meal and their companions. If your windows face the sun, you must invest in window shades. Tinted glass can help with the glare and reduce the potential fading the sun can cause to furnishings. Often, more solid decorative shades are necessary. If you have solid shades, be sure to lower them when the sun strikes the dining room and raise them when the problem has passed. It is distracting to have the shades down when they are not needed.

**Flickering lights**   I have been in several restaurants where the lighting level fluctuated repeatedly. An occasional surge is not unusual, but recurring brightening and dimming will drive your guests crazy! If you notice this problem, consult your electrician or public utility to find a solution. Allowing it to continue will eventually empty your restaurant.

**Harsh lighting**   Lighting that glares or casts harsh shadows makes both people and food look bad. Control all the lights in the restaurant by dimmers so you can adjust the lighting intensity to the most flattering levels. Bear in mind that you may have to continually adjust the lighting levels as the sun rises and sets.

**Poorly lighted stairways or hallways**   Dim lighting causes people to feel less secure, and insecurity leads to a lower state of mind. Carefully design and control the lighting throughout the restaurant to enhance the guests' sense of well-being.

**Clutter and junk**   Cleanliness is an important factor in guest satisfaction. Junk and clutter make cleaning impossible and contribute to a feeling of dirtiness in the restaurant. Your guests can conclude that you maintain your kitchen in the same condition and choose to dine elsewhere.

**Personal items of the staff stored in view**   Your guests come to the restaurant for a complete change of environment. Personal articles are a distraction from that escape. The most satisfactory solution is to provide a staff locker room for personal items. If you can't do that, create a secure space for personal articles out of sight of the guests. Remember that you cannot store personal items in the food preparation areas. Personally, it bothers me when I find purses stored in the service stations. Your guests probably won't see that, but it is not a good sanitation practice and may point to the need for lockers.

**Light glaring from the kitchen**   Lighting sets the mood of the dining room. Lighting levels in the kitchen are far brighter. You must baffle kitchen light carefully to prevent destroying the atmosphere for your guests. This problem becomes more acute if you have an exhibition cooking area or an open pass-thru window from the kitchen.

**Seasonal decorations still up weeks after the holiday**   Unless this is part of your concept, the holiday celebration is not over until you have packed the decorations and safely stored them for next year. Timing is everything when you are talking about holiday decorations. Usually the decorations must be removed the morning following the main holiday celebration. Be sure your planning includes scheduling the timely removal of seasonal items.

**Chipped paint on windowsills or door frames**  The trim takes the most abuse and it can get away from you. Make a point to examine the windowsills, baseboards, and door frames with a critical eye at least once a year. Repaint as necessary to keep the room looking fresh and attractive. Door frames take a particularly heavy beating. Clean them regularly to prevent them from becoming soiled or sticky.

**A messy pile of newspapers or magazines in the waiting area**  Particularly if your restaurant is a breakfast destination, you will accumulate the newspapers your guests leave behind. Making these available to other diners is a homey touch that can be a plus for you. The problem is having a place to keep used newspapers neatly available. The greeter is the most likely staff member to handle this task. Be sure you support their efforts with a rack, box, or table where they can place the papers.

**Carrying trash through the dining room during meal hours**  My first restaurant in San Francisco was on the third level of the shopping arcade of a major downtown development. The only route from the kitchen to the dumpster was through the dining room, across the patio, and down the elevator. My second restaurant was on the second floor of a building in Sausalito where the only route for trash was down the main entry stairs. Believe me, when you have this challenge, scheduling is essential! Be sure to remove all trash during the slack periods, no matter how small the quantities might be. If you don't stay on top of this, you'll find your production capacity choked on garbage in the middle of the rush!

**Bus tubs full of dirty dishes**  This is particularly annoying next to guest traffic lanes. If you use bus tubs, see how creative you can be about keeping them out of sight. Admittedly, concealing bus tubs may create additional cleaning requirements. Still, you can control cleaning more easily than you can control the reactions of your guests when you keep your garbage on display in the dining room.

**Pictures on the wall not level**  Maybe it is the rotation of the earth that causes pictures to tilt after awhile. Of course, you can solve the problem by screwing pictures directly to the walls. If you hang pictures more conventionally, check them regularly to be sure they are level. Small pieces of adhesive velcro attached between the picture and the wall can help.

**Jumbled pile of tray stands in the dining room**  Constant use is not an excuse for disorderly storage of tray stands. The solution is to make sure a specific place is set aside for tray stands and that staff returns all stands to this spot. Your sales people and bussers can identify the most convenient locations. Be sure the spot you choose is convenient or you only make the problem worse. Once you determine the location, do something to make the stands less visible to your guests. Perhaps placing a tall plant on each side of the spot will be enough. The answer depends on your decor and traffic patterns.

**Inconsistent elements of decor**   How seriously would you take a Moroccan restaurant with a log cabin decor? This may be an exaggeration, but you get the point. I usually see this problem when a restaurant has been recycled from one concept to another and the owner has tried to save some money. The theory is good, but the practice is not. Inconsistent decor creates uneasiness in your guests and is false economy. They are less likely to perceive your operation as a completely new restaurant, and you may be saddled with the sins of the previous operation.

**Fluorescent lights in the dining room**   Fluorescent lights are terrific in the kitchen but disastrous in the dining room. You cannot dim fluorescent lights except with very expensive controls, so you have no control of your lighting level. Worse yet, the light spectrum from some fluorescent tubes can make your food look off-color and unappetizing.

**Cigarette machine a focal point in the dining room or lounge**   I discussed this in a previous chapter and it is worth repeating. Cigarette vending machines are designed to catch the eye. They are a distraction, particularly for nonsmokers. If you have such a machine on the premises, place it away from the major traffic flows. The hallway to the restrooms is often a good choice. Don't create a diversion in your prime revenue-producing space.

**Tables not promptly cleared**   The most attractive decor in a dining room is people on chairs, not dirty dishes on tables. The excuse I often hear for a dining room where most the tables remain uncleared is that the rush just ended. If so, why isn't the dining room staff busy clearing tables? When the rush is over, only the amateurs take a break. The professionals get the room ready for the next rush before they take a break.

**Continual renovation or construction**   Constant upgrading is important to keep your restaurant competitive, but do the major work as quickly as possible. Remember that you are investing the money to create guest comfort, not inconvenience. Dining in a construction zone is not most people's idea of a relaxing evening and they may take their business elsewhere until you complete the project. If the work goes on too long, they may develop other dining habits.

**Shades hanging unevenly in the dining room**   Assign some-one the responsibility to monitor the appearance of the dining room throughout the day. You might want to make this a task for the last person who reported for work. New arrivals are more objective than someone who has been in the room all day. Remember your guests are always new arrivals and will notice anything that is out of order.

**Soiled or faded drapes**   We take draperies for granted because their changes are so subtle. Draperies exposed to strong sunlight will change color over time. This will be most noticeable if there are similar drapes in the room that are not subject to direct sunlight. All drapes become soiled. Slap them with your hand. If you see a cloud of dust, it's time to vacuum them or send them out for cleaning! Drapery cleaning is not an overnight project, so do it when you close the restaurant for a short time, a rare occurrence for most operators. The most effective defense is a good offense. In planning the restaurant, make all windows in a room the same size. Then buy a spare set of drapes. This allows you to rotate draperies and clean them one at a time. You never have to close for cleaning and your drapes will last longer.

**Draperies hanging off the track**   Make this inspection part of your morning routine. Most drapes attach with hooks and they can come loose if anyone disturbs the material. Operate each drape before the res-taurant opens to check the integrity of the mountings and take care of any problems at once. It is a small detail in a business where you measure success by attention to details.

**Soiled, faded, or peeling paint or wallpaper**   Wallcoverings deteriorate so gradually you may not notice their condition until the prob-lem is extreme. Make a thorough inspection at least quarterly to note de-ficiencies and to schedule their correction.

**Sloppy, handmade signs**   Wall signs may be appropriate in casually themed operations but are rarely proper in more upscale restaurants. If you choose to have signs in the dining room, be sure they have the same level of finish as the rest of the decor. Use a professional sign painter to make any signs that you plan to display for more than a few days. The cost is surprisingly small. You can reuse signs for daily specials that repeat every week. In any case, verify spelling with a culinary dictionary.

**Staff disturbing the dining room**   A staff break room is just a dream for most operators. If the staff eats standing up in the kitchen, it is a health department violation. The only option for most operators is to use the dining room. If the staff eats in the presence of guests, they must conduct themselves in the same manner as your guests. If they are raucous or disruptive, it will reflect poorly on your restaurant. Guests will sense a "Jekyll and Hyde" nature to your crew and trust them a little less.

**Broken wallboard or plaster**   You must maintain the physical integrity of your establishment. You do not always have control over those events that cause damage to the walls, but you always have control over the repair efforts. In the food preparation areas, broken walls are a health hazard. In the guest areas, broken walls deliver a message that you run a shoddy operation. Make all repairs at once. If a guest sees the same problem two visits in a row, there may not be a third chance. After you make the repair, analyze the cause of the accident to see if you can prevent a recurrence. Rolling carts cause many wall problems. Often bumpers on the carts or corner protection strips will avert future damage.

**Repairs that are obvious amateur efforts**   Fixing problems yourself is an economic necessity for many independent restaurateurs. If the local building codes allow it and you can make the repair to professional standards, save the money and do the work yourself. If the repair is illegal or so poorly done that it is a distraction for your guests, it can be an expensive savings. Do everything in your restaurant to the same professional standard. You don't cut corners on your food; don't cut corners on the physical integrity of your building.

**Burned out light bulbs**   Checking and replacing light bulbs is a daily duty whether you like it or not. The difficulty is usually that you don't know if a bulb is out until you need to turn the lights on. When it is time to turn the lights on, it is too late to replace the bulbs. To stay ahead of burnout, keep a supply of bulbs on hand. If access is difficult or awkward, such as with recessed lights in a high ceiling, invest in a bulb-changer. This is essentially a suction cup on the end of an extension pole. Bulb changers allow you to replace inoperative bulbs without the need to drag a ladder into the dining room.

**Duct tape holding carpets together**   Thank goodness for duct tape! Without it, most restaurants would fall apart! Include duct tape as a standard part of every foodservice tool kit. Be aware that duct tape is available in several colors besides the standard silver. If you must use tape for a temporary repair, pick a color that matches the material needing repair. At the same time, make a call to someone who can make a permanent repair. Duct tape will work in emergencies but is only an acceptable long-term solution on ducts!

**Leaks in the ceiling**   Unfortunately, the only way you find out the roof leaks is when the water comes through the ceiling. The roof is part of the building you seldom see and, consequently, seldom think about. While it is fresh in your mind, call a roofing contractor and find out how often your particular roof needs recoating. Include this expense in your long-term capital budget and repair the roof before it becomes an annoyance to your guests.

**Disintegrating carpet**    There comes a time in the life of every carpet when it must be replaced. Conscientious operators make the replacement before the need is too obvious. Trying to stretch an extra six months from a deteriorated carpet can defer a few hundred dollars of capital expenditures at the expense of alienating a few hundred guests.

**Broken tiles on the floors or walls**    Broken tiles are unsightly and pose a cleaning problem as well. Take a minute to examine the physical integrity of the tiles at least once a day. Repair cracked tiles promptly. If you retile, be sure to keep some spare tiles on hand for replacements.

**Deferred maintenance**    Deferred maintenance is a polite way of saying that you have let the condition of your restaurant slide to a point where it is noticeable. Decisions to delay upkeep activities always make sense at the time. The problem is that eventually the work must be done. The longer you delay the repair, the more expensive it is likely to be. Meanwhile, your business starts to feel shabby.

When the restaurant is drab, guests do not feel as good about being there. The longer the condition persists, the fewer guests return. The fewer guests return, the less likely you can afford the repairs. The only way out is never to get into this position in the first place. Do what you have to do to make your restaurant a reflection of your professionalism.

**Broken windows**    Almost any town in the country has a 24-hour glass company. Since you know that eventually you will replace some glass, establish a relationship with a glass company before the emergency arises. Have them look over your restaurant to get familiar with your needs. If you learn that replacements for your windows are a special order, you won't be surprised if you have to do it sometime. In any event, you must repair broken glass at once. Besides being another distraction you don't need, broken glass can cause injury to your guests and encourage break-ins.

**Offensive decor**    Avoid decor that will alienate your guests. Many people are disturbed by stuffed animals, snakes, and so on. They may have an objection to killing animals, have an allergy to the fur, or think the trophies are dirty and present a sanitation problem.

# Obnoxious Noises

Noise has a role in restaurants and it depends on the function you want your establishment to serve. Crowded restaurants are more noisy than less populated restaurants. Gathering spots usually have a higher noise level than an operation designed to be a sanctuary from an active world. There are extremes in both directions and finding the right sound level requires that you know your guests.

**Background music that intrudes on conversation**  The appropriate music level depends on the type of restaurant. Still, even a lively place can have sound so loud it causes people to complain. People go to restaurants for social reasons and every element of the operation ought to enhance that social motive. Music so loud that it interferes with conversation will only be attractive to people who do not want to talk. The more formal the restaurant, the more subdued the sound.

**Loud entertainment**  The bar is usually the loudest area of a restaurant. If you want simultaneous activity in the bar and the dining room, consider insulated walls between the two areas. If your bar gets busy after the dining room closes, a sliding partition will let you to expand into the dining room.

**Kitchen noise that reaches the dining room**  Kitchens are noisy by nature. Clanging pots and pans, shouted orders and instructions, machines whirring, and food sizzling all add to the noise level. If your restaurant has an exhibition cooking area, this problem can be even more severe. In new construction, you can position the kitchen to reduce the problem or sound transfer. In existing operations, the solution is more elusive. If you have a problem with noise transfer, insulate the dividing walls or place acoustical tile on the kitchen ceiling. Check the mountings of dishwashers and ventilation fans to be sure they don't vibrate and cause extra noise.

**Radios blaring from the kitchen or dishroom**  Is there something genetic about kitchen workers that they need to have music blasting in their ears at all times? This is a constant struggle in many restaurants, particularly where the production crew feels disconnected from the activity in the dining room. Help them understand that the reason to prohibit kitchen radios is the noise pollution it creates for the guests. The solution may be to extend the restaurant sound system is into the kitchen or allow the use of personal tape players with headphones.

**Harsh acoustics in the dining room**  There is a difference between loud sound and harsh acoustics. Loud sound is a function of volume. Harsh acoustics are irritating at any level. Hard surfaces create harsh acoustics. If your restaurant has a "clean look" with stark walls, hard floors, large windows, and bare tabletops, your dining room will likely be noisy. The solution is to break up the reflective surfaces. Discuss the most effective way to do this with an acoustic specialist.

**Having television sound and background music on simultaneously** This is noise pollution in the extreme. The cacophony created by two conflicting sound tracks is unbearable to many people. Wiring the television sound through the house sound system an effective solution. This assures that only one source of sound is being broadcast at a time. It also permits all guests in the room to hear the television without the sound blaring.

**Irritating background music** Sound type and sound quality determine the irritation factor of music. The appropriate type of music depends on the formality of your restaurant and the primary market you attract. The quality of the amplification system and speakers in your system determine the sound quality. The louder the volume level, the more you will want to spend on components. Low quality, low power components pushed to extremes will distort the sound and irritate your guests, even those who like loud music.

**Clattering dishes** Train your staff to clear and set tables quietly. The noise is distracting to everyone in the dining room. Working silently is especially important when clearing extra place settings from a table occupied by a single diner. Clattering dishes will only call attention to the lone diner and may make them uncomfortable.

**Dropping china, silver, or glassware** Accidents happen but the crash of breaking dinnerware is particularly jarring. If the staff applauds the accident, it only shows their insensitivity to the impact of excessive noise on the diner's enjoyment. It further shows their lack of awareness of the cost of serviceware and the potential impact of that cost on the profitability of the restaurant. Coach your staff in proper methods for handling serviceware and the importance of not trying to carry too much at once. Perhaps carts are a workable solution for your operation. It might be worthwhile to create an incentive for your crew to reduce breakage.

**Blaring television sets** The speaker system is the weakest part of a television set. When you increase the volume, acoustic distortion can cut some people like a knife. If you want to broadcast television sound throughout a room, tie it in through the sound system. The easiest way to do this is to route your television signal through a VCR. You can then tap the audio outputs on the back of the VCR into your sound system. The quality of sound will be better and you can service all your guests without irritating sound levels.

**Crying babies and disruptive children** The more you understand what children want and provide it for them, the more you will reduce potential problems. Chapter 14 offers suggestions for making your restaurant more responsive to the needs of families with children. You can't stop children from being children, but you can take steps to reduce potential disturbances. As a general precaution, do not seat families next to couples or elderly diners. If unruly children create a disturbance for your other guests, though, you must restore order in the dining room. Talk to the parents and ask for their help in quieting their children. They know their youngsters are creating a disturbance. Insensitivity and failure to act can alienate your other clientele.

# Unsettling Odors

The only smell you want wafting through your dining room is the wonderful aroma of your food. When other fragrances enter the air, the result can be disastrous.

**Sour smell in the dining room or bar carpet**   The smell comes from bacteria acting on spilled food and beverage and indicates the carpet needs cleaning. Carpet may be an inappropriate flooring choice in areas where spills are a regular problem. In a high volume bar or a restaurant catering to families, hard flooring will be easier to clean and maintain. Still, carpet is the flooring of choice in most operations. Clean all spills promptly. Be sure to vacuum the carpet daily and have a schedule for regular carpet shampooing. If you stay ahead of the problem, you can avoid the problem.

**Seating smokers beside nonsmokers**   Without separate dining areas, expect complaints any time you have to put smokers and nonsmokers next to each other. It is an immutable law of nature that smoke will always move toward those who cannot tolerate it, despite your ventilation system!

**Murky or smelly water in the bud vase**   Fresh flowers in a vase on the table are a real delight in many restaurants. However, if the same flower sits in the same water for a few days, it starts to smell like low tide in Boston Harbor! If you use fresh flowers, make changing the water part of your nightly sidework and you'll be fine.

# Frustrating Feels

The final dimension of dining room atmosphere determines how your guests feel while they are dining. I have discussed several of these points before and they are important enough to mention again.

**Uneven heating or cooling**   Seating a guest in a draft will guarantee their discomfort, particularly an elderly guest. If the problem is with your heating or cooling system, have it adjusted. If the draft comes from the front door, create a vestibule or build a low divider wall. You can solve the problem if it is important to you. I guarantee that it is important to your guests.

**Wobbly tables and chairs**  If you thought matchbooks were invented just to level dining room tables, you know the problem. Wobbly tables and chairs are constant distractions throughout the meal. Your guests will remember the uncomfortableness longer than they will remember your fine food and service. Self-leveling feet are available for dining room tables. Ask your restaurant supply house or look for them at a trade show.

**Slippery floors**  Slick flooring makes guests fear for their safety. Unmarked slick floors can cause physical injury. Neither situation enhances the dining experience. Except for emergency cleanups, mop floors only during slack periods. Always put out warning signs to alert guests and staff to a potentially slick floor.

**Overcrowded tables and chairs**  In some concepts and in some cities, crowded tables are the rule and guests hardly notice. However, a Denver restaurant with a New York City seating density will be uncomfortable and unnerving. Guests not conditioned to having other diners within inches of them will feel their privacy has been violated. This is particularly true in more upscale concepts. Overcrowded tables usually mean tighter traffic aisles that create problems for all diners. Passing patrons and staff can constantly bump and jostle a guest seated next to the aisle. Guests in wheelchairs may find the dining room inaccessible. Whatever seating increases you may gain from crowding tables together is more than offset by the number of guests who will not return.

**Sharp edges on tables, booths, or chairs**  Nobody wants to have their clothes ruined, particularly on a social occasion. Even if you do a superb job of handling the situation, the inconvenience that this causes the guest will not encourage a return to your restaurant. If you are responsible for damage to a guest's clothing, there are two things you must do. You must pay the value of a replacement article on the spot. Be generous and don't negotiate the price. You also must compensate for the "hassle factor"—the inconvenience of having to shop for a replacement. I suggest this take the form of a free meal or a gift certificate for the restaurant. It costs you a little less and helps maintain the guest's habit of dining in your establishment.

**Being seated at a bad table**  Many restaurants have "good tables" and "bad tables." The good tables are usually by the windows. The bad tables are by the traffic lanes, the kitchen door, or the restrooms. Guests seated at good tables are far more likely to enjoy themselves than guests relegated to the less desirable tables. If you have undesirable tables, change your layout to eliminate them. If you can't solve the problem, remove the table and put in a plant! You cannot afford to seat guests unless you can give them a quality dining experience.

**Torn coverings on seats or booths**  The physical integrity of your guests' dining environment can determine whether their dining experience is pleasant or annoying. Inspect booths and chairs for damage after every business day. Order immediate repairs when you find a problem. You can't ignore rips and tears because they will only get bigger and more ugly. Ask your upholsterer to recommend a good vinyl repair kit for temporary patches to vinyl seating. When ordering new seating, design the cushions to be removable and order a few spares. This will keep all your seating in service while repairs are being made.

**Dining room that is too hot or too cold**  Proper temperature in the dining room is essential to guest comfort. As the room fills or as guests become more active, room temperature increases due to body heating. Be sensitive to these changes and adjust your thermostat to compensate. Be alert for guests who don sweaters or jackets. Watch for patrons wiping their foreheads. When in doubt, ask your guests if the temperature is comfortable for them.

**Broken or rickety chairs**  If your guests think their chair may be unsafe, they will spend the entire meal waiting for it to collapse. In this condition, they cannot appreciate your restaurant and will leave feeling dissatisfied. Some chair designs are more durable than others. When considering new seating, ask for the addresses and phone numbers of other restaurants that are using the same chair. Ask the managers of these operations for their experiences with the product before you make a final commitment to purchase. Remove broken chairs from service immediately and replace them with a spare chair. You *do* have spares, don't you? Send broken chairs out for repair or throw them away at once; otherwise, they will pile up in your storeroom and choke your operation.

**Small table in the middle of a big room**  The smaller the table, the more important that you place it against a wall or a divider. A small table in the center of a large room makes the guest, particularly a single diner, feel adrift and uncomfortable. If your clientele is predominantly couples and you have many deuces, break up the dining room with low divider walls or planters. Place the two-tops against the dividers. This provides the necessary intimacy and often increases seating capacity. In any event, an uncomfortable table makes for an uncomfortable evening.

# Bonus Points

Everybody likes pleasant surprises. These little unexpected touches are opportunities to improve your score and put your guests in a better mood. They help make up for any lapses in the operation and give people something to talk about to their friends.

**Individual volume controls**   When I designed the new athletes' dining room at the U.S. Olympic Training Center in Colorado Springs, I included two big-screen television sets at the end of the room, easily visible from every table. I wired the television speakers through the sound system and placed 13 separate speakers in the dining room, each with its own volume control. The athletes could turn the volume up to hear what was playing or turn it down if they did not want to be disturbed. We did not have to turn the television volume up to the threshold of pain to have it project to the back of the dining room. Also, the sound quality was much better.

**Tableside phones**   This is a particular attraction to sales people who do most of their scheduling by phone. Some restaurants have free local telephones permanently mounted at many of their tables. Cordless telephones can be an easy solution when the dining room layout makes it impractical to install wired tableside phones. Several companies even offer cordless phones that link to a computer to provide a printout of charges for both local and long-distance calls. If you provide tableside phones merely as a gimmick, their benefit will be short-lived. If they are an amenity that provides an unexpected service or convenience to guests in need, they will add to your reputation for guest service.

**Divided dining areas**   Smaller dining areas create a sense of intimacy and comfort that most guests don't experience in a more open room. Low dividers, half walls, planters, plants, and level changes give the dining room visual interest and break up the space.

**Individual light dimmers**   Many people need bright light to read the menu and prefer more subdued lighting during the meal. Some solo diners like to read or work while they enjoy their meal. Obviously one preset level of illumination will not be universally satisfactory. Particularly if your dining room has high-backed booths, consider wiring the table lighting through individual dimmers. This will allow each guest to have the lighting just the way they want it.

**Private dining rooms**   There are many reasons that people go out that could be enhanced by privacy. Small business meetings, special occasion celebrations, or a romantic evening can become more enjoyable and unique in a private setting. Private dining rooms can open new markets for business. When they are not needed, you can close them off to make the dining area appear more full with fewer people. You can open them into the main dining room for use during peak periods. They are an effective way to make odd spaces more productive. If you are remodeling your dining room or planning a new operation, give this idea some thought.

**Professional design**   When professionals have designed a restaurant's interior design, lighting, sound, and layout, the result can be breathtaking. This level of design assistance is not within everyone's budget, but it is worth considering. Even if you do not employ a professional to do the design, pay a small consulting fee for their input before drawing plans. You also can ask for their reactions to a particular design. Remember that the goal is to create a restaurant where all your guests will always feel comfortable. What is it worth to you to get that result?

# 6

# Menu Missteps

Your menu is your blueprint for profit. It determines your image and defines your concept. The menu is the shopping list your guests use to spend their money. Often it is your best (or worst) sale-maker.

Your menu is a merchandising tool. It ought to help you sell the things you want to sell and be written in such a way that it is entertaining, informative, and representative of your restaurant. Often, prospective guests may decide whether or not to visit your restaurant solely on the basis of seeing your menu somewhere. What it says to them and what it contributes to your success is a critical element of your profitability.

# Poor Presentations

What you see is what you get in menus. Placing the menu in your guests' hands sets the mood for the evening. If the menu is exciting and interesting, the evening will have more promise. If the menu creates problems for diners, they will be more apprehensive.

**Menu print too small to read easily**   Your guests cannot order what they cannot read. This is a particular annoyance for older diners who dislike reminders that their eyes are less sharp. The options are to either raise the lighting level or use larger type on the menu. Sometimes, changing the paper or ink colors on the menu will improve the contrast and make it more readable. Watch your guests as they read your menu. Be alert for signs of difficulty and take any necessary action.

**Menus that are difficult to understand**   Many menus are so disorganized that you cannot even begin to understand what the restaurant offers. The problem is that you create a confusing image in the minds of your guests and they don't know what to make of you. Advertising bombards Americans with thousands of messages every day. To be memorable, you have to stand out in their minds. A clear menu is a major advantage in creating that mental position.

**Printed menus with handwritten changes**   Image is everything. If you make a change, print a new menu. This includes changing the year of vintage on wine lists. Handwritten changes are not a professional look. Fortunately, with computer desktop publishing and laser printers, menu changes are easier than ever for some operators. The return of clear-covered cafe-style menus also makes alterations more simple. If you like color on your menu and still want ease of change, print four color shells and overprint the individual selections on the computer.

**Specials board showing yesterday's offerings**    Promoting expired specials suggests that you are not paying attention. Make it a routine responsibility after the meal to erase the special from the board. It is part of shifting your perspective to see everything in the restaurant from your guest's point of view.

**Illegible blackboard specials**    Using a blackboard to list specials can be an effective marketing aid. It is an easy solution but only if your guests can read what is on the board! Be sure the person writing your specials has neat, easily readable handwriting. Don't make guests guess or it could negate the merchandising value of the board.

**Recitation of daily specials that goes on . . . and on . . . and on**    Limit verbal presentations of daily specials to two or three items. Your guests can't remember any more information anyway. Presenting more choices wastes the sales person's time and makes the diner impatient. I recommend a mini menu explaining the day's specials that you can leave on the table after you give the verbal presentation. Then your guests won't have to feel uncomfortable because they can't remember what you said.

**Misspelled or grammatically incorrect menu copy**    Menu writing is more than simply listing your entrées. Verify the spelling of entries with a culinary dictionary and carefully proofread the final copy. Avoid long and glowing descriptions in favor of a simple listing of ingredients. After all, who really believes "broiled to perfection" anyway?

**Menus that are too big to handle easily**    Menus make a statement—just be careful what you're saying. Menu size has a relationship to the amount of information you want to present and the size of your tables. It is awkward for your guests if the menu is too large to set down on the table. You must usually make large menus of a heavier material to prevent them from folding.

**Mimeographed or flimsy menus**    If your menu looks like a tenth copy made with used carbon paper, you will look like an amateur, no matter how skillful your food and service. Mimeographed menus may make your guests think of grade school quizzes—probably not the memory you want to evoke. Most copy centers can typeset your menu on a computer for a small charge. You can then make changes and have crisp copies made as often as necessary.

**Unidentified items on the line**    The days of "mystery meat" are over. Guests will not order what they cannot identify. Unlabeled items mean you miss an opportunity to merchandise the items on the line. Admittedly, it can be like a full-time job trying to stay on top of item labeling, particularly as you make frequent substitutions. Decide if the results are important enough for you to make the extra effort. In my book, if it increases your sales and makes your guests happier, it is always worth doing.

**No English translations**   Formality is one thing, snobbishness is another. When a restaurant does not print the menu in the native language of their guests, it is pretentious and rude. Even if you just explain the items in subtitles, having a menu your English-speaking guests can read is just common courtesy. Unless you have more business than you can handle, most restaurants cannot afford to alienate any potential patronage.

**Antiquated menu presentations**   If your menu looks like 1950 and your restaurant doesn't, you may have a problem. Outdated menus can lead to an image that you are an outmoded restaurant. I'm not suggesting you should change the items on your menu, just look at how you are presenting them. Often a fresh look can give your operation a boost in the market.

**Soiled or wrinkled menus or table tents**   Menus with creases, stains, or beverage rings look unappetizing. Menus that are greasy, dog-eared or sticky get the meal off to a bad start. The condition of your menus can cause patrons to draw conclusions about the cleanliness of your kitchen. If that conclusion is unfavorable, everything you do will be suspect. Inspect all menus before the meal and throw out all those that are not perfect.

**No daily special insert**   Everything you do in the restaurant must reflect your concern for guest gratification, attention to detail, and professionalism. An incomplete menu makes a statement. The lapse creates an additional annoyance for your guests and the staff who have to correct the error. Coach your greeters to check each menu to be sure the inserts are in place. Consider changing the color of the menu inserts each day to make it easier to spot outdated ones. You don't need the embarrassment and your guests don't want the inconvenience.

**Listing items guests can't order at the time**   It is annoying if your guests have to consult their watch when reading your menu. When it is noon and the menu lists items that are not available after 11:30 or items that are not available before 5:00, you lose points. Be sure your menu tells your guests what you *can* do for them, not what you *can't!* I understand the desire to save some money on printing, but at what cost?

**No relationship between the menu board and the items on the line**   You know how it happens. The items on the line and the menu board are in perfect agreement when you open. As the meal progresses, you sell out of some items and replace them with others. The exchange happens on the line but nobody takes the time to change the menu board. How are your guests going to know what to order? If the menu board lists beef burgundy when beef stroganoff is on the line, your guests will notice something is wrong before they notice how good the stroganoff looks. The easiest solution is to have a menu board that uses preprinted cards instead of changeable letters. It will make changing the board easier. Easy jobs get done while the difficult jobs are put off. Do yourself a favor and make it as easy as possible to do the job easily and correctly.

**Entrées that don't look like their photos**   Full-color photographs can be an effective way to market your entrées. Photographs create expectations in your guests and entice them to order; however, if the item you serve does not live up to the advance billing, you will not have met guests' expectations. They will be disappointed, no matter how good the item turns out to be.

**Not bringing a menu for dessert selections**   When it is time for dessert, presentation is everything. Oral descriptions can only do so much. Remember that your guests will not remember more than two or three verbal presentations. You could bring back the dinner menu, but it includes information that is not relevant to a dessert decision. Even in casual restaurants, have a separate dessert menu. This menu can merchandise not only desserts but also after dinner drinks and special coffees. There is more to gain than to lose. Even if you have an attractive dessert tray, a separate dessert menu can still be a valuable sales aid.

# Policy Problems

As always, management policy creates many menu problems. Whether the decision is overt or by default, the way management has chosen to operate the restaurant can create irritations for your guests. Have any of these diner disasters ever happened in *your* restaurant?

**No children's menus**   Children appreciate having something just for them because they are always having to work with other people's standards. Adults appreciate the simplicity of knowing what you have in children's portions.

**Not enough menus for all guests**   Asking guests to share menus makes a poor first impression. The first step in the solution is to realize that lack of menus slows service and makes your guests less trusting of your professionalism. Find out if the shortage is because of too few menus or simply a failure to get them back to the greeter after the guests have ordered. Peak period demands will determine how many menus you need. During the rush is when you are least flexible and when a menu shortage can most easily affect your timing. Always have spare menus on hand in a sealed package. At least once a week, count your menus to be sure you still have enough in service. If you need to break into the reserve package, you will know to order more menus printed. Also, if you find you are losing menus to souvenir seekers (or local restaurateurs), print small promotional menus. You will get the exposure and save money simultaneously.

**Ordering the *description* of an item and getting something else**  Be sure menu copy properly describes the item and makes it attractive to your patrons. Because people who write menu descriptions have a tendency to say what sounds good, wording is often misleading. Phrases like "grilled to perfection" are trite and rarely accurate. If your guests believe what they read, they will be disappointed when they don't get it. Consider omitting sentence descriptions entirely. Instead, give your entrées an exciting name and simply list the ingredients.

**Small portions and big prices**  People may not go out to eat just because they are hungry, but you can bet they don't go out to eat if they *aren't* hungry! Small portions at high prices can work briefly in trendy restaurants. Still, how many 20-year old trendy restaurants have you seen? In the end, you must provide value or lose your patronage. Smaller portions at *smaller* prices, on the other hand, may just be the direction of menus in the next decade.

**Only dinner-sized portions at lunch**  Most Americans still eat their larger meal in the evening. They are conditioned to accept larger portions (and the accompanying higher prices) later in the day. Failure to offer more traditional luncheon-size portions at midday effectively makes the menu unworkable. Guests are in a no-win situation, they must either order something they don't really want or get up and leave.

**Charging 50¢ extra for blue cheese dressing**  I know that blue cheese dressing costs a little more than the average. I also know that some dressings cost a little less than the average. To keep from confusing (and annoying) your guests, base your prices on the average and keep it simple. If you want to tip the scales a bit, develop a tasty, low-cost house dressing and feature that as a signature item.

**Fixed-price menus with surcharges for anything, except perhaps caviar**  If you advertise a fixed-price menu, that is what your guests expect. If your "fixed-price" menu becomes like buying a car with all the added extras, you will be remembered as fondly as the stereotypical car sales person! Fixed-price menus can be attractive to diners. Just don't run the risk of making your guests feel cheated by trying to run the tab up on them.

**Menus that completely change every day**   A completely fluid menu can confuse your market about what to expect from your restaurant. This general idea has worked in some small restaurants but the danger is still there. If you think this style has some promise for you, consider a weekly menu instead. Perhaps two or three solid signature items backed up with two specials can satisfy your need for a limited menu without becoming confusing for your guests.

**Failure to offer nonmeat options**   A growing number of people in the country are choosing to reduce or eliminate their meat consumption. Additionally, many more are watching fat and cholesterol intake and find nonmeat entrées a more frequent menu choice. By reflecting this preference on your menu, you become a viable destination for these diners. An added advantage of meatless entrées is that your profit margins are often more attractive.

**Violations of "truth in menu"**   In many areas, the law requires you to present an accurate picture of your menu offerings. Despite the law, honesty is always the best policy. If you have to lie to your guests to keep their business, you are living on borrowed time. You must have the trust of your patrons to be successful and you will not earn that trust by mis-leading them. Make sure that what you say is accurate.

**Boring menus**   If price increases are the only menu changes you ever make, you risk restaurant death by boredom. When your menu becomes stale, your entire operation gets dull. Adjust your menu at least twice a year to remove less popular (or less profitable) items and add variety. Don't make radical changes, just tune it up a little. Your staff will appreciate the change as much as your guests.

**Negative comments on the menu**   I had lunch at a restaurant whose menu contained the following notations:

- We reserve the right to refuse service to anyone.
- Sales tax will be added to all taxable items.
- Not responsible for lost or stolen items.
- Please refrain from smoking pipes or cigars.
- Sorry, we do not accept checks.

The first thing I noticed was how negative the menu was. I am sure this was not their intent but it was the result they got. There may be legal reasons why your menu has to include certain statements. Whatever you want to say, pay attention to how you say it. You may be making a different statement than you intended.

**No heart-healthy choices on the menu**   I believe this may be the direction of the future. All things being equal, I believe many diners would prefer low-fat choices, *provided* those choices are tasty. It takes some experimentation to modify menus to lower the fat, cholesterol, and sodium without losing taste, but you can do it. With the nutritional content of restaurant food under suspicion, three or four healthy choices on your menu can help you become the restaurant of choice. One group particularly concerned with nutrition are long-haul truck drivers. As a result, you are likely to find low-fat choices at most American truck stops! If you want more information on the subject, contact your local chapter of the American Heart Association.

**Too many (or too few) items on the menu**  See that your menu offers enough of variety to give guests a reasonable choice and not so many items that it is confusing. Guests do not come to your restaurant to become students of your menu. They should be able to find a choice that interests them within a reasonable period of time.

**Too many choices and the endless discussion it takes to make them**  An enjoyable and effortless dining experience creates the good time your guests want. Logic says that the more choices you give a guest, the more likely they are to get exactly what they want. This could be true, but the process of making all the choices can be cruel and unusual punishment! Giving people unlimited choices does not enhance their dining experience. In fact, it may only allow them to eat what they would eat at home and restaurants ought to be more special than that. There is a lot to recommend a unique house dressing, signature soups, and distinctive side dishes. It is easier on the kitchen, faster for the service staff, and more interesting for the guest.

**No signature items on the menu**  What are you going to be famous for? What are your guests going to tell their friends about? Signature items create an identity for your restaurant in the minds of your market. Advertising bombards people with hundreds of slick advertising messages every day. They tune most of them out. Signature items help you create an image in people's minds and help them remember you when they make the dining decision.

Signature items do not have to be your most expensive menu offering. They do not even have to relate to your main menu theme. They just have to be special preparations that you do better than anyone else . . . and that your guests rave about. For example, locals know San Francisco's Tadich Grill as much for its creamed spinach as for its fish.

# Wine List Weirdness

A menu by any other name is still a menu. Wine lists may be the object of intense study, an afterthought prepared by a wine sales person or somewhere in between. A full discussion of wine list design could be an entire book but one that would apply to a limited number of restaurants. For now, here are a few common errors to consider.

**No wine descriptions**    Unless your guests are wine experts (and most are not) they may need some help in choosing wines that are unfamiliar to them. Wine lists are typically arranged by color, import/domestic, and sometimes by the type of grape. This is a start but it is of little help to those unversed on the wines you offer. Guests understand the differences between sweet and dry wines. Full-bodied and delicate also are distinctions your guests understand. If your patrons are generally not very wine literate, consider restructuring your wine list along these lines. A user-friendly wine list encourages patrons to experiment and makes them more comfortable ordering wine. The more comfortable your guest become with wines, the more they will develop the habit of drinking wine with the meal. Combined with thorough staff training and tastings, this approach can increase your wine sales significantly.

**Lack of balance**    Effective wine lists offer something for all tastes. Specific requirements for cellar composition depend on your menu. A steak house wine list would likely offer more red wines than a seafood cafe, where the wine list would feature more white wines. Balance requires a range of choices between red and white, sweet and dry, full-bodied and delicate. Balance also requires a graduated range of prices with selections for every budget. Having your best-selling wines available by the glass is also a plus.

**More than three items not in stock**    If you are going to offer it, you have to stock it. Maintaining a wine list is a continual process. The more extensive the list, the more time required to support it. This is another area where desktop publishing can help you present a more professional face to the public by updating your wine list as your inventory shifts. If you cannot reprint as wines or vintages change, choose wines where you can count on a reliable supply.

**Few moderate-priced selections**    Many operators price themselves out of the market by trying to price wine with the same percentage markup they use for liquor at the bar. Wine is the only item in the restaurant that you present in the same form as your guests can purchase it themselves. If they know they can buy a particular wine for $10 at the wine shop, they will resent your trying to sell the same bottle for $35. Reasonably priced wines will increase wine sales. Higher sales bring in more dollars and dollars are the way you pay the bills. A fair pricing formula you might consider is to start with the *retail* price of the bottle. (Your price, of course, will be less than retail.) Add a standard dollar amount, perhaps $5 to $7, to provide your profit. The sales price will be fair, higher priced wines will be more of a bargain, and your reputation will spread among wine lovers.

**Too many selections**   Like menus, wine lists can have so many choices that they become a full-time study in themselves. Carefully created and maintained wine cellars are a delightful enhancement of fine dining. Those restaurants with the clientele and staff to appreciate and maintain the wine list make a special contribution to our industry. For most operators, though, the care and feeding of an extensive wine list can be a struggle. You complicate the problem when there are many not-in-stock items.

The wine list is a complement to the restaurant's food menu. Most casually themed restaurants will be well served by a modest list that is within their ability to understand and service. More upscale restaurants can justify a more extensive list. Many operators at the lower end of the market can make do with interesting house wines. As with any menu, the attraction of a wine list is not what you write but what you can deliver.

# Bonus Points

Everybody likes pleasant surprises. These little unexpected touches are opportunities to improve your score and put your guests in a better mood. They help make up for any lapses in the operation and give people something to talk about to their friends.

**Menus in braille and foreign languages**   You wouldn't offer your English-speaking guests a menu written in Chinese. Yet we think nothing of presenting an English language menu to a Chinese guest. It is only courteous to give your guests menus they can understand. Your local organization for the blind will help you prepare braille menus. Ask your multilingual guests to help you translate your menu into other languages. Include English subtitles so your staff can follow along. It is a small gesture of respect for a small segment of your market but a true measure of your passion for guest gratification.

**Extensive heart-healthy menu options**   This trend is still in its infancy, offering a real opportunity to gain a controlling position in the market. With the right recipes, food items, and equipment, you can prepare low-fat dishes that are as tasty as any conventional offering. Of course, not all selections have low-fat versions. For example, I have designed a well-balanced restaurant menu where 75% of the items meet American Heart Association standards . . . including hamburgers and french fries! All it takes is wanting to do it.

**Imaginative dessert selection**   There is always room for dessert. It is only the *idea* of dessert that gives guests pause. It is interesting that many diners will carefully order low-calorie entrées and follow up with a massive dessert! You can most always sell a dessert for two diners to split, provided you capture their imagination. To do this, offer some signature desserts—items so unique and mouth-watering that your diners just can't refuse. Present them either in person with a dessert tray or in heartfelt word pictures. Assume that nobody can pass up your special peach cobbler. It helps if you make your desserts on the premises instead of purchasing them from outside sources. Back all this up with an attractive dessert menu. Since most people don't bake exotic desserts at home, you can offer your guests something truly special that they can't get anywhere else.

**Smaller portions at smaller prices**   Dieters and elderly diners appreciate this option and it can work to your advantage. You can offer half the portion for 60% to 75% of the menu price and still maintain respectable margins. This approach also allows entrées to be attractive as appetizers. Half portions will make you more attractive to the growing number of diners who prefer grazing to ordering a full meal.

**Basic nutritional information**   Your guests want to know what they are eating. Basic food cost and portion control principles require the use of standardized recipes. Any high school or college nutrition student can do a general analysis of your recipes. Many hospital dietary departments have sophisticated computer programs for recipe analysis. Make a few friends in the right places and you may be able to provide information to your guests that will give you a competitive edge. Analysis also helps you find ways to improve the nutritional content of your entrées.

# 7
# Service Stumbles

Your service staff takes the largest responsibility for guest satisfaction, because they are the principal point of contact. They orchestrate the dining experience. Their attitude, presence, and skills will highlight or destroy the efforts of the rest of your crew.

I caution you, though, that it is too easy to lay the blame for service problems at the feet of the service staff. Service staff attitudes only reflect the attitudes of management. Operators who have denied this relationship are the ones with a high staff turnover and perpetual guest relations problems. They believe it is impossible to find qualified workers. In the same market, other restaurateurs consistently have excellent staff. It is not easy to acknowledge our own role in problems. Still, by taking responsibility for staff attitudes, we can change our level of guest service.

We call this phenomenon "the shadow of the leader." The good news is that we can change ourselves—in fact we are the *only* person we can change. When our outlook changes, the outlook of our staff follows suit. It is not the place of this book to go into lengthy discussion of how to do this. I mention it here only to give the serious manager something to think about as we explore the many opportunities to destroy guest service!

## Annoying Attitudes

Attitudes are mind-sets. A "bad attitude" is a belief that the needs and convenience of the restaurant staff are more important than the needs and convenience of the guests. It is a disease. Here are a few signs that tell you that this virus infects your organization.

**Needing to be the center of attention** The need to be the focal point suggests an individual with an ego problem. It implies that what is happening for them is more important than what is happening for anyone else. These people cannot make your guests feel important until their priorities shift. Fortunately, their attitudes can turn around if they adopt a guest-oriented stance to their jobs. That change will not happen for them until it happens for you.

**An "I'm doing you a favor" attitude** It is easy to find arrogance and indifference in the world. People don't need to come to the restaurant to experience it. Besides, the guests are doing *you* a favor by patronizing your restaurant. They have many other choices . . . and they will make other choices if you don't earn (and show them you appreciate) their business.

**Socializing with some guests while ignoring others** Good service is fair and equal. Human nature being what it is, you will insult the slighted guests and they are unlikely to return. The solution is training, coaching, and support for your staff to help them become more sensitive to the needs of all their guests.

**Being too familiar or excessively chatty** Guests come to the restaurant for their own reasons. When staff members interject themselves into the guest's world personally, they are intruders. This familiarity will create withdrawal and resentment in your guests. The staff member probably thinks they are just being friendly. Remember that good service is always defined from the guest's viewpoint.

**Making a fuss about a dropped dish** Accidents happen and nobody likes to be embarrassed. By calling attention to a mishap, you drop your guest's level of well-being immediately. This usually guarantees a negative outlook for the rest of the meal. The most effective way to handle a spill is to treat it as the everyday occurrence it is. If you must say anything, a passing comment like "Don't worry about it. It happens all the time," will take the pressure off your guest and salvage the evening for everybody.

**Having a visible reaction to the amount of the tip** Non-verbal statements are often more devastating than verbal ones because everybody in the room can read them. Two items are of concern here. It is appropriate to coach sales people about not displaying their reactions to the amount of a tip. A more significant question is, why is their first action to look at the amount of the tip? Although a counseling session is in order, be sensitive to the possibility that the sales person may be under some financial pressure. There is a chance that they feel unappreciated on the job. In any case, there is always more going on than you know about.

**Ignoring obvious attempts to get attention** When this happens, it is insulting to the guest and suggests sales people with control issues. *They* are the ones in charge of the dining experience, not the guest. They will not tolerate anyone telling them what to do. It is impossible for these individuals to give responsive service unless they can find some humility. Help them get their priorities straight.

**Making light of a guest's complaint** How a restaurant handles complaints says more about its service orientation than almost anything else. Giving guests what they want is important to your success. Take all guest complaints seriously. Service staff who do not treat every complaint as a significant opportunity to assure guest satisfaction will discourage the very feedback essential to their success.

**Refusing to take payment to the cashier** This attitude reflects an organization (or an individual) where guest service is an imposition.

The fault most likely lies with the attitude of management. Precede any staff discipline actions with serious self-examination.

**No sense of humor**   There are many unexpected events in the restaurant business and a sense of humor is often the lubricant that makes an evening flow smoothly. Mike Hurst, owner of Fort Lauderdale's 15th Street Fisheries, always asks job applicants, "What's the funniest thing that's ever happened to you?" He asks the question with a straight face and watches their reaction. Their answers are not important. He wants to see a laugh and an animated response. He figures that people who can laugh at themselves are the "sparklers" he wants to hire.

**Protecting the house**   This usually happens when the guest has a legitimate complaint that goes against a house policy. The sales person ignores the well-being of the guest and defends the policy. This problem can only arise when there is more pressure to follow the rules than to please the guests. Though you have every right to set these priorities, you must also pay the price such arrogance brings. Not only will it cost you guests, but you are likely to lose any service-oriented staff members as well.

**Expecting guests to know the restaurant's procedures**   It is easy to get irritated when a guest asks about something that, to you, is obvious. We assume that what is basic knowledge to us must be equally evident to everyone. The safest attitude is to treat every guest like a first-timer and take delight in telling them details they didn't know about your restaurant.

**Giving a disgusted look following an exchange with a guest**   This is an insult to the guests that everyone in the dining room can see. Remember that guests *always* have good (to them) reasons for their comments and questions. Mocking them only shows your ignorance and insensitivity.

**Calling guests by their first names**   Using a guests' first names can sometimes be a plus, provided you know them personally and they have asked you to use their first names. However, the practice is offensive when there is no prior personal relationship and the staff member gets the guest's first name from a credit card. For example, my first name is William. My friends call me Bill. People who address me as William plainly do not know me. Instead of coming across as friendly, they impress me as arrogant. When you get a guest's name from a credit card, use only their last name and be safe.

**Presuming the tip**   Always bring the change back to the table. Never assume a tip. A tip is a voluntary transaction between the guest and the service staff. If you take away the voluntary aspect, you will lose the tip and lose the guest as well. Servers who engage in this practice may be insecure about their abilities and afraid they won't get a tip any other way.

**Refusing a request to change tables**  Is this another control issue coming to the surface? If guest gratification is truly Job 1 in the restaurant, this sort of problem is unlikely to surface. If it does come up, you know where to point the finger first.

**Using a condescending tone of voice**  Elderly guests, the handicapped, and minorities are particularly sensitive to condescending voice tone. Just because someone is different does not mean they are stupid or undeserving of excellent service. These groups often receive poor treatment. They will appreciate your responsiveness and respect.

**Different treatment for different people**  Beware of prejudice in all its forms. Do not draw conclusions just because a guest is young, arrived with a bus tour, is not wearing their best clothes, or has a coupon. There are no second-class guests in a legendary restaurant . . . and becoming a legend is a worthy goal to strive toward.

**Rushing guests off the table or out of the restaurant**  Repeat as necessary: "This restaurant exists for the enjoyment and pleasure of our guests, not the convenience of the staff or owners." If you hurry a party just so you can get an additional seating at the table, you may never see them again. What's more, their negative word-of-mouth will offset the good comments of five other parties. The implications of the math are not difficult to grasp.

# System Slipups

Many problems point to breakdowns in the restaurant's systems. The only effective way to solve these problems is to identify the weaknesses in the system and then fix the system. If you try to solve these problems by fixing *people,* you will never receive another suggestion from anyone on your staff. No one will point out a problem if they think they will be blamed for it.

**Wet plates or trays**  If plates or trays are not air drying, it may mean your dish machine's final rinse is not up to temperature. If there is no temperature problem, the dish crew may be stacking the pieces too quickly after they come out of the machine. The reason could be as simple as training or as involved as lack of space in the dishroom. Whatever the cause, wet serviceware gets the meal off to a bad start for your guests.

**Running out of a menu item**  You need effective forecasting and inventory control to reduce the problem of outages. On the other hand, never being out of stock may signal excessive inventory levels. The solution is attention to inventory management . . . and the right choice of words. When you *run* out of something, guests think you don't know how to run your business. If you *sell* out of something, guests think you have highly desirable items. If you cannot provide what the guest orders, always suggest alternative choices.

**Running out of china, silver, or glassware** You can't talk your way around this situation! Small inventories can be false economy. The immediate problem is inconvenience to the guest and the potential loss of future business. When you finally do buy the additional stock, if it is still in stock, it probably will cost more. Purchase enough china, glassware, and silver so that you can make it through the rush without having to wash dishes. You won't have to worry about running out and you can save valuable labor hours as well. With enough dishes, a few bus tubs, and some racks to hold them, you can accumulate dirty dishes during the meal period and not have to operate the dish machine at all. Use your entire kitchen staff on the line during the rush to get the meals out quickly. When the pace slows down, assign several people to the dish room and you can clean up all the dirty dishes in about half an hour!

**Orders that arrive incomplete** You have to get it right the first time or you will throw off the timing of the entire meal. In fast-paced operations, an expediter can be invaluable in assembling and checking orders. Incomplete orders cost you points with your guests and create additional work for your service staff.

**Sitting at the table without being acknowledged** From the guest's perspective, the immediate availability of the server is usually not critical. Guests just feel more comfortable when they know the server is aware they are waiting. Even if you are busy, at least let the guests know you have noted their presence. Stop at the table within 1 minute of the guests' arrival, focus your attention, and let them know you will be right back. Talking to the table while on the move without stopping will only irritate the guests. Be sure your system makes time for this important first step of good service.

**Not providing service in the order of arrival** People become territorial. They expect that if they arrived first, they should be served before parties arriving or seated after them. It is not an unreasonable expectation. Your greeter can help smooth out potential point loss by rotating parties between stations. This assures that a server does not get two or three new parties simultaneously. If that is not possible, work out a means of communication so the service staff is clear on which parties arrived first.

**Not getting coffee until after dessert arrives** Many desserts are hardly edible without coffee. Delivering coffee before dessert maintains the flow of service between clearing the main course and serving the desserts. It also assures your guests will gain the most enjoyment from the efforts of your pastry chef. Since it takes longer to drink a cup of hot coffee than to eat most desserts, you also may turn the table a little sooner.

**Wrong pacing—meal service too fast or too slow**  Appropriate pacing varies with the type of restaurant and the meal period. In quick service operations, speed is always the most important factor. In table service, rapid service is usually more important at breakfast and lunch than in the evening. A possible exception is guests who are enjoying a pretheater meal. They will be watching the clock closely. The more you know about the motives of your guests, the easier it will be to adjust the pace of service to be responsive. The higher the check average, the more time your guests expect to spend at the table.

**Not serving all guests at the table simultaneously**  Hot food must be hot. If you do not serve all guests at the table at once, some guests will sit with their food cooling while they wait for you to serve their companions. It is a socially uncomfortable experience that will not enhance your guests' enjoyment of their meals or of your restaurant.

**Not providing a place for meal debris**  Give some thought to what guests are going to need to get through the meal comfortably and be sure they have it. For example, where are they going to put clam shells, bones, cracker wrappers, and so on? Always have a spare plate or bowl for bones and shells. To solve the problem of cracker wrapper clutter, just place the full cracker basket inside an empty one. When bringing the crackers to the table, separate the two baskets. You will have created a receptacle for the trash . . . and created a pleasant point of difference from your competition.

**Not being able to get through breakfast or lunch in 25 minutes**  If your operating system cannot regularly meet this timing, feature two or three items you can prepare quickly, perhaps with a guarantee of timely service. Remember that the critical timing is from the time your guests arrive until the time they are out the door. This is different from the length of time it takes to deliver their orders.

**Food sitting visibly in the pickup window or on a tray stand**  This has to be a frustrating experience for restaurant guests. I have even seen guests get up and serve the plates themselves! If your system cannot move hot food while it is still hot, consider a runner system. Under this structure, sales people do not leave the dining room. The next available runner delivers hot food to the table when it is ready. If the sales person is busy, the runner can serve the entrées following the seat number codings on the guest check.

**Having to wait for coffee to brew**   Everyone appreciates a fresh cup of coffee, but nobody likes to wait for it. Particularly in fast-paced restaurants, you may want to assign someone to just brew coffee. The Regas Restaurant is the oldest and most prestigious restaurant in Knoxville, Tennessee. They brew coffee in small batches throughout the day and have earned a reputation for the best coffee in Knoxville. They have a fulltime staff member who does nothing but grind and brew their coffee. The coffee person is an important point of difference for the Regas.

**Necessary condiments that don't arrive before the food**
Don't make guests wait for a condiment while their food gets cold. An effective operations system always allows the necessary accompaniments to arrive at the table before the entrée is served. This assures that hot food will not sit on the table while you fumble around the service stand looking for the steak sauce!

**Guests having to get their own coffee**   Americans expect prompt coffee refills. When their frustration reaches the point where they get up and get it themselves, you are losing points rapidly. Either add enough bussers to keep up with demand or consider insulated coffee carafes that you can leave on the table.

**Endless waits in the drive-up line**   When fast food isn't fast, your point total suffers drastically. Many franchise operators have adopted cordless headsets to speed communication between the guest, the order-taker, and the production line. The idea is helping. If slow service is a problem, involve your staff in identifying the lapses in the system. Give them the opportunity to suggest ways to improve your accuracy and speed.

**Serving food ordered by another table**   Getting the orders confused is embarrassing for everyone. The guest doesn't know whether to eat the food or not. The service staff shows their ineptitude. The guest who originally made the order doesn't get served. An additional problem is what to do when you realize the mistake. You can't pick food up off one table and serve it to another.

The proper solution, if there is one, is going to be costly. I suggest you first acknowledge the mistake to both parties and apologize for the error. Leave the item as a complimentary gift to the incorrect party. Bring a complimentary replacement to the person whose order you misdirected. If you try to talk your way out of the error or avoid responsibility for correcting the error, you will only irritate both parties. The cost of a few entrées is far less than the cost of losing two groups of potential regulars.

**Mispacked take-out orders**   This is the number one reason for dissatisfaction among quick service patrons. Statistics suggest that fast feeders improperly assemble one out of three orders. This is particularly irritating at the drive-up window, since the guests won't discover the error until they are away from the property.

**Bringing food the guest did not order**   People love surprises. Bringing them something special at no cost is a good way to gain points. However, bringing them something by mistake only shows how haphazard the restaurant's systems are.

# Horrible Habits

A problem with hiring "experienced" servers is that you don't know the content of that experience. Many experienced staff have only succeeded in learning someone else's bad habits. Fortunately, you can overcome bad habits through diligent coaching, provided you know what to watch for.

**Lack of eye contact**   One of my favorite pastimes, especially in coffee shops, is to see if the waitress can make it through the entire meal without ever looking me in the eye. It is discouraging to see how often it happens. Coach your staff in the importance of smiling eye contact. The idea is simply to start the relationship with all new guests by looking them directly in the eye and giving them a big smile. Nothing warms the heart like smiling eye contact. When it doesn't happen, guests think you have something to hide. They trust you less and are more critical of the restaurant.

**Different service for groups perceived as low tippers**   Age or genetics do not decide tipping tendencies. People will tip when they feel they have received service worth the gesture. Your job is to be sure that every guest in the restaurant has a delightful experience. Often, single diners will appreciate your caring and be particularly generous. Many teenagers work in restaurants and understand what it is like to work for tips. They can be surprisingly liberal in their tipping if you treat them well. Seniors *may* not have as much money as other diners, but they are more likely to develop a dining habit than most other groups. If you treat them well, they will give you most of their business. Older diners grew up when service standards were higher than they are today. They appreciate good service and will reward your respectful efforts with their regular patronage.

**Picking up the menus too quickly**   If you have the story of your restaurant on the menu, give the guest a chance to read it. A personal history provides information that can help make your operation unique in the market. It offers an excellent opportunity to tell guests of policies and priorities that are difficult to convey any other way. Invariably, just as the guest is getting interested in this dissertation, the server snatches the menu away and leaves the guest empty-handed! If the guests are reading the menus, leave them. Single diners will appreciate having something to read. The more familiar guests are with your menu, the more reasons they have to return.

**Talking to the order pad**   Coach your staff to look at the guests, not their pads, when taking the order! The habit is irritating because it makes your guests feel that understanding what they want is less important than the process of writing it down. The lack of personal focus works against the goal of guest gratification.

**Pointing at each guest with the pen**   Your guests are not at the table to perform for you. Unfortunately, this is the impression you give when you point at each guest with your pen when asking for their orders. It makes the dining experience less personal and irritates your guests. Unlike verbal mistakes, pointing with the pencil is an error you can detect from across the dining room. This also makes it easy for management to discover. Just being aware that this unconscious habit can be irritating is an important first step toward breaking it.

**Repeating each item as the guest orders**   This is particularly annoying when you repeat the order as a question. It sounds like this: The guest says, "I'd like the club sandwich, please." Server: "Club sandwich?" Guest: ". . . with a side of french fries." Server: "French fries?" Can you hear how silly that sounds? You sound like a broken record and it is very distracting for your guests. If you are unsure what the guest said, repeat the order back just before you leave the table.

**Naming each item as you serve**   No comment is necessary when you serve an item. If you feel you must say something, comment on the item or the preparation. Saying "This salmon came in fresh this morning and we grew the dill for the sauce in our own garden" will elevate a guest's mood. Just saying "salmon with dill sauce" gains you nothing.

**Addressing a woman as "the lady"**   People are people, not objects. Watch your words. Always talk to each guest individually and personally, regardless of their sex or age. Asking the male companion what the woman wants to eat will probably insult her.

**Loosening the caps on condiment bottles**   I'm sure this practice seems like a courtesy to those who do it. The problem comes when a guest instinctively gives the bottle a shake before using it. You do not pick up points when Worcestershire splatters all over your dining room and your guests!

**Thumbs on the plate during service**   Serious lapses occur when you are not paying attention. A need for speed never justifies careless service. Many guests will not say anything about a thumb on the plate. This does not mean they do not notice the error. Rather than risk a confrontation, they will talk about it to their friends. If the rest of the meal experience was marginal, a misplaced thumb could be the reason they start dining elsewhere. Hold serviceware with the side of the thumb, not the tip.

**Stacking or scraping dishes in front of the guests**    Once you remove a plate from the table, whatever you scrape off it is just garbage. You wouldn't bring garbage to the table at the beginning of the meal; don't do it at the end. Handle your garbage away from the table and avoid creating a negative memory for your patrons.

**Harsh, grating, or loud voices**    Some diner concepts are doing very well with an insulting, abrasive manner of service. Unless this is your operating style, you will lose points with your guests if the sales person's voice is not pleasant and well modulated. The more relaxed the pace of the restaurant, the more refined the appropriate style of speech.

**Approaching a table with another table's dirty dishes in hand**    This is like shoving garbage in your guests' faces. How receptive do you think they will be to your skillful dessert dissertation if they are looking at the remains of someone else's lunch while you are talking? Never address a table unless your hands are clear and you are entirely focused on the guests.

**Using jargon when addressing guests**    Each restaurant has its own verbal shorthand. It means something to you but sounds like another language to your guests. You wouldn't address your guests in German if you knew they couldn't understand it. Why would speaking in jargon be any different? For example, don't tell them you have a 4-top by the window, just say you have a wonderful table with a view. If you say their chick sand is almost ready, they may think you are talking about women on the beach instead of a broiled chicken breast sandwich! You get the point. Using these phrases can be an unconscious habit until you are aware of what you are saying.

**Entering the guests' conversation without invitation**    If your guests want you for a buddy, they will invite you over after work! If you overhear one person at the table say the Lakers won 110-102 and you know the score is wrong, resist the urge to correct them. If they want your opinion on something, they will ask for it. By the way, knowing the game results can be an important plus if you have a sports-oriented clientele. Just don't offer your guests information they have not requested.

**Interrupting or asking questions while the guest's mouth is full**    I hope it is unnecessary to point out how rude this behavior is or how uncomfortable it makes your guests feel. If the restaurant is on fire, you have a duty to interrupt them. Otherwise, there is nothing you have to say that is so important that it is worth irritating your patrons. When you approach the table, don't say a word. Stand there quietly until your guests finish what they are doing and they look at you. Then say what you need to say. It is far more respectful and enhances their dining experience.

**Leaning on or over the table**   This habit may be an invasion of privacy. You can reach over to pick up a menu and give it to the guest, provided you do not stay draped over the table. Leaning on the table is always a poor practice. By not violating their airspace, you show your guests more respect.

**Handling silverware by the eating surfaces**   This is a terrible habit that all your guests will notice. Failure to handle silverware properly puts your guests in fear of your sanitation practices. Whether there is a basis for their concerns or not, they may just decide not to take a chance and take their business elsewhere. Coach your staff thoroughly on the importance of handling silverware only by the handles.

**Holding glasses by the bowl or rim**   The same rules of proper handling apply to glassware. Never let your crew handle a glass by the bowl or rim. It not only leaves fingerprints but also is like sticking your fingers in the guest's mouth! Many diners will send back glasses if you handle them this way. You don't need the aggravation . . . and neither do your guests. Train your staff to handle glassware only by the stem or the lower third.

**Sweeping crumbs onto the floor**   If you have only told your staff to clear the table, this is what you may get. They need to understand that they have a responsibility for maintaining the ambiance of the dining room. Crumbs on the floor will be a distraction to your guests for the rest of the evening and will lower their opinion of your restaurant. Eventually you must pick up the crumbs anyway. Marvin's Law of Creative Laziness says to never do any more work than necessary to accomplish what you want. Why clean up the crumbs twice? If crumbs *do* get on the floor, consider a cordless "dust buster" for a quick cleanup.

**Placing a tray on the table**   If the tray is large, put it on a tray stand. Hold a cocktail tray in your hand. Remember that the table is the guests' private domain. You have permission to enter it with food and beverage, but they will resent your claiming a portion of their space by placing a tray on the table. If the table is empty, it is still poor practice to place a tray down. Other guests may not feel the bottom of a tray is particularly clean and that placing it on the table dirties the table. Use a tray stand and avoid the problem.

**Not facing the bills when giving change**   This simply means that all bills are face up, with the picture right side up and in order by denomination. It is part of treating money with respect. A jumbled pile of currency makes guests feel that you are treating their money casually. Bear in mind that the change is their money unless they decide to make some of it a tip. Proper handling of currency shows your professionalism and makes people more comfortable about entrusting you with their cash.

**Language that is too formal or too casual**   I have discussed the value of consistency in the execution of a restaurant concept. Language is another element of that consistency. The language expectations are different in a Burger King than they are at Le Cirque. The more formal the restaurant, the more formal the language used needs to be. Inconsistencies will make guests feel that something is wrong, though they may not know why they feel that way.

**Not serving everything at the table from a tray**   At home, people carry plates and glasses to the table in their hands. If we want to make dining out a more pleasant experience than dining at home (and I hope we do), this is a good place to start. The way it looks to your guests, trays are clean and professional whereas hand-carrying is dirty and amateurish.

**Placing fingers inside glasses, cups, or bowls**   I have discussed the dangers of fingers on the plates when serving the table. Proper handling of cups, glasses, and bowls is even more critical. Mishandling these items places the fingers on a surface guests may put in their mouths. Proper handling is essential when setting the table and it is also important when clearing a table. Mishandling soiled cups, glasses, and bowls is also like putting your fingers in someone's mouth! You can remove glasses faster when you put your fingers inside them. The question is what do you do after that? Guests do not know if you washed your hands before you pick up the clean serviceware. How realistic is it to think you will wash your hands in the middle of the normal clear and reset cycle? Your guests are far more sensitive to poor sanitation practices than you may realize.

**Placing a bus tub on a chair**   The situation is similar to the example of the tray on the table. Guests may not think bus tubs full of soiled dishes and food scraps are clean. They are probably right. Your other dining room guests may think that placing a bus tub on the chair makes the chair dirty. They are probably right, too. The patrons in the dining room start to wonder about the chair *they* are sitting in. To avoid lowering your diners' security level, always place bus tubs on a cart or a tray stand.

**Taking something off one table and immediately placing it on another**   If a table wants ketchup, go to the service stand and get it. Resist the urge to take the bottle from the table next to them. It may appear more responsive but your guests do not see it that way. The guests from whom you take the ketchup will feel diminished because you have taken something away from them. The table you give it to will feel short-changed. For whatever quirk of human nature, guests think items coming from the service stand are clean, safe, and acceptable. They view items taken from another table with suspicion and are uneasy when it happens. Perhaps it is because they know you and they don't have the same level of trust with the stranger in the next booth.

**Not bringing enough small bills and change for the tip** Although it is poor form to assume a tip, it is reasonable to be prepared for one. If a guest chooses to leave a tip, they will appreciate having the proper change to do it. It is annoying to have to ask for quarters or change for a $20 bill. It slows down the guest and requires an extra trip to the table for the service staff. When bringing change to a guest, consider what the guest is likely to need for a tip and structure the change that way.

***Telling* the guests in what order their meal selections will be taken** It is not the servers place to dictate how the order will be taken, particularly if the guests have other wishes. When serving large parties, it is often helpful to ask permission to start at one end of the table and take the orders in sequence. The important point is to ask permission first and be open to alternatives. Dictating to your guests will only build resentment that can interfere with their enjoyment of your restaurant.

**Asking men for their orders before asking women** Proper etiquette is to handle service in the following order: children first (since they won't wait), women, elders, then gentlemen. If the guests at the table want to give you their orders in a different sequence, do not argue about it. Serve the entrées in the order suggested if you can. Some guests may consider it rude or insulting if you alter this sequence.

**Fussing over a single diner** Single diners are people like anyone else—they just happen to be dining by themselves at the moment. Singles usually appreciate a little more personal attention from the service staff. However, making a fuss only embarrasses your unaccompanied guests. Be sensitive to their signals. Give solo diners the care and respect they deserve and you can gain a loyal regular guest.

**Asking a man for the woman's order** Perhaps you could get away with this 15 years ago. Today you stand a good chance of offending your female diners. More than ever, you must treat all guests as equals, regardless of age, sex, or physical condition. Anything less will create more problems than you are ready to handle.

# Frustrating Focus

Focus is another name for presence. Presence is simply the absence of distractions. When you have high presence, your guests feel well served.

When you are distracted, when your mind is on something else, your guests become annoyed. It is as simple as that.

Have you had a conversation with someone who was doing something else while you were talking to them? Even though they may have heard everything you were saying, how did their lack of focus make you feel? If you are like most people, you would have found the experience irritating.

It is no different in the restaurant. If the service staff is thinking about something else while interacting with guests, the guests will feel irritated. Your diners may not understand why, but they will experience that the service was poor and will not be in a hurry to return. When you clutter your staff's minds with a long list of things to remember, no matter how well-intentioned the list, you sow the seeds of your own destruction because when service people are thinking about your pithy points, they are not focused on the guests. With your staff in this distracted state, good service is impossible, even if your crew followed your list to the letter. On the other hand, when your service staff is in a state of mind free from distraction, your guests will feel well served in spite of the circumstances. When a staff member has a high presence, long lists on how to provide good service are irrelevant. The implications and applications of these notions are discussed in Robert Kausen's breakthrough book, *Customer Satisfaction Guaranteed*.

Here are some variations on this theme to help you better understand the point I am making. The same distracted state of mind is behind all of these problems.

**Not having total focus when at the table**  When your mind is somewhere else, it is impossible to give good service. Distraction in the server creates irritation in the guest. It is the feeling of glib insincerity you get when someone is mouthing words and you know something else. It is even more annoying when you know that what they are thinking about has nothing to do with serving you. When you are at the table talking with guests, there is nothing you can do about bringing coffee to Table 17, emptying the bus tub, or making an appointment with the dentist. Do not allow these thoughts to be distractions.

**The feeling of being "processed"**  You create this feeling when you do all the mechanical steps correctly but fail to connect with your guests on a human level. Coach your staff about the results you want to achieve and give them as much latitude as possible to figure out how they want to do it.

For example, I told the staff in my San Francisco restaurant that I wanted to be sure our guests enjoyed themselves. One night I was walking through the dining room when I saw one of my waiters sit at the table to take the order. I almost fainted . . . and the guests loved it! It was just Sam's style. He knew when it would work (and when it wouldn't) and he used good judgment. He was one of my most productive and popular waiters.

I would never suggest that you tell your service staff to sit with the guests, but it worked for Sam. He did what I asked him to do—his guests had a wonderful time. Who knows what your crew could come up with if you gave them the chance?

**Not really listening when spoken to**   Talking to someone who is not listening will create rage in even the most reasonable person. Anytime you are talking with guests, drop all other thoughts from your mind. Hear what they are saying, but pay particular attention to how they are saying it. Be aware of their tone of voice—the message is always in the tone.

**Being too hurried to be attentive**   The quality, not the duration, of the contact creates guest satisfaction. A good example of what I mean is when a small child is pulling on your trousers wanting attention. If you try to push the child away or say you are too busy, they won't leave you alone but keep begging for attention. On the other hand, if you stop what you are doing, clear your mind and give the child your total concentration, the result is amazing. After about 20 seconds of undivided attention, most children will run off and play happily for hours. Children just want the connection with you. Your guests (and your staff, for that matter) are no different.

**Not establishing rapport with the guests**   Rapport is that warm human feeling of connection. Rapport comes easily when you are in an undistracted state of mind in a business climate that reflects a passion for guest gratification. To help establish rapport with your guests, pause as you approach the table. Drop whatever else is on your mind, focus on the table and wait until they look up at you. When they make eye contact, smile. Let yourself be touched by the opportunity to "make their day." Say what you have to say, find out what you need to know, smile, and go on your way. This takes no longer than the scattered approach you see every day. The results, however, are dramatically different. Operating in this manner, you keep perspective and control of your station. You hardly notice events that others would call emergencies. You can easily handle your job in a relaxed and professional manner.

**Not informing the guests of service delays**   Focus makes you more naturally empathetic. As such, you are more likely to be sensitive to your guests' experience. You are more likely to want your guests to know of any delays in preparation or service because you know it matters to them. The details that are important to your guests become important to you.

**Appearing stressed or out of control**   Lack of focus causes the events of your life to look overwhelming. As we discussed earlier, feeling stressed or out-of-control is just a symptom of a busy mind. When you learn to drop distractions, you automatically start to take things more in stride.

There are no skills to learn. Events will just look different to you. You will instinctively know what to do. The first step toward dropping distraction is simply to become aware of your busy mind. When you find your mind cluttered with thoughts or you feel yourself getting stressed, recognize what is happening. Relax, take a deep breath, and get on with your day. If you do not take your thoughts too seriously, you will be on your way to greater control of your life.

**Being insensitive to the needs of your guests**     Every guest has special needs. Some are more obvious than others. Groups such as the handicapped or the elderly may need special treatment. Teenagers and families have their own problems and priorities. Business guests need a different style of service than romantic couples. Groups that are celebrating a special occasion want a festive experience. There are so many possibilities that you may feel overwhelmed. Relax. If you are undistracted and empathetic, you will instinctively do what works. All it takes is a focus on pleasing your guests and a clear mind.

**Not bringing something the guest requests**     Poor memory is a symptom of lack of focus. When your thinking is scattered, you try to remember everything at once and end up forgetting it all. Give your mind a break. Realize that efficiency comes from lack of distraction, not from increased activity. If your goal is to assure your guests have an enjoyable experience, keep a clear mind. With a clear mind, you are less likely to get behind. If you seldom get behind, it is easy to handle requests as they come up.

**Providing inconsistent service**     You may have accepted the idea that there are "good days" and there are "bad days." Did you ever wonder why? The good days happen when the staff has nothing much on their minds except their guests. The bad days are when the staff is so distracted they don't connect with anyone. The organization always reflects the state of mind of the person in charge. If your staff is losing it, you know where to look first.

**Doing work at the table that doesn't involve the guest**
Never do anything at the table that does not involve the guests. If you need to add up a check, do it in the service stand, not on the table. Do you expect your guests to stop their conversation and just watch quietly while you do something that doesn't include them? Your inconsiderate behavior will only cause them to think less of the meal, the service, and the restaurant. To assure that your guests feel served, avoid a distracted mind when you are at the table.

# Poor Policies

Many service problems arise from well-intentioned but misguided management policies. Your staff is in an awkward position when they have to defend policies that stand in the way of guest gratification. If they displease you, they could lose their jobs. If they displease their guests, they go against all their instincts. The only way out of this dilemma is to make pleasing the guest the most important job in the restaurant. Give your staff the authority to do what they need to do to assure that your guests have a memorable dining experience. Making sure your guests enjoy themselves *is* the most important job in the restaurant.

### Failure to resolve a complaint promptly (in favor of the guest!)

If you are serious about guest gratification, there is no negotiation when if comes to a guest complaint. The only approach that will work is to apologize for the situation and fix it immediately. Do not ask the guest what they want you to do—it puts the guest on the spot and makes them uncomfortable. When you understand the nature and source of the problem, propose a generous solution that will make the guest happy. Remember that you are not just solving a problem, you are making an investment in securing a regular patron.

### Failure to honor menu prices

If you give a guest a menu, honor whatever it says. Some restaurants charge less for an item at lunch than they do at dinner. If this is the case and you give a guest a lunch menu in the evening by mistake, honor the prices. You can never win an argument with a guest.

### Stacking plates up the arm to carry them to the table

Many diner-style concepts and coffee shops use this operating style. The look may be traditional, but when the bottom of a plate sits on top of a guest's food, the novelty quickly disappears. If you are going to use this approach, coach your service staff that sanitation considerations are as important as how many plates they can carry in one trip. It is preferable to make two trips rather than alienate guests because they feel you have soiled their food.

### Not bringing the full one before taking the empty one away

This is such a simple touch and it is so often overlooked. If you take the empty roll basket away and come back with the full one, your guests feel deprived for a period. If you reverse the order, you do the same amount of work but show far more sensitivity to the guests. This awareness creates another point of difference from your competition.

### Failure to accommodate special requests

In his book *It's Not My Department*, author Peter Glen offers a simple approach to guest gratification. He suggests you find out what people want, how they want it . . . and then give it to them just that way! The idea is not complicated. People with special requests will give their business to those restaurants who can meet their needs.

**Presenting untotalled guest checks**   I have been in restaurants where the cashier totals the check and adds the tax. I'm sure there was a good intention behind this policy, but it was probably to make it easier for the server, not the guest. From the guest's point of view, they still do not know how much the meal is going to cost when they head to the cashier. Without knowing the total, the guest cannot calculate a tip. This means the diner must either guess how much to leave, return to the table or just stiff the server. None of these alternatives is particularly convenient or comfortable.

**Confusing service format**   A team service format can be effective, provided you explain it to your guests at the beginning of the meal. Without an idea of what is happening, having several service staff at the table can confuse your guests. In a team service restaurant recently, I had three staff members ask me the same question. I gave the same answer to all three and none of them filled my request! I didn't know whom to be upset with. If you are going to use a team service format, be sure your guests understand what you are doing and how it works. Give them one person to go to if there are problems.

**No fresh fork for entrée or dessert**   You don't set the table with dirty utensils. Why would you hand a dirty fork back to your guest during the meal and ask them to reuse it? The easiest approach is to be sure there are enough forks in the place setting. You may prefer the look of presenting the fork with the dessert. In any event, don't ask the guest to reuse a soiled utensil. Some guests will ask for a fresh fork; some will just remember it wasn't a memorable meal and go elsewhere.

**Pouring coffee from glass pots in an upscale restaurant**
In coffee shops and casually themed restaurants, guests expect you to pour coffee from the glass pot. When the check average climbs, though, a more formal presentation is appropriate. Make your coffee service a point of difference and you can give your guests a reason to think of you every time they dine somewhere else.

**Failure to make a big fuss for special occasions**   If you are going to celebrate a birthday or anniversary, then *celebrate* it! Have candles or sparklers for a cake, preferably a complimentary cake. Make up a special song instead of falling back on the stale standards. Get your staff involved. Make the celebration tasteful and appropriate to the mood of your dining room, but make it a celebration!

**Refusing to heat baby food or a baby's bottle**   If guest service is your most important job, then service your guests. If your kitchen has a microwave oven, heating baby food or formula is a simple task. There is no reason to treat a parent's request for this service as an imposition. If there are very young children at the table, offer the service to the parents before they have to ask. They will recognize and appreciate your caring.

**Three-foot peppermills**   Perhaps oversized peppermills were unique in the 1960s and 1970s, but they are trite today. The idea of offering fresh ground pepper is still a nice touch, just think about your presentation. How about small salt and pepper mills on the tables? If your service staff brings the peppermill, perhaps it might contain white pepper. Take another look at this practice and see how you can give it a fresh twist (no pun intended!).

**"Do-it-yourself" doggie bags**   If you pack your guests' leftovers for them to take home, do it with the same care and attention you give everything else in the restaurant. I have seen servers simply leave a container or bag on the table and expect the guests to do it themselves. This a good example of a practice developed for the convenience of the staff instead of the convenience of the guest. Stamp out this short-sightedness before it puts you out of business. Don't ask your guests to handle their leftovers.

**Not advising the guest of a service charge policy**   The debate over service charges versus tipping continues to swirl around the industry and can create some confusion for diners. If you impose a service charge instead of voluntary tipping, courtesy requires you to note this on your menu and on your guest check. I also recommend you have your service staff verbally inform your guests of the policy. If guests feel they were not properly notified, they may suspect a ploy to gain a double tip. It may work once, but when your guests find out what happened (and they will), they will feel cheated. You can't cheat people and expect to keep them as a patrons.

**Slow morning coffee service**   For most Americans, it takes a cup of coffee or tea to start their day off right. If guests get the coffee promptly, they will wait for the rest of the meal service more patiently. How you address this need will depend on your operating style. If your sales staff cannot keep up with it, perhaps the bussers could fill coffee cups. You might place insulated carafes on the table to take the pressure off. Whatever you do, find a way to get a hot cup of coffee (or tea) to your breakfast guests right away. You will have happier guests.

**Anyone other than the guest adding a tip to a credit card slip**   A brewpub in Park City, Utah, had the nerve to do this to me . . . once. They will never get a second chance. If a guest signs the credit card receipt, does not indicate a tip, and leaves the slip untotaled, that's the luck of the draw. If you add a tip without permission, you have lost that guest forever. Even if the cardholder intended to leave a tip and just forgot to do so, they will not forgive your arrogance. If you feel it was an honest oversight, have the house pay the tip. It will cost you far less than alienating a potential regular guest.

# Coaching Concerns

Although all the points in this chapter are legitimately the responsibility of management and therefore coaching concerns, some are more obvious than others. As a manager, your job could easily take the form of finding and correcting faults. If you approach your job like a coach, the job becomes one of finding and developing the strengths of your staff. The shift is subtle but it will make all the difference in helping your crew recognize and correct these annoyances.

**Not removing extra place settings**   Don't have anything on the table that the guest does not need. This includes extra place settings. If you don't remove extra settings, your guests also may wonder what is going to happen with the place setting after they leave. Will it just stay there for the next diner? If that worry enters their mind, they may start to wonder about *their* silverware.

**Inability to answer basic menu questions**   Your guests want to know about your food and you must be able to tell them. Thoroughly train sales staff so they can knowledgeably discuss recipe ingredients and preparation methods. If they know some interesting fact about the dish, even better. This information has the most impact when it comes from personal experience, not memorization. This means your service staff has actually *tasted* everything on the menu and has watched your cooks prepare it. Include greeters, cocktail staff, and bussers in the classes. You never know who the guest will ask. The money you invest in training meals for your staff will pay regular dividends.

**"Canned" communications**   Scripted communication is worse than no communication at all. Guest enjoyment is created by the human dimension in service, not the mechanical content. The message is always in the tone of voice and the warm human connection with the guest. It is appropriate to make sure you communicate certain points to the guest at various times during the meal. It is more effective to specify the desired *ends* and leave the *means* to the discretion of the service staff. This allows them to be themselves and respond more appropriately to what the guests want. Anything less is about as satisfying as making love through an interpreter!

**Clattering dishes**   Professional restaurant staff does not call attention to themselves or distract the guests' dining experience. Clattering dishes are usually a sign of an eager busser who does not understand that their behavior forms a part of the guest's dining experience. Reset tables as quickly as possible but not at the expense of diner enjoyment. Show your bussers what to do and help them understand why the way they do it makes a difference.

**Memorized entrée descriptions** Guests can tell when you are speaking from experience and when you are repeating something you learned. When you speak from certainty, your sincerity and personality come through. Your tone and bearing deliver an entirely different message than an intellectual dissertation. The difference is difficult to describe but your guests will instantly recognize it.

**Being out of something and not suggesting an appropriate alternative** When you have sold out of an item, the situation is already awkward. You only make it worse if you do not suggest alternatives. How are guests supposed to know what else they can order? By not making a suggestion, you place them in an uncomfortable position.

**Failure to make suggestions or recommendations** Your mission is to help your guests have a good time. Part of that task is informing them about the unique and exciting choices your restaurant offers. If you don't tell them, how are they going to know? Even the most well-written menu is a poor substitute for an enthusiastic and knowledgeable suggestion. Always offer two alternatives when making a recommendation to avoid appearing like you are pushing something. If guests want something other than what you suggest, they will ask about it. The important point is to be sure they are comfortable during the process.

**Pushy sales techniques** Skillful salesmanship can help your guests have a more enjoyable evening. Insensitive, memorized sales pitches will make you sound like a used car huckster and alienate your diners. The goal is to make people eager to buy, not to try to sell them something. The less distracted you are while at the table, the more personal and effective your check-building efforts will be.

**Not giving prices when presenting oral specials** Just because you present the specials orally does not mean the price information is not important to the guest. If you find it awkward to mention prices, complete the presentation by handing the guests small menus with the specials written out and the prices included. This also will help them remember what you said when making their dinner choices.

**Not knowing what brands are carried at the bar** How often can you say "I don't know" before you feel stupid? Basic service staff training must include a thorough knowledge of the bar operation. This includes the brands you carry and the ingredients of your specialty drinks. If you have signature drinks (and I recommend you do), be sure your staff has tasted them and can describe them in an appetizing and accurate way.

**Placing a cocktail napkin or plate with the logo askew or upside down**   Always place an item with the restaurant's logo so the logo faces the guest. Haphazard placement only shows your lack of concentration and inattention to detail. Human nature being what it is, your guests will notice a crooked placement. They may *not* notice if you do it properly.

**Not warning about hot plates or beverages**   Refilling the coffee cup is part of good service, but make sure the guest knows that you've done it. If not, you take the chance they will burn their mouth on a cup of coffee suddenly much hotter than expected. It is also a good idea to get permission before refilling the coffee, particularly if the guest uses cream and sugar. It is annoying to alter the balance of the cup when your guests have it adjusted just the way they like it. Hot plates are a different issue because in a great restaurant, hot plates are the rule. If you can hold a plate of hot food without a towel, the plate is not hot enough. Serving hot food hot requires hot plates. Make sure you do it and make sure your guests know you are doing it.

**Serving a bowl without an underliner**   Bowls hold liquids and liquids often spill. The only question is whether the spill is going to go on the underliner or on the table! If it falls on the underliner, nobody notices. If it falls on the table, it affects the guest's enjoyment of the meal and creates a cleaning problem. Marvin's Law of Creative Laziness says to never do any more work than necessary to accomplish your goal. Give everyone a break and make underliners standard practice in your restaurant.

**Dropping plates instead of presenting them**   You show your respect for the work of your kitchen staff by the way you handle their food. Train your staff to present the plates at the table. Place plates in front of the guest with respect, entrées closest to the diner. If there is a logo on the plate, be sure it faces the guest. If you distribute the plates like you are dealing a hand of cards, expect your guests to be less enthusiastic about their meals.

**Not bringing all the serviceware needed for the menu item**
A bowl of soup without a soup spoon is useless. If you forget, the soup will cool while you find the spoon and return to the table. Meanwhile, your guest feels awkward and uncomfortable. They can do nothing but sit there and look at the soup. As with condiments, it is often helpful to bring the necessary serviceware before you serve the menu item. This way you can be sure to serve hot food while it is still hot.

**Serving with the elbow in the guest's face**  When you serve from the left with the right hand or from the right with the left hand, your elbow is in your guest's face. Serving from the left and clearing from the right is still the preferred convention but sometimes it is neither possible nor practical. Booths, for example, require a different approach. In whatever way you choose to serve the table, be consistent in your approach—do it the same way each time. For smoother service, use your left hand when serving from the left and your right hand when serving from the right. This will prevent your imposing on your guests' comfort by putting your elbow in their face.

**Inconsistent service methods**  People are creatures of habit. They are more comfortable when they know what to expect. To create maximum guest comfort, always approach the table from the same position. Always serve and clear from the same sides. Whether that is the classic "serve from the left, clear from the right" or not is less important to smooth service than consistency.

**Not serving children, women, or elders first**  Serve children first. They have not developed social graces and will not wait their turn. Serve women next starting with the oldest. Finally, serve the men, older gentlemen first. The arrangement of the table or the size of the party may dictate a different order of service. Come as close as you can.

**Not warning about potential food hazards**  There may be some legal implications in this point, but it is just common courtesy to advise your guests of potential hazards in your menu items. For example, "boneless" fish could still contain some bones. Raw fish and shellfish could contain bacteria harmful to some people. If there is a potential hazard, you are only being polite when you alert your guests to it.

**Refilling water or coffee after each sip**  This annoyance happens when you have only told bussers to keep the water or coffee full. If they are eager to please, they will do just what you told them and do it aggressively. They must have a sense of what makes a good dining experience for your guests and know how their job fits into it.

**Not moving with the "speed of the room"**  Good service is almost invisible. Guests should only notice what is going on at their table and not be distracted by other movements in the room. If you are moving fast in a slow-paced dining room, you are a distraction. If you are moving slowly in a fast-paced restaurant, you are a distraction. The speed at which you move is different from the speed at which you do your job. You can still be very quick and efficient in a slower-moving dining room. The quality of your movements is just different. The process is like the martial arts master whose power comes from a state of focused relaxation. If you can move with the speed of the room, you can give responsive service and your guests will hardly notice you are there.

**Unsupervised buffets or salad bars**   The major complaint against salad bars is that they are unsanitary. Some of the people you serve are very sensitive to sanitation practices and some are unconscious. Children are legendary violators of salad bar etiquette. They will stick their fingers in the dressing to taste it. They will nibble at something and put it back. They will refill a dirty salad bowl and spread your salads all over the floor. By the way, children come in all ages and sizes. Unless you supervise the salad bar closely, these practices will drive away many of your guests. You also run the risk of passing a foodborne illness to the ones you don't scare off.

To have a successful salad bar, a knowledgeable staff member must constantly attend the table. Display items in small quantities and allow them to run down before changing them. To prevent cross-contamination, do not pour new product on top of old and put out clean serving utensils when you change the containers. Wipe up spills promptly. The attraction of salad bars is their striking presentation and that does not happen accidentally.

**Not checking back within one minute of serving the entrée**   If there is a problem with the entrée or if guests need anything, they won't know that when you serve the item. So, asking if they need anything else at the time of service is rude. After two bites, the guests will know what they think of the food and what they may need to go with it. Give them a minute and then ask if everything is prepared the way they like it.

**Not visually checking each table regularly**   The situation on your station can change quickly. A rapid visual check will provide eye contact with any guest who is trying to get your attention. You also will identify new parties that have been seated since you left. If a guest is trying to get your attention and feels ignored because you do not notice, they will become irritated. Irritated guests do not tip well or become regular patrons.

**Making guests ask for salt, pepper, or basic condiments**   Have salt and pepper on the table before seating the guests because they need these items throughout the meal. You will only look foolish if you must bring them later and it is impolite to make your guests ask for them. During the breakfast period, be sure sugar is on the table. At lunch and dinner, however, you can create a point of difference by bringing the sugar when you serve the coffee.

**Not clearing one course before serving the next**   You cannot serve a meal gracefully if you are trying to set a plate down with one hand and slide another out of the way with the other. Besides, nobody wants to look at soiled plates and fresh food in the same glance. Give yourself a break and do your guests a favor. Always clear the previous course before serving the new one.

**Condiments or utensils from one course left on the table after that course has been cleared**  Once your guests finish a course, remove everything from that course. If they need a particular item again later in the meal service, bring it back at the appropriate time. Keeping the table clear of unnecessary items makes the table less cluttered. A clean table will make the meal service and the restaurant feel cleaner to your guests.

**Removing plates before all guests are finished**  Many people are slow eaters. It is embarrassing to them, and the others at the table, when they are the only ones with a plate in front of them. I'm sure there are well-intentioned motives to remove a guest's plate as soon as they finish. Still, the practice places more pressure on the diners who are still eating. If a guests want their plates removed, they will let you know. Otherwise, it is more considerate to clear the entire table at once.

**Uncleared tables**  The most attractive decor in a dining room is people on chairs, not dirty dishes on tables. The problem is more irritating if the staff is taking a break. The excuse I often hear for a dining room where most the tables remain uncleared is that the rush just ended. If so, why isn't the dining room staff busy clearing tables? When the rush is over, the amateurs take a break. The professionals get the ready for the next rush, *then* take a break.

**Clearing plates without permission**  You are there to enhance the guest's experience, not intrude on it. Common courtesy dictates that you wait until you have the guest's permission before taking anything from them, particularly something as personal as their dinner plate. Be sure not to grab for the plate while you are asking the question. Your eagerness and lack of sensitivity will cost you points.

**Not clearing plates promptly**  Nobody likes to linger over soiled plates once they are through eating. As the last diner finishes, pause a few beats and then quickly clear the table. The pause is important to prevent your guests from feeling rushed.

**Not thanking the guests when they leave**  People go to businesses that appreciate their patronage. Thanking guests as they leave is not just courtesy, it is an investment in their future patronage. When guests feel you are sincerely grateful for their business, they feel better about giving it to you. Gratitude is so uncommon that your guests will remember your appreciation and return for more.

**Vanishing waiters**   Why can you never find a waiter when you want one? Most restaurant guests have had this frustration. The best defense is a good offense. Make a visual check of each table at your station every time you enter the dining room. If you are on break while you still have occupied tables, be sure someone else watches your station closely.

If your shift is over and you must leave while you still have occupied tables, don't just walk out. Explain to your guests that you must leave and tell them who will see to their needs. Be sure to thank them for their patronage. Reassure them that your departure will not affect the quality of their evening. The substitute sales person should present themselves to the guests a few minutes after you leave the table. The problem of disappearing waiters is particularly acute when guests are trying to settle the check and be on their way. If you need an incentive, recall that this is when guests are deciding how much of a tip to leave!

**Not continuing to service the table once you have presented the check**   The meal is not over when you place the check on the table. The meal service has not ended until the guests are in their cars and on their way home. Sometime between when you first present the check and when the guests leave is the time they decide how much of a tip to leave. They may need more coffee. They may decide to order after dinner drinks. Anything could happen and it is your job to be right there to handle it smoothly. If there are guests at the table, you are still onstage.

**Clumsy or improper handling of credit card charges**   When you deal with a guest's credit card, you are handling their money. In effect, your hand is on their wallet. This is a position of trust and requires you to take particular care to avoid making the guest uneasy. Be sure all staff know the proper procedures for handling credit card purchases. It is equally crucial that they handle the card itself with respect. This means never leaving a credit card unattended or tossing it around casually. A credit card is a blank check on your guest's account and they have trusted you with it. Make sure your behavior shows your patrons that you take your responsibilities seriously.

**Giving *all* one-dollar bills as change**   If you appear to be angling for a tip, you may irritate your guests. Make it as easy as possible for them to leave a reasonable tip but don't overdo it. The exception to this rule is when you make change for a blind guest. In that case, returning only singles will assure the blind guest that they have the proper change.

**Watching while the guest completes the credit card slip**
The tip is a personal decision by the guest. If the server gives the impression they are looking over the guest's shoulder, the guest will feel you have invaded their privacy. The sensation of being spied upon is extremely uncomfortable. It also gives the impression that you are trying to rush the

guest, not a good thought to implant while the guest is deciding how much to tip.

# Professional Problems

The next few items relate to the skill and knowledge of your sales staff. Physical skills develop only with practice. Do not allow staff to serve your guests until they have mastered the basic moves of their trade.

**Dribbling wine on the table when pouring**   Proper wine service is smooth and unobtrusive. Dribbling wine is both annoying and unnecessary. Train your staff to roll the bottle slightly at the end of the pour. As a further note, skill in opening and pouring wine only comes with practice. Ask your wine supplier to help you find a supply of foil caps so your staff can practice foil cutting. An "Ah-So" wine opener will allow you to recork the bottles. Drill your crew until they are confident in their abilities to handle wine service smoothly. The more comfortable they are with the process, the more likely they are to suggest wine to your guests.

**Incorrect change**   If you return the wrong amount of change, your guests may think you are either incompetent or trying to cheat them. Neither conclusion works to your benefit. To be safe, coach your staff on proper cash handling procedures. Be sure they know how much money the guest gave them. Train them how to count the change when they take it out of the drawer. If you have a cashier, be sure the cashier counts the change again when handing it to the guest. If you return the change to the table and counting it out would be distracting, fan the bills and place the change on top. This way the guest can quickly be sure you have returned the correct change. You cannot be too careful when you handle your guest's money.

**Little knowledge of community attractions**   Newcomers to the area want some good "inside advice" about where to go and what to do. It is helpful when all your staff can respond knowledgeably to these questions. Contact your local Chamber of Commerce or Visitors Bureau for information on events, attractions, and activities. Remember, the longer visitors stay in town, the more opportunities they will have to dine at your restaurant.

**Asking guests to help with the service**   People do not come to your restaurant to serve themselves. If you need help, ask another staff member. Do whatever it takes to make the service as smooth as possible for your guests. After the shift, review the situation and figure out the training needed to avoid future repetitions.

**Resting the wine bottle on the rim of the glass**   Never touch the glass with the bottle. The outside of the bottle is not clean and many guests are very sensitive to what touches the surfaces from which they eat or drink. This is a simple training problem that may be caused by the server being unaware of their actions or trying to avoid dripping wine on the table. Teach them to twist the bottle at the end of the pour.

**Spilling food or beverage**   Sloppiness is the sign of a distracted sales person in a rush. Part of the job of management is to help the service staff maintain their composure. If a staff member is getting rushed, give them a hand and take the pressure off. Spilling food or drink is unprofessional and you can usually avoid it.

If an accident does occur, try to take it in stride. Apologize, clean up the mess, and continue the meal service. Don't get dramatic about the incident. If you have spilled something on a guest, make it right at once. Give the guest more than enough cash to cover the cost of cleaning and something extra to make up for the inconvenience. I recommend a gift certificate for the next time the guest comes into the restaurant. It is a generous gesture and helps be sure the guest will return to give you another chance.

**Losing or damaging a credit card**   When you handle a guest's credit card, you are handling their money. If you damage the card, a portion of their funds will be unavailable to them until they can get a replacement card. If your guests are from out of the area, the problem is more serious. Vacationers who lose the use of their credit card may not be able to continue their holiday. You must make a management decision about how to handle this situation if it occurs. Work out your plan of action now, before the emotion of the moment. You may offer to cash a check so they can continue with their vacation until a new card arrives. Take responsibility for finding a solution that works for them.

**Unreadable guest checks**   People are always more comfortable when they know what is happening. An illegible guest check is uncomfortable because the diners cannot tell how much they owe. They may not even be able to tell if you have given them the proper check for their meal.

**Illegible credit card forms**   Illegible credit card forms can be more unnerving than illegible guest checks. Guests may be uneasy if they worry that the card company might charge their account for an improper amount. If you have ever tried to resolve a charge error, you know how frustrating a process it can be. Keep your guests' minds at ease. Write carefully and legibly.

**Not knowing how to handle advertised specials or coupons**   Special promotions are an effective way to create excitement and generate new business for the restaurant. Promotions create a sense of expectation that draws new guests to your door. If people arrive in response to an advertised offer and you do not know what they are talking about, it creates an unpleasant situation for everyone. Since many people responding to your special offer will be first-timers, they won't know if you are incompetent or just confused. In either case, it is not a desirable first impression. Be sure to train your staff thoroughly on the content, goals, and procedures of your promotions *before* you advertise your specials.

**Wet, stained, or misadded checks**  Be sure everything you place on the table reflects the professionalism and care you want guests to associate with your restaurant. Messy food checks are the mark of an amateur.

# Cafeteria Calamities

Just because an operation does not have table service does not eliminate the need for service. It is possible to be the restaurant of choice . . . even if your patrons do not have another choice. All it takes is the same service orientation we have been discussing. Here are some details to avoid.

**Awkward replenishing of buffets**  I was at a Thanksgiving buffet at a major new hotel. Since I hate lines, I waited until the main surge had gone through the buffet line before going up for my meal. I was the last person in line when an overzealous staff member cut in front of me to replenish and rearrange the buffet line. I asked if she could let me go through before she continued but she ignored me. I stood there with hot food on my plate for several minutes before this thoughtless individual finished her work and left. Unless someone decides to buy my meal, I will not be back.

**Pouring old product on top of new product**  This practice is a bad habit developed for the convenience of the staff. It is repulsive to informed guests because it provides an opportunity for cross-contamination; that is, if the older product is tainted, it will contaminate the fresh new product. Avoid it. Present items in small quantities. Attend your line constantly so you can replace empty containers at once. Your line will look better, your guests will be happier, and your food will be safer.

**Not changing serving utensils when changing food containers**  Always bring clean serving utensils when replacing containers of food. Placing a soiled spoon into a crock of fresh product provides an opportunity for cross-contamination. Your guests will appreciate the gesture. It is also annoying to have to use a serving utensil that has food smeared on the handle from a previous patron. Replace soiled utensils, don't just wipe them off. It is more professional and increases your guests' confidence in your operation.

# Truth Is Stranger Than Fiction

A while ago I got the craving for a really great hot turkey sandwich. I immediately thought of a local diner-style restaurant that prides itself on being authentic by making real mashed potatoes. I figured if I would find a world-class hot turkey sandwich anywhere in town, this would surely be the place. I could already taste the thick slabs of real turkey breast as I sat in the booth and ordered. When the sandwich arrived, it was made with shredded turkey! I had never even *seen* shredded turkey before. The waitress came back a few minutes later to inquire about my meal. I told her the hot turkey sandwich was not at all what I expected and that I was seriously disappointed. She said, "Yeah. A lot of people tell us that," and just walked away!

# Bonus Points

Everybody likes pleasant surprises. These little unexpected touches are opportunities to improve your score and put your guests in a better mood. They help make up for any lapses in the operation and give people something to talk about to their friends.

**Remembering what a guest likes**   In an ideal world, everyone in a restaurant would always know exactly what I want, how I want it, and when I want it. I could just sit quietly and everything would happen effortlessly. Of course, it is not an ideal world, but the goal of always giving people what they want is worth pursuing. You can take some significant steps in this direction if it is important enough to you. For example, The Rattlesnake Club in Detroit has biography cards on all their regulars that contain everything the restaurant knows about what their guests like. Each day they review the reservation list and study the cards of the diners they expect that evening. How's that for improving your odds?

**Knowledgeable suggestions**   Skillful salesmanship helps the guests know the wonderful choices they can make at your restaurant. Selling is not a dirty word if your intent is to help the guest have a more enjoyable experience. Remember that people do not go out to save money, they go out to have a good time. They won't take you up on every suggestion. Still, you know what the restaurant has to offer. If you know what your guests want, you can help your patrons find items that will delight them.

**Anticipation of needs**   There are few touches more impressive than the service staff arriving with just what you want almost before you realize you want it! If you understand the meal process and look at everything from the guest's perspective, you can more easily anticipate needs.

**Refolding an absent guest's napkin**   This is such a small touch but it is so uncommon that it is impressive. When guests leave the table, they usually place their napkin on the table or on the seat of their chair. Just casually pick up the napkin, refold it quietly and place it over the arm of the chair. By the way, this only works with linen napkins!

**Placing the coffee cup handle at 4:00**   In standard American service, you place the coffee cup to the right of the diner. With the handle in the 4:00 position, the handle is just where it needs to be for the typical right-handed guest to pick up the cup. It is a small detail, but it shows your awareness of the guest's needs. If you notice the guest is left-handed, imagine their delight if you place the coffee cup on the left with the handle placed at 8:00!

**Extra napkins for gentlemen with beards or moustaches**
Understand that men with facial hair have an additional problem when eating some foods. Speaking from experience, if you have a beard, an ice cream cone can last all day! Particularly if you are serving a messy item like barbecued ribs, bring an extra napkin and let them know it is for their moustache. Your sensitivity will be so unexpected that they will remember you for a long time!

**Cafeteria self-service**   When I took over the foodservice program for the U.S. Olympic Training Centers, I inherited a standard military-type cafeteria operation. The athletes were fed but were not very excited. We made many changes; one of the first was to turn the service spoons around. I made the entire operation self-service, allowing the athletes to make their own selections. They could take as much (or as little) as they wanted. Some very unexpected things happened.

The first change I noticed was that my cost per meal dropped almost 15%. When they could take whatever they wanted, the athletes took less food than we were giving them before. The most pleasant surprise was the change in the relationship between my staff and the athletes. Freed from their serving duties, my crew's main job was to keep the line replenished and looking attractive. Their conversations with the athletes changed from task-oriented ("do you want peas?") to being more personal. Everybody had a more enjoyable time. This approach may not work for everyone, but it worked for our Olympic athletes!

# 8
# Attitude Errors

Staff demeanor has an important role in guest gratification. The way your staff conducts themselves says a lot about your restaurant and your attention to detail. As always, all the problems noted are the responsibility of management. Many of them are traits to be alert for during your screening and hiring process. Some are training-related. All are important to your success.

You cannot prepare first-class food with goods of inferior quality. You cannot provide first-class service with mediocre staff. The good news is that people can change their attitudes if they see a bigger picture. The bad news is that we are not in the rehabilitation business. You must help your present staff to develop and grow, but you can be more selective with new hires. Remember that the majority always rules. If most of your staff take pride in their work and are serious about expanding their professional skills, the professional level of everyone on your staff will improve. On the other hand, if most of your crew sees nothing wrong with cutting corners and taking home an occasional steak, new workers will follow their example.

The quickest way to take the temperature is to see who is quitting. Are you losing your good workers or your troublemakers? The real professionals will not stay long in an organization that does not operate to their standards. The slackers will be uncomfortable if their peers demand they produce at a high level. You can determine the direction your company will take by which attitude you allow to predominate.

# Horrible Habits

Habits are unconscious behaviors. Your staff may not even be aware of what they are doing or its impact on your guests. Eliminating these actions increases the chances of having delighted diners.

**Eating or drinking at work stations**   Other than routine tasting by the cooks, eating at work stations is a serious violation of basic sanitation rules. Eating puts your fingers around your mouth, contaminating your hands and increasing the risk of transmitting foodborne illness. Even if you wash your hands immediately after eating, you are still placing the restaurant and your guests in peril. The habit is a major distraction for the guests, particularly the ones who understand proper sanitation.

For example, my wife will never return to a restaurant where she has seen this behavior. I have heard the same comment from many other diners. Eating in the work stations brings you unfavorable attention and diverts the guests' focus from their experience. When it is time to eat, sit and enjoy your meal. You will be doing yourself and your guests a favor.

**Uncovered heads in the kitchen**    All health departments require some form of hair restraint in the kitchen. In many jurisdictions, a hair net or hair spray is enough to keep stray hair from falling into food. For kitchen workers who are visible to the public, there is another consideration. To feel comfortable, guests must be able to *see* that the cooks' hair is restrained. The only sure way they can do this is when the kitchen crew are wearing hats. The style of head covering will depend on the style of your restaurant. Just make sure your cooks are wearing something the guests can see.

**Chewing gum**    Chewing gum makes you look like you are eating something. Seeing staff eating on the job is repulsive to many diners. In some diner concepts, gum-chewing is part of the look for staff. Personally, it is a reason I do not patronize many of these operations. Regardless of the concept, there is no excuse for food preparation staff or bartenders to be chewing gum. Your safest route is to prohibit all staff from chewing gum on the job.

**Poor personal sanitation practices**    Don't think the public doesn't know, doesn't care, or doesn't see poor sanitation practices. The habits most often mentioned are the following:

- Touching your hair and then touching food without washing your hands
- Handling cash and then handling food without washing your hands
- Paying undue attention to your face and not washing your hands
- Coughing or sneezing and not washing your hands
- Scratching various body parts and not washing your hands
- Clearing a table then handling clean dishes or food without washing your hands

You can see the importance of handwashing in preventing potential point loss. It is also sound sanitation practice. Have conveniently located hand sinks and make sure you are in the habit of using them. If these sinks are partially visible, your guests can see you wash your hands and may feel more comfortable.

**Standing around doing nothing**    If there is time to lean, there is time to clean. There is always something to do in a restaurant. A restaurant is always in motion and a person who is not moving becomes obvious. When you stand out this way, you become a distraction to your guests. The distraction is worse if your hands are in your pockets. To be safe, always be in motion.

**Sharing guest restrooms and not washing hands**    I cannot overemphasize the importance of handwashing. It is your single most important way to prevent the spread of foodborne illness. Guests are particularly sensitive to handwashing in the restrooms. Even if it were not a health department requirement, it is only common courtesy. When you share the guest restrooms, everybody is watching you closely. Be sure to wash your hands and be particularly thorough about it. Your conscientious cleaning will make your guests feel more confident.

**Poor personal hygiene**   Your appearance must be as appetizing as the food you serve. Your guests will notice dirty or untrimmed fingernails. Dirty hands are always a major turn-off. Body odor or bad breath will drive away even the most loyal patron. Be sure to shower before coming to work each day and wash your hands after you arrive at the restaurant. The preshift inspection is an old idea but a good one. Be sure your staff knows the standards of your restaurant. If they do not measure up, send them home to clean themselves up. They will do what you *inspect* of them, not what you *expect* of them.

**Speaking a foreign language in front of the guest**   Guests find this behavior insulting, no matter what the actual content of the conversation. If your staff talks in another language, train them never to look at the guests while they are having a conversation. To do so will make their conversation appear to be about your diners. You do not want to offend your guests this way.

**Using poor grammar when addressing a guest**   When interviewing job applicants, pay attention to their speech, particularly if they are going to be in direct contact with your guests. Guests will form an impression and memory of your restaurant from the tone and grammar of your staff. The ability to do the job includes not only physical skills and knowledge but the ability to leave your guests with a good impression.

**Whistling or singing with the background music**   I hope your restaurant is a place where your crew feels cheerful enough to sing. Happy staff always make for a more pleasant dining experience Unfortunately, singing or whistling rarely makes your guests feel happy. Vocalizing may work in some concepts, but it must be an overt part of the operating style. It is seldom a positive point elsewhere. Singing or whistling may just be unconscious habits but the result can be distracting to your guests. If you feel the urge to break into song, hum to yourself with a smile on your face.

**Not moving at the "speed of the room"**   Good service is almost invisible. Guests should only notice what is going on at their table and not be distracted by other movements in the room. If you are moving fast in a slow-paced dining room, you are a distraction. If you are moving slowly in a fast-paced restaurant, you are a distraction. The speed at which you move is different from the speed at which you do your job. You can still be very quick and efficient in a slower-moving dining room. The quality of your movements is just different. It is similar to the martial arts expert whose power comes from a calm and relaxed state rather than frenetic movement. If you can move with the speed of the room, you can give responsive service and your guests will hardly notice you are there.

**Pointing in the dining room . . . ever**    Directing a guest by pointing is rude. It is always preferable to say "let me show you" and lead them where they want to go. Pointing the way to the restrooms, in particular, can embarrass your guest. If you can't lead them there yourself, be sure you can give discrete directions that don't require waving your hands. Bear in mind that usually the only guests who will not know the location of the restrooms are people who have never been in the restaurant before. Train your staff to let you know of any first-time guests so you can personally welcome them to the restaurant. If a guest asks the location of the cigarette machine, coach your crew to offer to get the cigarettes for them. Don't let a pointing finger become a substitute for responsive guest service.

**Unintelligible speech**    To feel comfortable in your restaurant, guests must easily understand what you say. Do not speak to the table until you have the guests' attention. Speak at a moderate pace in a clear voice and pronounce your words carefully. Use complete sentences as much as possible. Watch your guests' reactions as you speak and be sensitive for signs that they don't understand what you are saying. If you see guests with furrowed brows or quizzical looks, stop and regroup. It is rude to continue if you have lost the people you are trying to serve.

**Rattling pocket change**    Keep your hands out of your pockets. It always looks unprofessional and is even more annoying when accompanied by jangling coins. Male managers are most likely to have this nervous habit and it can drive your guests up the wall! If you can't keep your hands out of your pockets, at least keep your pockets empty.

**Clicking a ball point pen**    This is another unconscious nervous habit often seen when servers are waiting for guests to make their meal decisions. The best solution is to recognize that impatience works counter to responsive guest service and strive to become sensitive to anxiety when it appears. Remember that good service operates on your guests' time schedule, not yours.

**Walking past items dropped on the floor**    Anytime a member of the staff ignores debris on the floor, it shows a lack of pride in the restaurant. Rather than addressing the behavior directly, look for the cause of this attitude. Poor behavior usually suggests a low level of personal security and a feeling of not being a part of the company. If so, all the lectures in the world will not solve the problem. If you can help your staff feel better about their role in the success of the restaurant, the problem behaviors are likely to disappear.

**Interrupting another staff member**   Unless you have to evacuate the building for an emergency, never interrupt the flow of service at the table. This habit is inconsiderate to both the staff member and the guests. If you break in on another staff member when they are talking with a guest, you are saying that your needs are more important than your diner's.

**Answering a question with a question**   Your guests ask questions because they want answers. If you want them to enjoy themselves, give them answers. You may need more information, but don't ask for it until you have given them some recommendations or reassured them that you can solve their problem. Also be sure that you are answering the *concern* reflected by their question. For example, a person who calls on the phone to ask how busy you are really wants to know if (or how long) they will have to wait for a table.

# Irritating Appearances

How you look is important to your success and the prosperity of the restaurant. Your appearance delivers a message from across the dining room. Guests will draw conclusions about you and your professionalism from the details.

**Kitchen staff loitering in the dining room**   Your restaurant is a place of business, not a social club. Do not let your kitchen staff loiter in the dining room while the service staff is working. There is a difference between loitering and taking a scheduled break. Designate an area for your staff to take their breaks so they will know what you expect. If the dining room is the only place a worker can sit, staff on break will be in view of the guests. This makes them part of your dining room decor. Establish standards for staff appearance and behavior that will enhance your guests' impression of the restaurant rather than diminish it. The gathering must be purposeful instead of random. It must be obvious that the workers are there for a legitimate reason. Their appearance must be pleasing. If the kitchen crew is wearing shredded Harley Davidson T-shirts with filthy aprons, your guests will get very nervous.

**Soiled or ill-fitting uniforms**   If you invest in uniforms to provide a more professional look, get serious about your appearance. Be sure uniforms are spotlessly clean and fit properly. Looking neat is good but looking crisp is better. You and your guests can tell the difference. Be sure your shirt tails are tucked in. Never wear a soiled tie. Issue enough uniforms that your crew can have a clean one every day and replace them before they start to look dull. An investment in attractive, well-constructed uniforms makes a bold statement about the way you do business. Presenting a professional image to the public makes your guests more confident in your skills. Don't forget to provide uniforms for your managers.

**Smoking in uniform**   Staff smoking in the restaurant just looks like hell! Smoking is not a clean activity. Anything that makes your guests feel that your restaurant is less clean will hurt you. Staff standing behind the restaurant smoking presents almost as bad an impression. The only safe place to have a cigarette in the restaurant is either in a designated smoking break room or in your car. Your restaurant's uniform is part of your restaurant's image with the public. When you smoke while you are in uniform, smoking becomes part of that image also. It is not the impression you want to leave in the minds of your market.

**Unkempt hair**   Staff working in foodservice operations must have neatly arranged hair. Hair must be clean and off the shoulder. Longer hair must be tied back. Food handlers must keep long hair tucked inside their hats. Remember that neat hair also applies to facial hair. If you allow male staffers to sport beards or moustaches, they must be neatly trimmed and attractive. Unshaven faces are rarely appealing to your guests.

**No staff uniforms**   In the 1970s, we wanted people to be natural. We thought if we let the staff wear their own clothes, they would feel more comfortable and provide better service. It might have worked in the 1970s. Today, though, allowing the staff to wear anything they want gives the restaurant a haphazard appearance. Without uniforms, it can be difficult for guests to tell your staff from other guests. A less obvious advantage to uniforms is what they do to help your staff attitude. When people dress for work, their thinking changes. Like actors getting into costume before going onstage, your crew starts to "get into character." Their performance will likely be more professional when they look the part.

**Filthy footwear**   Dirty running shoes caked with food spills will not cause your guests to remember you fondly. Footwear is an important part of creating a professional appearance that many restaurants overlook. For safety reasons, restaurant footwear must be grease-resistant. This gives better traction and helps avoid slipping accidents. It also lets the staff move faster in the kitchen and dining room. To prevent fatigue and lower back pain, footwear should be comfortable and provide proper arch support. To enhance the professional image of your uniforms, be sure all footwear is clean, shined, and of the same design.

The only sure way to do this is to specify what footwear you will allow to be worn on the job. If you do this, you must become involved in the purchase. You might require your staff to buy a particular style of shoe and repay them over some period. You also could buy the shoes through the restaurant and deduct an amount on each paycheck until they have paid for the shoes. If they stay a certain length of time, you might repay them for the full cost of the shoes. Bear in mind that you cannot reissue footwear. Your state laws may have a bearing on what you do or how you do it. I can only tell you that attractive footwear is attractive to your guests. What you do with that information is up to you.

**Slouching or poor posture**    People who stand erect convey a more professional image and instill more confidence in your guests. During the screening and interviewing process, notice how job applicants stand and move. When job skills and willingness to work are equal, the person with the best posture is likely to get the job.

**Silly-looking uniforms**    We have uniforms so the crew will look sharper and more professional. Be sure to consult them when making the selection of what to wear. If you require them to wear uniforms they hate, they will feel self-conscious and look uncomfortable. Why would you do this to people you respect? You accomplish the opposite of the intended result and waste money.

**Inability to speak basic English**    Communication is the heart of good service. There are wonderful opportunities in this industry for people from all ethnic backgrounds, but they must have the ability to talk easily with our guests. If guests must struggle to make themselves understood, they will not have a pleasant experience.

**Distracting accessories**    All restaurant staff must look clean and professional. Remember that your role is to enhance the dining experience of your guests, not to make a personal statement. Any time your appearance distracts your guests' attention from the reasons they went out to eat, their level of well-being goes down a little. As their level drops, they become more critical of their experience.

I am not suggesting you do not have a right to your personal beliefs and affiliations. I only want to point out that making personal statements on the job is inappropriate and counter to the best interests of your guests and the restaurant. The most common distractions are the following accessories:

- Excessive or gaudy jewelry
- Brightly colored nail polish
- Wristwatches
- Union buttons
- Political buttons
- Religious symbols
- Heavy perfume or aftershave scent
- Ornate belts or belt buckles
- Dark or tinted glasses
- Chipped or worn nametags

**Sitting on the counters**    A culinary professor of mine always admonished us not to put anything on the counter we didn't want to eat! He made his point. Take your breaks only in your appointed break areas, not on the tables. It looks unprofessional and unsanitary. Sitting on the tables only reflects lack of coaching or a feeling of detachment from the restaurant operation.

**Obvious hangovers**   People do not come to the restaurant to hear your problems. They are not interested in whether you stayed out all night and drank too much. Your physical impairment only draws the focus of attention away from your guests. Since the secret to assuring guest satisfaction is reducing distractions, you can figure out the problem.

**Bandages on the hands**   How safe would you feel if a person preparing or serving your food had a dirty bandage on their hand? Do you think your guests are any different? If a food handler in the kitchen has a bandaged wound, have them wear thin rubber examination gloves like medical professionals use. These are more sterile than plastic gloves and provide a secure grip when handling knives. Give staff with bandages on their hands a job out of the public eye and be sure the bandage is protected from food contact.

**Sleeveless tops**   Tank tops may be the hot look in your area, but they are not a good choice of attire for restaurant staff. Sleeveless tops are simply too revealing for foodservice operations. Nobody comes to the restaurant to look at your staff's underarms. The look may be sexy but it is not appetizing, particularly on men. Sleeveless tops often expose part of women's brassieres, another unpleasant distraction. Be sure uniform tops have sleeves long enough to maintain decorum.

**Smelling like cigarettes**   People who smoke may not realize that everything they own smells like cigarettes, especially to nonsmokers. Even the smell from a smoker's automobile can permeate clean uniforms on the drive to work. There is not much you can say about what your staff does after work. Still, be aware that nonsmokers are very sensitive to the smell of smoke. The safest course is to have staff who smoke work only in the smoking section.

**Dour faces**   If you are having a good time, notify your face! Guests have a better time when the restaurant staff is enjoying themselves. It is particularly important that guest contact staff have naturally pleasant facial expressions. People who smile easily usually see life in a more positive, friendly way. They are more likely to help your guests have a pleasant evening.

**Unattractive staff**   You cannot usually make personal appearance a valid job requirement. Still, restaurants are a visual experience. We spend a lot of time and money to prepare beautiful meals in a striking environment.

If your service staff does not look equally appetizing, you lose much of the impact.

I am not suggesting every staff member must be a candidate for a magazine cover. Attractiveness involves more than physical beauty. Weight, skin tone, posture, and fluid motion figure into perceptions of attractiveness. Workers with naturally pleasant facial expressions and a ready smile appear more attractive than people whose faces are in a perpetual frown. Remember that your staff is also part of the environment of your restaurant and will have an effect on your guests' experience.

**Food handlers who are ill or have a cold**   Guests have a legitimate concern for their health when they see ill food handlers. If you are too sick to work, you ought to be recovering at home. If you are well enough to work but should not be handling food, do a job where you will not pose a hazard to your guests. There are always storerooms to clean, trash cans to wash, and other essential tasks to do that can help the restaurant.

# Attitude Atrocities

Attitudes also can be unconscious habits. Unlike habits, though, they have more personal force behind them because they appear to be more overt.

**Excuses . . . for anything . . . anytime**   Apologizing or making excuses for the food, service, or policies of the restaurant will make you seem like an amateur. If you are not proud of it, don't serve it. If you don't agree with a policy, get it changed. If you can live with it, live with it. If you can't live with it, leave. A successful restaurant sets high standards and brings its staff up to meet them. When you hear your crew make excuses to your guests, it may mean they have higher standards than you do.

**Profanity within earshot of guests**   Profanity peppers modern speech and you must be constantly alert to avoid accidentally offending your guests. The safest practice is to refrain from using profanity anywhere in the restaurant. Assume that guests can hear *everything!* The staff will reflect the example of management. There cannot be a double standard about profanity in the workplace.

**Personal conversations loud enough for guests to hear**
Part of what makes the restaurant experience special is its removal from the routine affairs of the day. Conversations between staff members, particularly if they are personal (nonbusiness) and loud enough for guests to hear, break the spell. Keep conversations in the dining room to a minimum. Use a quiet voice and limit the topics to those affecting guest service. Kitchen staff also must be sensitive to their conversations. It is easy to forget how far voices can carry in some restaurants. In the heat of the rush, normal

kitchen conversation can become shouts. Just because the guests are out of sight does not mean they cannot hear what you say.

**Whining or complaining**   Never complain to anyone who cannot solve your problem. Nobody likes a whiner. Complaining to your co-workers is bad enough. Whining to a guest is even worse. People don't go out to eat to hear your problems. Griping to them only ruins their opinion of the restaurant . . . and of you.

**Arguments or displayed anger**   Few events can destroy a pleasant mood as quickly and as thoroughly as the eruption of anger. You cannot always prevent arguments among guests at the table. Because of the pressure of business, it is more likely that a staff member will get angry. It is helpful to understand that the more positive a person's mood, the less likely they are to have a dispute with anyone. The way to avoid anger in the restaurant (and the damage it can cause) is to maintain a high state of mind. You do this for your guests by avoiding the momentous minutiae in this book. You do this for your staff by giving them thorough training, consistent support, and the authority to do their jobs in a way that works for them.

**Flirting with the guests**   Making advances to your guests can create all kinds of problems. When you are flirting with one guest, you are ignoring the others and they will resent it. This behavior is self-centered and unprofessional. Your activities may give your restaurant a reputation you don't want. If you start having affairs with your guests, they will be uncomfortable about coming back. If your guests resent your intentions, they will never return. Flirting with guests is dangerous, particularly if either party is married. Be smart enough to pursue your social life away from the restaurant.

**Confusing or indirect communications**   People do not go to restaurants to hold long conversations with the restaurant's staff. They will not appreciate your trying to be too clever when you talk with them. You will make their meal more pleasant if you just say what you have to say clearly, directly, and with a smile in your voice.

**Pretentious captains, wine stewards, or service staff**   The most effective service staff are friendly, accessible, understanding, and professional. Arrogant, haughty, and aloof are not particularly attractive attitudes to most patrons. Staff who display these traits could have a control issue that will make it difficult for your guests to feel well served. Remember that it is the human connection, not the technical execution, that brings guest gratification.

**Losing patience or becoming abrupt**   There is never a good excuse for losing your patience with a guest. Difficult people are part of the job. Nobody *wants* to be difficult but we all get that way sometimes.

Just try to take events in stride and do the best you can. Getting defensive is especially unnerving to your guests. Guests ask questions because they want information. Sometimes they may use a tone of voice that sounds harsh. Don't take it personally, it has nothing to do with you.

**Yelling in the dining room** Unless this is part of your operating style (and very few concepts can get away with it), keep the noise down. Loud voices disturb the guests' dining experience and make you look like an amateur.

**"Stonewalling" when guests ask to speak with the manager or owner** The only real job in the restaurant is to make sure that guests get what they want. If they want to speak with the owner, they will only be happy when they speak to the owner. If a staff member tries to prevent that from happening, it will only make the guest more angry and determined. Often the server resists because the guest is going to complain about the service. Complaints are far less likely if guest gratification is the focus of the restaurant. Give staff members the authority to do whatever they feel is necessary to be sure your guests enjoy themselves.

**Lack of support for company policies** I recommend you have as few policies as possible. Policies usually just get in the way of guest service by providing a reason you can't do something the guest wants done. Management's job is to be sure everyone on the staff understands the reasons for company policies. The more they understand why you want something done a certain way, the easier it is for them to support the policy. When you see a conscientious worker having a problem with a policy, raise questions about the policy before you raise questions about the individual.

**Ignoring or not thanking guests as they leave** Gratitude is powerful. People cannot get enough of it, particularly when most events in their lives are so negative. People go to businesses that appreciate their patronage. Thanking guests as they leave is not just courtesy, it is an investment in their future patronage. When guests feel you are sincerely grateful for their business, they feel better about giving it to you. Sincere gratitude is so uncommon that your guests will remember your appreciation and return for more.

**No response to guest complaints** Most guests will not tell you their complaints. If they have a bad time in your restaurant, they will complain to their friends. They also will never return. When a guest cares enough to tell you about a problem, they probably speak for many others who have had similar difficulties. Treat it as a unique opportunity to identify and correct a flaw in your operating system. Never ignore a complaint. Usually guests do not expect you to solve problems on the spot. They just want to know that you are really listening and interested in what they have to say. Handling complaints properly can often create an enthusiastic regular guest for your restaurant.

# Bonus Points

Everybody likes pleasant surprises. These little unexpected touches are opportunities to improve your score and put your guests in a better mood. They help make up for any lapses in the operation and give people something to talk about to their friends.

**High staff presence**     There is something special about a person who is obviously thinking of nothing but your well-being. Your staff will follow your example. If you are distracted when you talk with them, they will be distracted when they talk to your guests. If you define the manager's job as maintaining a positive climate in the restaurant, high staff presence will be more common.

**Rapid communication among staff**     It always impresses me when I tell the waiter something and the manager arrives a few minutes later to follow up. It indicates a professional working environment with good teamwork.

**Smiling eye contact**     Nothing warms the heart like smiling eye contact. Coach your staff in the importance of starting the relationship with every new guest by looking them directly in the eye and giving them a big smile.

**"No problem"**     Here is another story to illustrate a point. In October 1981, I went to China to fly hot air balloons. There had never been a hot air balloon flight in China, so it was a pure adventure. I was in a part of the country not usually open to Americans and I was doing something that had never been done before. As you can imagine, the Chinese found many of my needs and requests very strange!

I had to ask for everything I needed through our interpreters. The first response to everything I requested was always "no problem." Sometimes I got what I wanted and sometimes it was something unexpectedly different. Still, I was impressed by how much the simple phrase "no problem" took the pressure off every situation. Professor Don Smith at Washington State University espouses a similar approach which he phrases as, "the answer is yes, what's the question?"

I won't suggest you can do everything your guests ask of you. Still, if the first words out of your mouth are "no problem," your guests will relax and be much more open to alternatives. Try it and see. Five billion Chinese can't be wrong!

# 9
# Vacant Verbiage

Language is powerful. The meaning of what you say is determined not only by the words you use but also by the tone of voice in which you say them and the prior experiences of the person who hears them. It is critical that you not only say what you mean but that you avoid any unwanted interpretations as well.

You can accomplish this through regular coaching. Training does not mean scripting. Scripting each interaction produces robotlike communication that is usually interpreted as lack of caring. To be effective, training ought to help the staff understand what responses are elicited by particular words and phrases. Without this awareness, you are likely to have well-intentioned but mindless conversations that do little to endear your restaurant to your guests. The easiest way to deal with these "dirty words" is to prohibit their use and challenge your staff to find more effective phrases. It makes for lively shift meetings!

## System Slipups

When you hear these phrases spoken in your restaurant, it indicates a breakdown in the operating system.

**"Who gets what?"** Establish a system so that anyone can read the guest check and know where each meal belongs. This is particularly important if anyone other than the sales person ever brings food to the table. A simple system of table and seat numbering can make all the difference in how guests perceive your professionalism.

**"It's against company policy"** Design company policies to enhance guest gratification. If they don't work for your guests, change the policy. In any event, tell guests what you *can* do for them rather than what you *can't!* Be alert for staff who are hiding behind policy rather than finding ways to help guests get what they want.

**"It's not my station"; "It's not my job"; "I'm on my break"** A response like this indicates a serious lack of focus on the needs of the guest. Creating and maintaining this focus is the job of management. Immediately talk with any staff member who uses phrases like these and watch them closely. They are a loose cannon!

**"I think this is the diet soda"** This arises when the order has two or more different draft beers, two scotches, and so on. Work out a system with the bartender to identify drinks that look similar. Don't show your amateurism by having to ask the guest to tell *you* what is in the glass.

**"You'll need this later"**   You don't set the table with dirty utensils. Why would you hand dirty forks back to your guests during the meal and expect them to reuse them?

# Negative Communication

Perhaps it is human nature, but it always seems easier to phrase things negatively. Unfortunately, negative expressions leave your guests feeling unserved. The phrasing and tone of many commonly heard expressions are as warm as an irate third-grade teacher berating an innocent eight-year-old!

**"We don't do that"; "We can't . . ."**   Explain what you *can* do and keep it personal. "I can . . ." is much more effective than "We can . . ." Positive communication is more pleasant, positive, and rewarding.

**"We don't have . . ."; "We've run out of . . ."**   If you *run* out of something, it appears that you don't know how to run your business. On the other hand, if you *sell* out of something, guests perceive that you have highly desirable items. Anytime you cannot provide what the guest orders, tell them at once and always suggest alternate choices.

**"Why didn't you . . ."; "You should have . . ."; "You have to . . ."**   Don't expect your guests to know your procedures. You are there for *their* comfort, not the other way around. If there is a problem, take care of the guest first and figure out what happened later. Your guests are intelligent adults—don't try to make anything appear to be their fault.

**"You made a mistake"**   A mistake by whose standards? Nobody likes to make a mistake. Take responsibility for the miscommunication, straighten it out to the guest's advantage, and get on with it.

**"Is that all?"**   This is too abrupt. How about "Is there anything else I can get you right now?" Keep your voice modulated and your tone soft. Guests will feel much more comfortable.

**"Yes, I know"**   This makes the guest's comment sound insignificant. Better to just say "thank you." Remember the goal is to be sure the guest has an enjoyable experience in the restaurant.

**"What do you want?"**   Just *try* to say this phrase in a pleasant way! It can't be done. Better to ask "how can I help you?" or something similar. If you can develop the habit of addressing your guests in complete sentences rather than choppy phrases, your speech will be smoother and your level of guest service will increase.

**"I'll try"** Either you will do it or you won't do it. "Try" says little or nothing and most people recognize this. Tell them what you *will* do for them.

**"I don't know"** It's your *job* to know! If you get caught on a question where you don't know the answer, avoid the phrase "I don't know." Say something like "Just a minute. I'll find out for you." Then be sure you do find out and promptly report your findings to the guest.

**"I'm sorry, but . . ."** If something goes wrong, apologize and suggest acceptable alternatives. Starting a sentence with this phrase puts your guests on alert that something unpleasant is about to happen. Rather than risk dropping their mood, find a more positive way to state your case. The appropriate phrasing will depend on the person involved and the degree of formality in your restaurant. A little humor can be of real benefit in these situations.

# Mindless Communication

When people aren't trained to be aware of the impact of their words, they often speak without thinking. Stale words make for a stale dining experience. Take responsibility for your words and their impact.

**"How's everything?"; "Is everything OK?"** Dennis Berkowitz, owner of Max's Diner and other creative San Francisco eateries, will give a free round of drinks if anyone on his staff says this. Ask questions that are more thoughtful and helpful to your guests. Outlawing the phrase forces your staff to be aware of what they are saying when they speak to your guests.

**"Just one?"; "Are you dining alone?"** Some people are self-conscious about eating alone. It is uncaring to use words that might make them feel worse about it. "May I seat you now?" will handle the situation more smoothly.

**"I'll be right back with your _____"** This phrase is just unconscious filler—mindless social noise. Only use phrases that say something to your guests. If you can't say something meaningful, you are probably wiser not to say anything at all! After all, if a sales person is truly *present* (not distracted) when they are at the table, comments are not always necessary.

**"My name is _____ and I'll be your waiter this evening"** This phrase has become a restaurant cliché. Unless you are prepared for a response of "My name is _____ and I'll be your guest this evening," think of another introduction. How about just a warm welcome to the restaurant and some enthusiastic suggestions?

**"Okay"; "Yeah"**    These slang expressions can sound flip or impolite. Be aware of your words and find something else to say. Phrases like "certainly, sir" or "that is correct" will sound much better and leave your guests feeling that you were polite and responsive to their needs.

**"Have a nice day"**    There has to be something more original and personal you can use than this cliché. Your guests hear the same thing in K-Mart! See if you can find a different way to show each party how much you appreciate their patronage. Pause, let your mind drop any other thoughts, and say what comes to your mind. You may not even remember what you said, but when it comes from your heart, the impact will be memorable.

**"I'll give you a few minutes"**    How wonderfully generous of you! First of all, it's not your time to give them. Second, if people are having difficulty making a decision, it's time for recommendations, not retreat. Third, the phrase is trite and only shows you are not paying attention to your guests' needs.

**"Enjoy"; "Enjoy your meals"**    These phrases are also worn and do not add anything to the guests' dining experience. You will improve your level of communication if you develop the habit of speaking in complete sentences. Put this to your service staff and get their suggestions. You may be surprised.

**"Who gets the check?"**    Does it make a difference to you? The question only serves to satisfy your curiosity and distract the diners. It is often impossible to tell who will pay the check. You risk insulting your female guests if you automatically give the check to the male diner. Place the check in the center of the table, thank them for coming, and continue to service the table until they leave.

**"I'll take this whenever you're ready"**    This is another filler phrase of unnecessary conversation. If there is any question about whether a guest should pay at the table or go to the cashier, print it on your guest checks. Even if your operation uses a cashier, if the guest places the check and payment on the table, take it up for them. Give the guest the service they want or risk losing them forever.

**"Guess what?"**    What a juvenile comment! Don't play games with your guests—it is not the reason they came to the restaurant. If you have something to say, state it clearly, get your answer, and move on.

**"Mathers party of two"**    Anytime you make the guest feel processed rather than served, you lose points. This phrase is another restaurant cliché that really irritates some diners. The most personal approach, of course, is to have a greeter go to the Mathers party personally and escort them to their table. If calling them on a speaker is the only solution, change your wording. "Mr. Mathers, your table is ready," "I can seat you now, Mr. Mathers," or words to that effect are more cordial.

**"How was everything?"**    This question usually comes after the meal as the guests are leaving. If you ask "How was everything?" the answer is invariably "Fine." If your reason for asking is to get a truthful answer, change the wording. Try asking if everything was done the way they liked it. Try asking them how you did. Better yet, ask how you could do a better job for them next time. You'll be amazed at the suggestions you will receive. Remember that nobody will say a word if they don't think you really want to hear what they have to say.

**"Your order is on the way"**    The only reason you would say this is that you want to say *something* but don't really have anything to say. The comment has no meaning and only distracts the guest. Save your words (and interruptions) for something that will enhance the dining experience.

**"Do you need anything else?"**    If you ask this when the entrée is served, the guest has no way of knowing the answer. Give them one minute (two bites) with the food and ask the question when they can answer it.

**"Everything is good here"**    When your guests ask the question, they want your recommendations. This response, even if it is accurate, is useless as a suggestion. Recommend two items. They could be your signature items, your personal favorites, or something that looks particularly good to you today. *What* you suggest is less important than *that* you suggest.

**"Are you done?"**    If your guest's plate is clean, the question is asinine. If the guest's plate still has food on it, they might interpret the question as rushing them. Just ask if you can remove their plate. The question is safer, the result is the same.

# Self-Centered Communication

The world does not revolve around us. Although we are always seeing from our own perspectives, we must be sensitive to the guest's point of view.

**"We have . . ."**    It sounds much nicer to say "You can have. . . ." Phrasing it in this way makes your comments sound more like you are providing a service than giving a lecture. Your guests feel better-served and you don't lose any points.

**"I need . . ."**    Who cares what you need? Find a way to phrase it in the guest's favor. If you are tempted to say "I need to know what dressing you want on your salad," try something more sensitive. Perhaps something like "You can choose any of our six special dressings for your salad. You can have . . ." Do you hear the difference?

**"We're running a little behind tonight"**    Your guests just *hate* to hear you say this! First of all, if guests call on the phone and ask if you are busy, they are trying to find out if they will have to wait very long. Don't tell them you have a line out the door! You might offer to put them on the waiting list and suggest they arrive in 45 minutes. Whatever you do, sell them on the idea that you can show them a wonderful time. Don't let them get away. They may never come back.

**"This is my first day"**    Everybody has to start sometime. It is reasonable to expect that the first few days on a new job will be a little less smooth. Still, this phrase is usually an excuse to your guests. Guests come to the restaurant expecting a good time and responsive service. It is not their problem if you are a rookie. In fact, they may feel less comfortable if they think management is asking them to break in the new crew. Be a pro and don't hide behind excuses—it can become a habit.

# Rude Communication

Often, we use phrases that are offensive to our guests without even realizing we are doing it.

**"Are you the roast beef?"**    No, they are your guests! Treat them as people or you will lose them. Perhaps you are used to thinking of your diners in terms of what they ordered, but I assure you that they don't think of themselves that way.

**"Follow me"**    There is no way to say this without sounding abrupt. At the least, precede it with a "please." It is smoother to tell them you have a wonderful table ready for them and lead them to it.

**"How are you guys doing tonight?"**    This is mindless at best and rude at worst, particularly when addressing a couple or a group of women where everyone is obviously not "guys." For many people, simply being asked how they are doing is an invasion of privacy. The easiest way around this is to avoid the entire phrase. Welcome them to the restaurant and get on with it!

**"Can't you see that I'm busy?"; "I only have two hands!";
"I'm only human!"**    This phrase is a sure indication of an overstressed staff member or one who needs a refresher in guest gratification. Get them off the floor and cover their station another way. They will only drive your guests away until they regain their composure. Better to have guests upset for something you *didn't* do than for something you *did*.

**"Folks"; "Guys"; "See ya"**   These slang expressions are impossible to say without a disrespectful tone. Be aware of this and avoid them. It will take some awareness and desire to break old habits. Eliminating these phrases from your vocabulary will instantly elevate the quality of your guest service. You will also make your restaurant more memorable to your guests.

**"What do you WANT?"**   The message is always in the tone of voice, never in the words. Think about it. If you are in another country where you don't understand the language, can't you always tell if someone is upset? Compassionate? Caring? Your communications are no different. If you inadvertently snap at a guest, recognize it, apologize, and try again with more humility.

# Ineffective Communication

Some phrases just don't work. Their continued use only reflects lack of training. The problem with these phrases is that they do not enhance the dining experience and are too easy to just say "no" to. In all cases, you are better off to make one or two specific suggestions. Jim Sullivan's book, *Service that Sells*, examines this topic in detail. For now, though, here are a few suggestions that may help.

**"Would you like a drink?"; "How about a cocktail?"**   How about "May I suggest something refreshing from the bar? Our special tonight is _____ or perhaps a frosty _____?" You get the idea.

**"Would you like an appetizer?"**   Very few people go out with appetizers on their minds, so this question could easily be annoying. Try something like "While we are preparing your dinner, perhaps you'd like to share an order of _____ or _____."

**"What do you want to eat?"**   This may be carrying the idea of straightforward communication to an extreme. Bear in mind that people don't go to restaurants just because they are hungry. There are many ways to satisfy hunger that have nothing to do with dining out. Be respectful and don't back them into a corner. Perhaps you could ask if they have had time to make a choice yet? This phrasing gives them a way to say no gracefully. This way, if they say no, it's because they haven't had *time* to make a choice, not because they haven't been *able* to make a choice. If they are uncertain, suggest two items you think they would like. If there is no ready response, quietly excuse yourself and check back in a few minutes or when they have put their menus down.

**"Would you like dessert?"**   This is another automatic "no." There are many ways to build dessert sales. "Have you ever tried our famous

_____?" will always open a discussion. Remember most people who won't select a dessert for themselves will usually share one with their companion. One dessert for every two diners is not an unreasonable sales target.

**"Nice"; "Good"**   Both are nondescriptive words. They are weak, say nothing, and sound trite. Your descriptions always have more impact when they come from your personal experience of the item.

# Unnecessary Communication

Guests don't come to the restaurant to have lengthy conversations with the staff. The following phrases are just unnecessary and do nothing to enhance the guests' dining experience. Don't even ask, just bring it!

* "Do you want cream with your coffee?"
* "Would you like more _____?"

# Truth Is Stranger Than Fiction

My favorite comment came in a small California coffee shop one morning. The waitress placed a glass of tomato juice in front of me and said, "Taste this and see if it's OK. It smells funny to me!"

# Bonus Points

Everybody likes pleasant surprises. These little unexpected touches are opportunities to improve your score and put your guests in a better mood. They help make up for any lapses in the operation and give people reasons to recommend your restaurant to their friends.

**Speaking in complete sentences**   The dining trend in the country is away from the formal dining experience and toward more casual restaurants. Unfortunately, this trend has also been reflected in our use of the language. Speaking in complete sentences is more respectful and does not have to be stuffy. It will be a strong indicator of your caring and professionalism. It will also set you apart from your competition. The Nassau Inn in Princeton, New Jersey, has an ongoing training program to encourage its staff to use full sentences, rather than curt phrases, when speaking to guests. They want to reestablish a style of gracious hospitality. They believe that proper language and polite manners will better convey their desire to be friendly and helpful.

**Using guests' names frequently**   Nothing is more pleasant to someone than the sound of their own name. Make it a game to find out the names of your guests and use them whenever appropriate during the meal. The greeter is in a perfect position to get the guests' names, either from the reservation list or just by asking them as they are seated. Remember always to use only their last name preceded by Mr. or Ms.

# 10
# Culinary Catastrophes

Opening the subject of food is taking a tiger by the tail. There are so many small points to make about different dishes. The nuances of their preparation, seasoning, and presentation are the subject of many books far more technical and scholarly than this one. Culinary details establish the character of a restaurant's kitchen and its reputation for fine cuisine. The more upscale the restaurant, the more food-related details figure into its success.

I will not even try to tackle the full spectrum of this subject. These decisions and judgments are properly between the skills of the chef and the palate of the guest. My focus here is on the more common annoyances of restaurant food preparation.

# Poor Procedures

When it comes to food, there are some things you just should not do. We see these basic culinary truths violated every day. If awareness is the first step toward solving a problem, perhaps the points in this section will help.

### Hot food that's not hot or cold food at room temperature

Hot food hot and cold food cold. If there is a cardinal culinary rule in the foodservice business, this is it. Still, restaurant cooks put hot food on cold plates or portion cold food onto plates hot from the dish machine every day. If you can prepare food at the proper temperature, how do you get it to the guest that way? It is simple thermodynamics. If the plate is hotter than the food, it will raise the food's temperature. If it is colder, it will cool the food.

To serve cold food cold, you must chill the food to start with. Cold plates are simply a matter of refrigeration. Other than preportioned frozen desserts, do not store cold food plates in a freezer. Frozen plates are *too* cold and can freeze moist foods. You might want to bring a chilled fork when you serve a cold plate. A crisp, cool salad is simple, elegant, and memorable. Mike Hurst of Fort Lauderdale's 15th Street Fisheries tells his guests that 43° is the perfect temperature for a salad as he serves a cool bowl of chilled greens. The statement creates a point of difference for his restaurant whenever his guests get a warm salad at another establishment.

Serving hot food hot becomes a little more involved. You must serve hot food at close to 200°F. Food cooked to order is usually at least that hot. Check the temperature of items held on a steam table. Stir frequently to be sure they are up to temperature, preferably at least 180°F. Plates that are hot enough to keep food from cooling on the way to the table are too hot to hold in your bare hand. If you are serious about hot food, heat plates in the oven to a minimum 250°F. Your staff must use a towel with 250° plates, of course, but your guests will get hot food. I also suggest removing your heat lamps. Your staff may think that heat lamps will keep waiting food hot. They will not. This can delay getting hot food to your guests. Without heat lamps, there is an urgency when hot food is up.

**Cold bread or rolls stale around the edges**   There is nothing like fresh, hot bread. People get stale rolls at home and dining out needs to be more special. If you can bake bread or rolls on the premises and serve them piping hot, you will have a big edge over your competition. To make sure bread is hot and fresh, you have several options. Bake it in small batches throughout the meal and bring it to the table hot from the oven. Keep it in a humidity-controlled warming drawer, making sure the temperature and moisture are correct. Reheat rolls in an injection steamer or a countertop pizza oven. The most effective method depends on the product and the physical limitations of your operation. Since every restaurant provides bread, you can make it a major point of difference for your establishment.

**Incomplete orders**   You have to get it right the first time or you will throw off the timing of the entire meal. In fast-paced operations, an expediter can be invaluable in assembling and checking orders. Incomplete orders cost you points with your guests and create additional work for your service staff.

**Hair or foreign objects in the food**   This is a difficult mistake to recover from. The only good solution is to avoid the error before it happens. Insist that all food handlers have hair restraints. Train everyone in the kitchen on proper techniques for storing, handling and preparing food. No detail is too picky if you want to assure the integrity of your food. If it does happen, remove the offending plate at once. Bring the guest a replacement meal quickly. Understand that they may want to order something different from the item you are replacing. In my restaurant, the entire meal would be complimentary and I would give them a gift certificate for a free meal on their next visit. When there is a problem, you must make it right and give guests another chance to experience a meal where nothing goes wrong.

**Making guests sick**   There are many documented cases of successful restaurants put out of business by an outbreak of foodborne illness. If you do not provide basic sanitation training to every member of your staff *before* you allow them to start work, you are gambling with your future. Approach sanitation with as much passion as you give to guest gratification. Devote a portion of every staff meeting to sanitation education. Make sure you have enough hand sinks and train your staff to use them frequently. Install hand sanitizers as a second step in personal hygiene. Get serious about sanitation.

**Half-melted ice cream**   Maintaining ice cream at the proper temperature is a challenge. If it is too hard, it is difficult to scoop and hard to eat. If it is too soft, it melts too quickly. Make sure to keep your ice cream cabinet properly adjusted and don't portion ice cream until you need it for service.

**Pouring old product on top of new product**   This is a bad habit developed for the convenience of the staff. It is repulsive to informed guests because it provides an opportunity for cross-contamination. If the older product is tainted, it will contaminate the fresh new product. Avoid it. Offer buffet items in small quantities. Attend your line constantly so you can replace empty containers at once. Your line will look better, your guests will be happier, and your food will be safer.

**Not changing serving utensils when changing containers of food**   Always bring clean serving utensils when replacing containers of food. Placing a soiled spoon into fresh product provides another opportunity for cross-contamination. It is also annoying to have to use a serving utensil that has food smeared on the handle from a previous patron. Replace soiled utensils, don't just wipe them off and put them back. It looks more professional and gives your guests more confidence in your operation.

**Frozen desserts too hard to get a spoon into**   Nobody enjoys struggling with their food. If you preportion frozen desserts, especially for a banquet, be sure they are not too hard to eat. Take them out of the freezer enough before service that they can soften to an edible consistency.

**Improperly prepared or improperly seasoned food**   The items on your menu create an expectation for your guests. If what you give them bears little resemblance to the item they expected, you will disappoint them. Serving your Steak Tartare medium rare is not likely to delight the patron who ordered it. The judgment of what "properly prepared" or "properly seasoned" means is still subjective. It depends on the diner's tastes and expectations, the prevailing customs in your market area, and the training of your chefs. To avoid problems, though, make sure that what you offer is what your guests expect to receive.

**"Tossed" salads that aren't**   The restaurant critic for the *San Francisco Chronicle* educated me about this 15 years ago. Unfortunately, he did it in print! I had listed a tossed salad on the menu. When he ordered it, he received mixed greens with dressing on top. In his review of the restaurant, he pointed out that a tossed salad requires that the dressing be tossed in the salad, not just dumped on top. He was right, of course. Tossed salads use less dressing and create a delightful balance between the dressing and the greens. If you do not truly toss the salad, call it a mixed green salad and be safe. If you care enough to present the item accurately, you can create a point of difference . . . and cut down on the amount of salad dressing you use.

**Ordering the *description* of an item and getting something else**   Menu copy and verbal presentations must accurately describe the item you are preparing. You will irritate your guests if the item on their plate does not contain the ingredients or preparation they expected. It is disappointing to order a crepe "filled with shrimp, crab, and scallops" only to find it contains a single shrimp. Guests also will be upset if the item contains ingredients they did not expect. Remember that many people have food allergies. Be sure that your menu, your servers, and your cooks are all on the same page. The only sure way to do this is to follow standardized recipes for every item on your menu. Do not allow your kitchen crew to get creative with the standard items. Use daily specials as an artistic outlet.

**Flavor transfer in fried foods**   When you can't taste the difference between the french fries and the fried fish, it's time to change the oil in the fryer. Flavor transfer comes from loose particles of one food item suspended in the oil and attaching themselves to another product. If you do a volume of different products, your safest approach is to have a separate fryer for each. If you can't do that, shake excess breading off before putting items in the fryer and regularly skim loose particles out of the oil. Strain the frying oil daily.

# Pathetic Presentation

People eat with their eyes. If your plate presentations are exciting and interesting, the evening will have more promise. If the plate looks depressing, the diner will be more apprehensive.

**Boring salad bars or buffets**   An advantage buffets and cafeterias enjoy over table service restaurants is that patrons can see the food before they make a selection. The possibilities for striking display and presentation are far more powerful than the best-written menu. Sadly, too few institutional operators have fully exploited the potential of presentation. Caterers have done a little better but have only scratched the surface.

**Poorly garnished (or ungarnished) plates**   Plate garnishing is another way to separate a plate of restaurant food from the same meal served at home. When I opened my first restaurant in San Francisco, we made plate garnishings a point of difference. While the majority of our competitors were dressing their plates with stray sprigs of parsley, we were presenting plates highlighted with colorful arrangements of fresh fruit. Fortunately, the industry is more conscious of garnishing now than it was in 1976. Still, there are always opportunities to make your plates memorable to your guests. Standardized plate garnishes will become boring for your staff and guests. Instead, tell your kitchen crew that the goal is to have a spontaneous, positive reaction from the guest when the plate is presented and watch the creative solutions they find!

**Nonfood items served on top of food items**   If a plate of food arrives with portion packs or ramekins stacked on top of the entrée, your guests will be annoyed. The contents may be edible, but the container is not. A good rule is never to put anything on the plate the guest cannot eat. This also includes placing food checks on top of the plates when the orders are ready for pickup.

**Messy presentations**   Unless they are part of your concept, avoid menu presentations that are messy for the guest to eat. It is irritating to be wearing good clothes and trying to eat a sandwich that is dripping down your arms. For example, hand-held sandwiches should not spill their ingredients or dribble sauce on the guest. You create the same problem when you put hard-to-cut items on a small plate loaded with vegetables and rice. Do not overcrowd your plate. Individual food items lose their identity and the meal is messy for your guests.

**Unappetizing plate presentations**   Plates that come out of a restaurant kitchen should have an impact on the guest. If you are doing it right, your patrons will have a spontaneous positive reaction when you present the plate to them. Tell your kitchen staff that achieving this reaction is the goal. Coach them with some suggestions to get them headed in the right direction and then stand back! You will be delighted at what they suggest. Plate presentation includes color, shape, and arrangement of the food. It involves selection of a complementary garnish. The cleanliness of the plate is also part of presentation. Clean up any spills before the plate leaves the kitchen.

**Salad bowl full of water**   A bowl full of water shows that the kitchen crew did not drain the greens before making the salad. The good news, I suppose, is that at least they washed the greens! A bowl full of water makes the last few bites of the salad an irritation instead of a pleasure for your guest. Greens stored in water will soften and deteriorate quickly. A more effective solution is to spin the excess water off the greens after washing and refrigerate them until you need them for preparation.

**Side dishes served on the entrée plate**   It sounds obvious, but side dishes are dishes that you serve on the side. That is where they belong. Like ramekins, the dishes themselves are not edible. Keep them off the plate. Separate dishes on the table encourage sharing and help expose the other dining companions to a wider range of your menu offerings.

**Foil on baked potatoes**   How did we ever start serving potatoes wrapped in metal? By now, most cooks don't even notice it . . . but your guests do. The rule is never to put anything on the plate that people can't eat. If you choose to cook the potatoes in foil, remove the metal before you serve the plate.

**Monocolored meals**   When planning your plate presentations, think in color. You probably won't get a spontaneous positive comment from a plate of french fries, breaded veal cutlet, and refried beans! Use vegetables and bright garnishes to give the plate more visual impact. When you plan a presentation, consider how it will look, not just what is on it.

**Butter floating in melted ice water**   Presenting butter on a bed of ice is an idea from the 1950s. The problem, of course, is that before the ice melts, the butter is too hard to spread. After the ice melts, the butter is soaking wet. The best solution is to find another presentation for your butter. (See the comments on page 137.)

**Dried out food on the buffet**   Cafeterias and buffets provide a unique opportunity for food presentation. Unfortunately, the longer the food sits at temperature, the more it dries out around the edges. To keep the line looking appetizing, present hot foods in smaller quantities and continually monitor their condition. Stir foods to keep them moist and distribute heat more evenly. Sauces on the steam table or in a chafing dish will thicken after 30 minutes. Be sure to add liquid to replace the moisture loss.

# Pitiful Products

People don't go out to eat just because they are hungry. Still, if they are not hungry, they probably won't be in your restaurant. This is still the foodservice business. Whatever the other elements of restaurant success, your food has to taste terrific.

**Mushy vegetables**   Unless you prepare vegetables to order, they are likely to be overcooked. This does not happen intentionally. Still, if you try to keep them hot on the steam table, they will get mushy. Most vegetables ought to have a fresh crunch to them. Cafeterias have a particularly hard time because the heat of the line continues to cook products while they await service. The solution it to put vegetables on the line a little under-cooked. Use smaller pans and prepare to meet the demands of the line.

**Food swimming in grease, butter, gravy or sauce**   Most people do not think this is an attractive presentation. Excessive grease or butter probably will make them think your food is not healthy for them. Too much sauce or gravy can overpower the dish. The goal is to make a balanced presentation where a guest is only aware of how tasty your food is, not the individual elements of the plate.

**Dried out food or condiments**    Particularly in dry climates, food items can get crusty around the edges if exposed to the air for very long. This drying makes the food look unappetizing and disturbs your guests. Stay ahead of the problem by keeping the tops on condiment containers. Cover portioned foods in plastic wrap until you need them for service. You can avoid this problem if you watch for it.

**Over- or undercooked meat**    This is particularly annoying the second time it happens to the same guest. If you cannot get it right, the guest may decide to dine at to your competitor. Part of the problem may be due to a difference of opinion about what a medium rare steak should look like. If you are having difficulties getting it right, have your guests order according to the color they want in the center of their steak. Rare is purple, medium rare is red, medium is pink, and so on. If the meat is not cooked the way guests want it, despite what they may have said when they ordered, make it right with them. Neither of you need the aggravation.

**Tough, brown, spotted, or wilted lettuce**    You present salad greens in their natural state. You cannot disguise a poor-quality product. To protect your professional reputation, use only top-quality produce. If you cannot get (or cannot afford) the quality you need, make a substitution. If you do not compromise your standards, you will gain the loyalty of your guests.

**Unimaginative salads with bottled dressings**    Every restaurant in the country has a salad. If you can create a point of difference with your salad, you have a marketing advantage. Offer a salad your guests can't make at home. Iceberg lettuce with cherry tomatoes, sliced cucumber, and Thousand Island dressing out of a jar is not the mark of a legendary restaurant. Use several different mixed greens, add interesting garnishes, develop signature salad dressings.

**Boring bread**    Bread presents another excellent opportunity to create a point of difference in the market. To become famous, never feature the same old bread or rolls as your competitors. Consistent with your concept, see what you can do that is special. Perhaps you can bake bread during the early morning hours when the kitchen is empty. Reheat the bread to order in a pizza oven the next evening. Bake biscuits, muffins, or quick breads in small batches throughout the meal and bring them to the table hot from the oven. How about fresh breadsticks, foccaccia, or hot garlic cheese bread? Lambert's Cafe in Sikeston, Missouri, is famous for its "throwed rolls" with sorghum. I don't know if the roll itself is unique, but the delivery system is certainly memorable.

**Surprise sauces**  Guests can be disturbed when sauces appear where none were expected (or desired), like on a broiled fish. This is another example of the importance of meeting your guests' expectations. If menu items come with a sauce, be sure to mention it when the guest orders. As a matter of policy, you might want to serve sauces on the side to give guests an option. Your diners may request this of you anyway.

**Soggy or greasy french fries**  French fries are the most popular menu item in America, probably because most people don't have deep fat fryers at home. McDonald's has built an empire with exceptional french fries and you can too, provided you take them seriously. Fries that are undercooked, greasy, or hard as a rock can be enough to send an otherwise satisfied guest down the road. Most of your competitors are likely to offer french fries. If their preparation is inconsistent, you can gain a market advantage by being picky about your fries.

**Old, overripe, or underripe fruit**  Fresh fruit offers an exceptional opportunity to introduce color to the table. If you select your produce carefully, you can gain points from an attractive fruit plate or fruit salad. If you use a product that is less than perfect, you risk disappointing your guests. You are wiser not to put an item out at all than to do it poorly.

**Overspiced foods**  Overspicing can be adding too much spice or adding spices to items where the guest was not expecting them. This is a particularly critical point for some older guests. If an item is spicy, be sure to warn guests when they order. Do not surprise them with seasonings they can't handle.

**Meat with excessive gristle or fat**  There are some wonderful dishes you can prepare with cheaper cuts of meat. You get in trouble when you try to make a poor cut work where you really need a more expensive one. Remember that the important point is whether your guests have an enjoyable experience, *not* what sort of food cost you can maintain. If you serve your guests tough or fatty meat, they will remember it long after they have forgotten your restaurant.

**"Can opener" cuisine**  In the quest to simplify operations, you can easily start to substitute prepared "convenience foods" for your own recipes. It is tempting to move in this direction when culinary talent becomes too expensive or too hard to find. You can purchase many items that are superior to those you can make yourself. The danger is that, over time, you can end up buying more products than you make yourself. In the extreme, you are not offering anything unique. Your competitors (and perhaps your guests) could duplicate your shopping list and through that, your menu. Add convenience products cautiously. Periodically, reexamine your production program to be sure you are still a restaurant and not just an assembly line.

**Moldy bread**  Treat your bread with care and never take it for granted. Make (or buy) your bread in small quantities so it will never be around long enough to become moldy. Train your staff to look for the signs of mold every time they handle bread. Your guests deserve at least that much attention.

**Too much dressing on the salad**  Why is it that so many restaurants want to drown the salad in dressing? The notion of "more is better" is simply not true. Dressings should complement the salad, not overpower it. The tastiest salads are tossed with the dressing, literally a "tossed salad." You use less dressing, create a point of difference in the market, and serve a tastier salad.

**Crushed or stale chips**  Nobody likes stale chips. Handle potato chips and tortilla chips carefully. Keep them in closed containers and don't open packages until you need them for service. Give serious thought about whether potato chips enhance your meal presentation or detract from it. Your guests can have the same product at home, so it is not very special. Make it a staff project to look for unique substitutes that could give your menu a fresh new look.

**A heavy hand with the paprika**  Many guests dislike restaurants that get carried away with the paprika. A light touch of paprika is a garnish. A heavy dose of paprika is a spice. Be sure your line staff knows and respects the difference.

**Undercooked eggs**  Just the *texture* of undercooked eggs is disturbing to some people. With the current concern about salmonella and raw eggs, the problem is more acute. To be safe, many operators now use pasteurized eggs for everything but fried eggs at breakfast.

**Things that *should* be crisp that aren't; things that *shouldn't* be crisp that are!**  Your guests expect certain foods to have certain textures. If the texture is different, it diminishes their dining experience. Crispness is a marketable texture. If you doubt that, look at the number of products that make claims of crispness. People know the difference between crisp and soggy. Don't disappoint them.

**Bread that can't hold up to the sandwich**  The messier the filling, the more substantial the bun must be to hold up to it. Nobody likes soggy sandwiches or disintegrating buns. Test your breads before you decide which ones to use for various sandwiches. Train your service staff to watch for problems at the table. Train your dish crew to pay attention to food left on the plates coming back from the dining room. If you notice a problem, fix it.

**Dried-out desserts**   The problem with cutting desserts in advance is that they can easily dry out. A moist cake is a true delight of the baker's art, but cakes are particularly susceptible to drying. If possible, do not cut a piece of cake until needed for service. Cover exposed surfaces with plastic wrap to keep them from drying out. It is more work, but it is the price you pay to serve a quality dessert.

**Powdered mashed potatoes**   The bane of institutional feeding is making an appearance in table service restaurants. Instant mashed potatoes can work in some operations, but don't try to save money with inexpensive products. If you use instant potatoes, get the highest quality product you can find. Better yet, use real mashed potatoes and create a point of difference.

**Sand in the spinach**   Fresh spinach is a wonderful product, but it can be sandy. If you use fresh bulk spinach, break the leaves apart and rinse them thoroughly in a sink full of fresh water. If you buy spinach in bunches, cut off the stems before you wash the leaves. You will lose a little spinach this way, but you will eliminate most of the sand (and the labor) that makes fresh spinach a problem. Spin the excess water from the leaves and store them under refrigeration until just before service.

**Unimaginative vegetables**   Vegetables ought to reflect the same creativity as your entrées. When they don't, it detracts from the meal. For example, I was in a restaurant recently and ordered Veal Piccata. The plate arrived with a creative garnish, a lovely piece of hand-crafted veal . . . and clump of cubed carrots that looked straight off a school lunch line! Don't undermine your culinary talent by failing to pay attention to everything you put on the plate.

**Fresh fish or seafood that isn't**   It is always a treat when you can offer your guests fresh fish. If your fish did not arrive in your restaurant unfrozen, though, don't lie to your guests just because it sounds better. "Fresh fish" that isn't fresh is the verbal equivalent of flowery copy on the menu.

**Poor-quality ice cream**   If people eat bargain ice cream at home, they want something special when they go out. If they eat premium ice cream, they know the difference. For ice cream to be a satisfying, restaurant-quality dessert, it has to be premium.

**Lumpy soups or gravies**   As more convenience food products enter the restaurant market, house-made products can be a point of difference for your establishment. If you are going to make it from scratch, make it properly. You don't need lumps to prove the item is an original.

# Prosaic Policies

You can create culinary problems by management decree. Fortunately, you can solve them the same way. Here are a few policy-related irritants to consider.

**Re-serving food**   A restaurant should not reuse unpackaged foods like rolls. When you remove a large basket of bread from the table, guests wonder what happens to the leftover rolls. A friend tells of having dinner one night with a federal health official. Suspecting that the restaurant was recycling bread, the inspector slit the side of a roll and inserted his business card. The waiter removed the roll basket. As the coffee arrived, they heard a shriek from the other side of the dining room. Another guest had found the card!

To provide responsive service and maintain cost control, serve rolls in small quantities. Explain to the guest that you will bring them more fresh, hot rolls whenever they want more. This way, the guest gets a better product, the service is more personal, and the restaurant does not waste food.

**Surprise substitutions**   If you cannot give guests exactly what they expect, let them know and give them alternative choices. An unrequested substitution, no matter how good the product, will irritate your patrons.

**Daily specials that aren't special**   Specials are a good way to provide variety for your regular guests and give the kitchen staff a creative outlet. Daily specials are an excellent vehicle for testing potential new menu items, covering more cost points and giving guests something to talk about. If your daily special is always (and only) a way to use leftovers, you are missing an opportunity.

**Butter so hard it rips the bread**   Rock-hard butter is annoying to your guests. It is impossible to spread without destroying the bread. Find a way to present butter so it has a consistency that does not detract from the guest's enjoyment of the meal. Do not serve butter directly from the refrigerator. To be spreadable, butter should be cool, but not cold. In most operations, it is relatively easy to serve foil-wrapped packets of butter or portion packs of margarine at proper temperature. Bulk or uncovered spreads require more sensitive handling. Remember that if you have it on your menu, you have to be able to serve it right.

**Repetitive sauces**   Every item on your menu ought to have several uses but variety is the spice of life. Vary the sauces you offer to protect your menu from an image of sameness. This is particularly important in hotels where a group may be meeting for several days. Review the group's entire menu to be sure you do not repeat similar sauces.

**Food spilled on the rim or bottom of plates**   Always wipe away food spills before the plate leaves the kitchen. This can easily happen when the servers stack plates up their arm. Food on the bottom of the plate also means that the bottom of the plate was sitting in someone's meal.

**Menu items that are difficult to eat**   Watch out for ingredients in soups or stews that are too big to eat in one bite and difficult to cut in the bowl. These presentations are awkward for your guests and detract from their enjoyment of the restaurant. Older diners are particularly uncomfortable when they have to wrestle with their meals. If you offer a chunky beef stew, put it in a shallow bowl instead of a deep dish. It will be easier for your guests to eat.

**Inconsistent portion sizes**   Standardized recipes specify portion sizes as well as ingredients. If your portions are inconsistent from one meal to the next, guests become less trusting. It is even more annoying when portion sizes differ among guests at the same table. Human nature being what it is, guests with the smallest portions will feel cheated. Inconsistent portion sizes also make cost control impossible. Portion control is the key to managing your food cost and avoiding unhappy guests.

**Excessive portion sizes**   For years, many operators' idea of good service was to "give them more than they can eat and keep the coffee cup full." There is no question that large portions are a marketing advantage for some restaurants. Still, there is a trend toward lighter meals. More diners have concerns about their weight and health. They are eating less but eating better. The popularity of grazing menus in many cities attests to the attraction of smaller portions at smaller prices. You can capitalize on this trend by offering half portions at 60% to 75% of full menu price. This will make your establishment more attractive to older diners who usually do not eat as much. People who are just being more careful about what they eat will also appreciate smaller portions. If these patrons cannot eat the way they want by dining out, they will just stay home.

**Inconsistent taste**   People are creatures of habit. If you want one of their habits to be dining in your restaurant, you must earn their trust. You will not build trust if diners cannot rely on the consistency of your food. When the lasagna is delicious one day and disastrous the next, people will stop ordering it. Neither will they risk the embarrassment of recommending your establishment to their friends unless they know what to expect from you. To achieve consistent product taste, develop standardized recipes for all menu items and insist that your production crew follows the recipes precisely.

**Remains of an unordered item on the plate**   I was in a local restaurant recently and ordered the daily special. The restaurant offered the item with mashed potatoes, but I asked the server to substitute french fries instead. As I finished my meal, I noticed mashed potatoes stuck to the plate under the spot where the french fries had been! I suspect the kitchen first put mashed potatoes on the plate instead of french fries and removed them when they caught the error. At least I *hope* that was what happened. I would hate to think the plate had mashed potatoes on it before the process started!

# Bonus Points

Everybody likes pleasant surprises. These little unexpected touches are opportunities to improve your score and put your guests in a better mood. They help make up for any lapses in the operation and give people something to talk about to their friends.

**Housemade croutons**　Poor-quality croutons out of a box can make guests forget an otherwise memorable salad. Croutons are easy to make and can be a point of difference in your salad presentation.

**Interesting jams, jellies, or preserves**　Most restaurants simply purchase jams, jellies, and preserves. If you make the product yourself, it brings a homey touch to your restaurant. You will enhance your image as a quality operation and gain a unique position in the market.

**Exceptional, piping hot bread**　Oh, the magic of fresh, hot bread! It is worth the effort to create a superior bread product and presentation. Every time your patrons eat in a competing restaurant, they will think of you when the bread arrives.

**Signature items**　To be successful in today's market, it takes more than just doing a good job. Be famous for something. Find items that you can do better than anyone else and use them to build your reputation.

**Housemade desserts**　Baking is a lost art at home. Exceptional signature desserts baked fresh on the premises are a major point of difference in the market. If you cannot bake your own desserts, personalize a purchased product with a signature sauce, fresh fruit, or something unusual. Don't just cut the cheesecake and put it on a plate.

**After dinner treat**　People love pleasant surprises. Instead of ordinary mints with the check, how about a chocolate-covered strawberry, a tartlet, or a fresh cookie? In Australia and New Zealand, it is common to receive a fresh chocolate with the coffee. See what you can come up with. Anybody can buy mints.

**Garnished food pans on the buffet**  Legendary restaurants garnish every food presentation to enhance its visual appeal for their guests. If you operate a cafeteria or buffet, you cannot garnish plates, but you *can* dress up the food display by garnishing the pans of hot food. Do an imaginative job of garnishing and you can lose your institutional image.

# 11
# Beverage Blunders

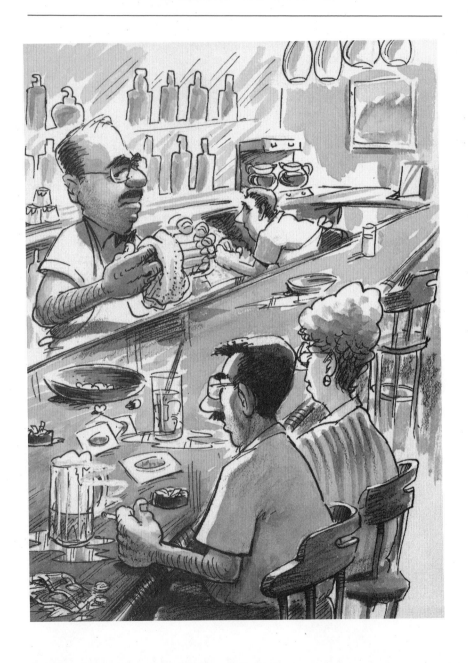

This chapter covers beverages of all types, not merely the alcoholic variety. Many restaurants are as popular for their bar operations as they are for their dining. You may not sell a meal to everyone who walks in the door, but you will surely serve them a beverage. You might as well do it properly.

# Procedural Paralysis

Often, the way you choose to do things is a clue to the source of your problems. Sometimes, *not* making a conscious decision on how you want to handle something has the same effect.

**Hot drinks in cold cups or cold drinks in hot glasses**  This is the same thermodynamic issue discussed in the previous chapter. Containers that are colder than the liquid will cool the drink. Containers that are warmer will warm the drink. The result can be a lukewarm Irish Coffee or a drink with melted ice. Either situation will irritate your guests.

**Unrefrigerated, spoiled, or scummy cream**  There are some people who prefer nondairy creamer to real dairy products for dietary reasons. Many operators use nondairy creamer only because it is easier to handle, not because it is their guests' preference. If you use real cream, half and half or milk, you must handle it properly. To avoid problems, keep real cream chilled and bring it to the table in small portions. Do not leave a pitcher of real cream on the table and do not add fresh cream to a partially full pitcher. Discard unused cream when clearing the table. Portion packs are even safer, but do not have the visual appeal of a small cream pitcher, particularly in upscale restaurants.

**Foreign objects in the beverages**  If you prepare drinks properly, they will have real visual appeal for your guests. Just be aware of what your guests see when they look at their drinks. Foreign objects in the glass can come from dirty glasses, impurities in the ice, or poor ice handling. Be sure glasses are clean. Store glasses upside down to prevent dust and dirt from getting inside. Install filters on the water lines to the ice maker. Keep ice bins clean. If you ever buy ice, be especially careful when emptying ice bags into the bin. Dirty bags can contaminate the ice supply. Use only clean buckets and scoops for ice transfers. Keep them properly stored so they will stay clean between uses.

**Improperly chilled beer or wine**  Improper chilling can mean a product that is too warm or one that is too cold. For example, room temperature beer works in Great Britain, but it doesn't meet the expectations of American beer drinkers. A crisp white wine is less enjoyable at room temperature. People drink beer and (some) wine cold because they taste more refreshing that way. If the beverage is not cool enough, it lacks the invigoration your diners want. On the other hand, if a beverage is *too* cold, it can lose its character. Beer that is too cold will be flat and cloudy. Do not chill beer below 40°F. The nearer it is to 45°F, the better it will taste. White wines have more bouquet and flavor at 45°F than at 35°F. If you keep white wine in a refrigerator you use to store food, it will be too cold for maximum enjoyment.

**Lemon slices too thin to squeeze**   Fresh lemon enhances the flavor of iced tea. I appreciate the visual appeal of a thin slice of lemon hanging on the rim of a frosty glass of fresh-brewed tea. But what can you do with a thin slice of lemon? It's too thin to squeeze and just dropping it in the glass does not add much lemon taste. Serve iced tea with a lemon wedge. At least your guests can do something with it! If you want a garnish on the glass, try a sprig of fresh mint.

**Drinks without a stirrer or straw**   Include a straw or a stir stick in every drink. Many women prefer to drink from a straw. A stir stick also gives guests something to do with their hands.

# Glassware Gaffes

The proper glassware makes a major difference in the impact of your beverage service.

**Improper glassware**   Using the right glass is the key to presentation and cost control in the bar. The proper glass is particularly important in wine service. The more expensive the wine, the more elegant the glassware ought to be. It would be a crime to pour a Chateau Petrus '82 into a water glass! Certain types of glasses are traditional for certain drinks. Varying too far from what your guests expect will disappoint them, even if you serve an otherwise excellent cocktail.

**Undersized glassware**   Small drinks are less impressive than large drinks, especially at high prices. Value is determined by a variety of factors but a large, attractive glass filled reasonably full is usually more appealing than a small glass filled to the brim.

**Soiled or scratched glassware**   You cannot present a drink attractively in a dirty glass. Also watch for glasses that have become scratched. Sparkling glassware accents the excitement of the tabletop. If glassware has been scratched or chipped, it not only looks terrible but is a safety and sanitation problem as well. Glassware styles change over the years. When it is time to order more glasses, look at what you are using and decide if it still reflects well on your restaurant. If not, make a change. It's a simple way to inject some new life into a tired dining room.

# Refreshment Relapses

Guests will not enjoy their drinks, alcoholic or otherwise, if you serve a poor-quality product. The list of potential drink errors is endless. Here are a few of the more common mistakes to avoid.

**Dried-out or slimy fruit garnish**   Fruit dries out after cutting, particularly citrus fruits like oranges and lemons. Storing cut fruit in its own juices can help maintain freshness longer. However, if bar fruit stays in liquid too long, it takes on a slimy feel. Don't cut more garnish than you need for the shift.

**Flat soft drinks**   Flat or metallic tasting club soda has probably ruined more drinks and cost bars more money than any other cause. Since the mixer makes up half to three-quarters of a highball, it is good business to serve good mixers. Soft drinks need sharp carbonation to be truly satisfying. Check with your supplier if you have a problem and adjust your system to correct it. Be sure to keep a spare cylinder of carbon dioxide on hand.

**Lukewarm coffee**   Always serve coffee at 190°F, especially at banquets. Lukewarm coffee is not enjoyable and irritates your guests, particularly coffee lovers.

**"12-hour" coffee**   Unaromatic coffee will send your guests packing. For a truly memorable cup of coffee, start with the highest quality beans you can find. Grind the beans just before brewing. Brew in small batches throughout the day and never hold coffee longer than 45 minutes. The difference between premium coffee and economy coffee is like day and night . . . for only a few cents more per cup. Legendary restaurants serve legendary coffee. Get serious and you can make your coffee a point of difference in the market.

**Tepid tea water**   If the water is not hot enough, it cannot brew a proper cup of tea. If tea drinkers cannot get a proper cup of tea, they will be disappointed. Since it is poor form to disappoint your guests, get serious about tea. Prewarm the teapot to keep it from cooling the tea water. Fill the pot with fresh boiling water and bring it to the table immediately. Legendary restaurants also serve legendary tea. Offer a selection of quality teas. Like premium coffee, the difference is only pennies a cup. Your reputation is worth it.

**Overly strong (or weak) coffee or iced tea**   Whatever you do, make a legendary brew. There is a proper balance between coffee and water necessary to brew a consistently excellent pot of coffee. Brewing great coffee takes clean water at the proper temperature and the right amount of coffee of the proper grind. The water flow rate must keep water in contact with the grounds for the right amount of time. If you try to save a few cents by using less coffee, your brew can be bitter because the grounds are over-extracted. Your coffee supplier can help you find the right balance.

Iced tea is often a brewing problem, also. Weak iced tea tastes like stale water. Brew iced tea slightly stronger than hot tea to allow for dilution as the ice melts. At his Max's Diner in San Francisco, Dennis Berkowitz prepares iced tea by pouring a pot of hot tea over a big glass of ice at the table. How's that for creating a point of difference on a common item?

**Draft beer that's all foam**   When draft beer is excessively foamy, it makes more work for the bartender and slows service to the guests. There are several potential causes for this condition. The keg may be agitated or too warm (above 45°F). The gas pressure in the system may be too high or the draft lines may be dirty. Improper pouring can also cause wild beer. If you hold the glass too far from the faucet or if the faucet is not fully open when pouring, the beer will foam. Draft beer can be a profitable beverage, but only if you train your staff to handle it properly. If you do not take quality draft beer seriously, you will only annoy your guests.

**Strong chemical taste in the water**   An off taste suggests a problem with the municipal water supply. If so, consider filters or softeners to treat the water and remove the impurities that create the taste. Some upscale restaurants are even bringing a bottle of mineral water to the table instead of using water from the tap. If this idea fits with your concept, it is a wonderful way to create another point of difference. The most potent points of difference are the ones you can create with items that everyone else serves. Water is perfect!

**Instant coffee**   Your guests drink instant coffee at home or on camping trips. Real restaurants brew real coffee. Fifteen years ago you could get away with using instant decaffeinated coffee, but no more. Decaf drinkers deserve the same quality beverage as regular coffee drinkers. Handling two brews takes a little more work, but happy guests are worth it.

**Beer with no head**   A detergent residue on the glass will prevent beer from developing a head. The neat collar of foam on a glass of beer makes the presentation more attractive. If you pour draft beer, you also use a little less product to fill the glass. The important point, though, is that your guests are happier when the glass looks inviting. Ask your supplier for a cleaner that can give you "beer clean" glasses and use it faithfully.

**Grounds in the coffee cup**   Be careful when grinding coffee and filling coffee filters. Loose grounds that fall between the filter and the basket can find their way to the bottom of the pot and into the cup. Train your staff to avoid emptying the pot at the table. If you leave a little coffee in the bottom of the pot, any loose grounds will stay in the pot. Throw out the remaining coffee and rinse the pot before refilling it. You will lose a little product this way but avoid the chance of irritating a diner with a mouth full of coffee grounds.

# Pathetic Policies

Many beverage problems are caused by a management decision to do (or not do) things a certain way. Changing the policy can solve the problem without much other effort.

**Drinking with nothing to nibble on**   People like something to munch on while they are drinking. Snacks make sitting in the lounge more of a social event than an alcoholic one. You could have simple bar snacks, an elaborate hors d'oeuvre spread, or an appetizer menu in the bar. Have *something* interesting to nibble on. It will make your guests more comfortable and increase your beverage sales.

**Charging for second pot of tea water**   This is an inane policy! I have even been in restaurants where they wanted to charge for another tea bag. This is a classic case of "penny wise and pound foolish." The cost of a tea bag or a pot of hot water is not worth the cost of losing the patronage of a potential regular guest. Take care of your guests and the profits will take care of themselves.

**Allowing someone to buy a woman a drink without her permission**   If you let this happen, it puts the woman in an awkward situation. In my restaurants in San Francisco, we had a policy that nobody could buy a woman a drink without her permission. We also trained the staff to be alert for any woman who looked uncomfortable with a gentleman's advances. When we spotted a problem, we would ask the woman if she was having a problem and defuse the situation. These policies made the bar safe for a single woman. We attracted women who wanted to be social but did not want to be harassed. The bar scene rarely got out of control because the men knew we would not allow any inconsiderate behavior.

**No fresh glass with a fresh drink**   When guests are drinking beer or wine, bring a fresh glass when you bring a fresh bottle. Whether they accept the glass or not, this touch is a mark of attentive service. Remember to replace any damp or damaged cocktail napkins on the table when you bring fresh drinks.

**Substituting a lower grade of liquor**   I suppose this still happens in sleazy taverns but I hope it never happens in a serious restaurant. Brand substitution is just cheating and it will come back to haunt you. The practice comes from an idea that the guest is too stupid (or too drunk) to notice the switch. Either notion is dangerous. If you believe your guests are stupid, you will not give them the respect they deserve and they will go elsewhere. If you are serving people who have had too much to drink, you are also flirting with disaster. It is illegal to serve an obviously intoxicated patron. Worse yet, you can create liability for your establishment if that person has an accident while driving home.

**No alcohol-free options**  With the increasing awareness of drinking and driving, many patrons are looking for alcohol-free options. Most of your guests go out to be social, not to get drunk. There are a lot cheaper (and safer) ways to get drunk than to do it in a restaurant. Americans are drinking less alcohol than in the past but they *are* drinking higher-quality liquor than before. If you can offer interesting alcohol-free drinks, you will allow guests to stay longer and spend more. Remember that drinking is primarily social. You can charge as much for alcohol-free signature drinks as you can for your regular well drinks. You have happier guests and more healthy profit margins. What a civilized idea!

# Sorrowful Service

Beverage service follows the same rules as serving food at the table. A well-trained staff providing unobtrusive service is the measure of a legendary establishment. As Don Smith would say, the coach makes the difference.

**Water, iced tea, or coffee not promptly refilled**  Americans expect free refills on coffee, water, and iced tea. Train your staff to be attentive but never to be overzealous. Bussers who refill glasses after each sip are annoying and intrude on the guests' enjoyment of their meal. Many restaurants are placing a carafe of iced tea, ice water, or coffee on the table. The restaurant staff can still provide the refills, but guests have the option of getting it themselves if the staff gets bogged down.

**Holding glasses by the bowl or rim**  Never let your crew handle a glass by the bowl or rim. It not only leaves fingerprints but also is like sticking your fingers in the guest's mouth! Many diners will send back glasses if you handle them this way. You don't need the aggravation . . . and neither do your guests. Train your staff to handle glassware only by the stem or the lower third.

**Coffee in the saucer**  This is just sloppy service. What is the guest supposed to do with a saucer full of coffee? If they try to drink, they will drip coffee on their clothes. Pouring it back into the cup is unappetizing. Pour coffee into the cup at the table instead of trying to carry the cup already filled. Be careful not to splash hot coffee on your guests when pouring.

Serve a coaster or cocktail napkin in the saucer to absorb any spills and act as a silencer.

**Pouring *anything* from a stained container**   You wouldn't serve food on a dirty plate. Why would you serve from a dirty container? Serving pitchers for water or iced tea must be as spotless as the glass you are filling.

**Awkward, improper, or inept wine service**   Proper wine service is smooth and unobtrusive. Skill in opening and pouring wine only comes with practice. Ask your wine supplier to help you find a supply of foil caps so your staff can practice foil cutting. An "Ah-So" wine opener will allow you to recork the bottles between exercises. Drill your crew until they are confident in their abilities to handle wine service smoothly. Train your staff to roll the bottle slightly at the end of the pour to avoid dribbling wine on the table. The more comfortable they are with the process, the more likely they are to suggest wine to your guests.

**Cold drinks without a coaster or napkin**   Cold drinks sweat and get the counter or tabletop wet. Without something to absorb this moisture, condensation will drip on guests when they lift the glass to drink. Your guests will appreciate your awareness of this problem if you bring a coaster or cocktail napkin to absorb condensation. If your napkins sport your restaurant's logo, it will remind your guests of your restaurant and reinforce your image every time they raise their glasses.

**Popping a champagne cork**   Champagne is a civilized beverage that deserves civilized handling. Only amateurs or college fraternities pop a champagne cork or shoot it across the room. The gaffe is particularly rude when the guest is paying more than $15 for the bottle. You can serve champagne properly without dampening the spirit of celebration at the table. Train your staff to release the pressure slowly when opening a champagne bottle. It is more professional and far safer.

**Pouring regular coffee into a cup of decaf**   This error is particularly annoying. It usually requires the service staff to replace the coffee cup and inconveniences the guest. To avoid the problem, have a way to tell which kind of coffee your guests are drinking. This is particularly true if someone other than the server pours coffee. Use different cups or different underliners to identify decaf drinkers.

**Scooping ice with a glass**   Using a glass to scoop ice is unsanitary and dangerous. From the public health perspective, scooping ice with the glass puts your hands in the ice and makes your guests uneasy. There is also a danger that the glass could easily break in the ice. If this happens, you must immediately empty the ice bin, clean it thoroughly, and refill it before service can continue. You can also count on the accident to happen in the middle of the rush! If a glass chips and you don't notice it, you could serve a piece of glass in a drink, causing serious injury to your guests. Don't take a bet you can't afford to lose. Always use a scoop to fill a glass with ice. Your guests will appreciate your professionalism.

**Not getting the order right the first time**    Guests are happier when they are eating and drinking. Do not make them wait while you shuttle between the bar and the table trying to get their drink order straight. Know your drinks and how they might be served. Ask the right questions when you take the order. Do they want it up or on the rocks? Do they want salt on the rim of their margarita? Be a pro and get it right the first time.

**Overfilling coffee cups**    More is not always better. Remember that many people like their coffee with a lot of milk or cream. Leave enough room for guests to adjust their coffee to taste.

**Iced beverages that are all ice and no beverage**    Unless you make iced tea by pouring hot tea into a glass of ice, don't fill the glasses full of ice cubes. If there is not as much liquid in the glass as your guests expect, you will upset them. You also create more work for the service staff, because they will have to provide refills sooner. If the drink is gone before the thirst, your guests get annoyed.

**Wet or sticky bartop**    I know your mom taught you not to put your elbows on the table, but you know everybody does it. If guests' elbows (or wallets, notebooks, or newspapers) *stick* to the bar top, watch out! How are they going to clean themselves up? What are they thinking about you while they are doing it?

**Refilling coffee cups without permission**    This is especially annoying for guests who take cream and sugar in their coffee. Just when they get it blended the way they want it, some well-intentioned server destroys the balance! If you leave carafes on the table, you can avoid the problem. If not, train your staff to pause with the pot by the guest's cup and wait for permission to proceed.

**Overfilling glasses**    Unless it is a small juice glass, never fill glasses any closer than within a half inch from the rim. This gap provides a frame for the surface of the beverage. It lessens the chance of a spill while carrying the glass and makes it easier for the guests to drink without spilling. Spills ruin the presentation of a great drink and diminish your guests' enjoyment of their evening.

**Not serving everything at the table from a tray**    At home, people carry plates and glasses to the table in their hands. If we want to make dining out a more pleasant experience than dining at home (and I hope we do), this is a good place to start. To your guests, trays look clean and professional whereas hand-carrying looks dirty and amateurish. How do you want to be remembered?

**Cocktail napkin with the logo askew**  Place a cocktail napkin or coaster with the restaurant's logo facing the guest. Haphazard placement only shows your lack of concentration and inattention to detail. Human nature being what it is, your guests will notice a crooked placement. They may *not* notice if you do it properly.

**Serving the wrong drink**  Getting the orders confused is embarrassing for everyone. The guest doesn't know what to do with the drink. The service staff shows their ineptitude. The guest who originally made the order doesn't get served. A further problem is what to do when you realize the mistake. You can't pick a drink up off one table and serve it to another. If a drink mix-up happens, acknowledge the mistake to both parties and apologize for the error. Leave the drink as a complimentary gift to the incorrect party or remove it promptly. Bring a complimentary replacement to the person whose order you misdirected. If you try to talk your way out of the error or avoid responsibility for correcting the error, you will only irritate both parties. The cost of a few drinks is far less than the cost of losing two groups of potential regulars.

**Not refilling snack bowls promptly**  Snack bowls are like water glasses. People expect you to refill them regularly. If people are eating, they are drinking. Avoid large communal snack bowls. People get nervous about sharing finger food, particularly if they are sharing with strangers.

**Depleted array of bar snacks**  If you offer a food buffet in the bar during happy hour, approach it as professionally as you do the rest of your food operation. Plan memorable menus. Decorate the buffet table attractively. Be sure to skirt the buffet table—it makes the presentation more impressive. Keep the buffet clean and neat. Replenish items on the buffet promptly right up to the end of happy hour. Think of the bar buffet as a sneak preview of the culinary skill guests can expect when they have dinner in the dining room. You may entice bar guests to stay for a meal.

**Not knowing the brands carried at the bar**  How often can you say "I don't know" before you feel stupid? Basic service staff training must include a thorough knowledge of the brands you carry and the ingredients of your specialty drinks. If you have signature drinks (and I recommend you do), be sure your staff has tasted them all and can describe them in an appetizing and accurate way.

**Not serving wine promptly**  Three years ago, on the infamous evening that led to this book, I went out for dinner on Cape Cod with my father and stepmother. The restaurant was *not* having a good night (and neither were we!) When the server asked us for a cocktail order at the beginning of the meal, we ordered a bottle of wine instead. The wine did not arrive until after the entrées were served! We knew we would not finish a bottle before we finished dinner so we sent the bottle back. Had the wine arrived promptly, we would have undoubtedly been ready for a second bottle when the meal arrived. If you serve the first bottle of wine promptly, you increase your chances of selling a second one. If you don't serve the wine until after you serve the entrées, you will just create resentment.

**Disappearing servers**   When guests' frustration reaches the point where they get up and get their own drinks, you are losing points. It is false economy not to schedule enough servers to keep up with demand.

# Bartender Boo-Boos

Bartenders are subject to most of the observations and suggestions in the chapter on service. They also have some unique opportunities to alienate guests. Be sensitive to the following mixology mistakes.

**Discussing a guest's previous companions**   Never mention someone's prior companions, especially those of the opposite sex and especially when the guest is with people you don't know.

**Pointing out prior impairments**   No matter how well you know the patron, never point out their drunken antics of the night before (or any other time). If someone has behaved poorly, they know it. Have the good taste not to mention it.

**Making guests wait while washing glasses**   Only undistracted, focused attention will cause your guests to feel served. By trying to do two things at once, you tell your guests that their arrival is not the most important event of the moment. I have seen more than one party walk out when faced with this thoughtless behavior. If you are involved in something else when guests arrive, at least acknowledge their presence with eye contact and a smile. Let them know you are aware they are waiting and assure them that you will be right with them.

**Inconsistent drink sizes**   Consistency is the mark of a professional. If bartenders give their friends a larger pour, they are not really making any friends. Guests who are not receiving special treatment will feel slighted. Those favored with the heavy hand will not have a good time, either. Most people drink to be sociable, not to get drunk. After being knocked on their cars a few times, people are likely to decide to patronize another establishment.

**Sloppy or inept moves**  The appeal of drinks prepared by a bartender over those from a service bar is the ability to watch the performance. Bartenders are part of the entertainment in the lounge. Practice makes perfect and a little choreography helps. Work with your bartenders to develop their style. While the antics of the bartenders in the movie "Cocktail" are a bit over the line, a few good moves can't hurt.

**Shortchanging the guest**  Never try to cheat or shortchange guests. No matter how much they have had to drink, the guests will eventually figure it out. Other guests at the bar also may catch on to what is happening. Your establishment will get a reputation from which you may never recover. Screen your staff well, train them thoroughly, and coach them consistently. Make guest gratification the most important job in the restaurant.

**Wiping the bar with a smelly or stained rag**  Using a dirty rag gives guests the impression that you are soiling the bar rather than cleaning it. Since guests sit at the bar while you are wiping it, pay attention to the cleanliness of your cleaning cloths. Do not use them for anything other than wiping the bartop. For example, do not clean a floor spill with the same cloth you use to wipe the bartop. Replace cleaning cloths when they get soaked or start to look dirty. Remember that wiping the bar with a wet rag makes it unpleasant to the touch. If you use a wet cloth on the bar, be sure to follow up with a clean, dry one to remove the dampness.

**Polishing glasses with a towel**  Polishing glasses only looks good in 1930s movies. The practice is unsanitary and will bother your guests. If bartenders are polishing glasses, it probably means the glasses were not clean enough after the washing process. Train your staff on the proper way to wash glasses and follow up to see that they have it right. Sparkling glassware is important. How you get it to sparkle is equally significant.

**Inconsistent taste**  Guests rely on the consistency of your products. If the daiquiris have a different taste from day to day, people will stop ordering them. To achieve consistent product taste, develop standardized recipes for all drinks and insist that your bartenders follow the recipes precisely.

**Handling beer by the mouth of the bottle**  Putting your fingers on something the guest will put in their mouths is a serious lapse. Handle beer bottles the same way you handle glassware. Use the lower third only.

**Wet change**  Yuck! If you hand the guest wet money or place change on a wet bar, your point total drops quickly. Some lesser life forms do this to encourage the patron to leave the money as a tip. Perhaps the inconsiderate bartender should leave!

**Not removing full ashtrays when clearing a table**   Your entire lounge may be a smoking area, but not all guests are smokers. While waiting for a table in a national chain restaurant, my wife and I (nonsmokers) were seated at a table in the bar. The staff cleared everything off the table except the overflowing ashtray from the previous party. Even if we were smokers, it would still have been disgusting. Perhaps it was just an oversight, but the cocktail crew didn't notice the problem. My suspicion is that nobody ever made them aware that such carelessness has an impact on their guests' experience.

# Bonus Points

Everybody likes pleasant surprises. These little unexpected touches are opportunities to improve your score and put your guests in a better mood. They help make up for any lapses in the operation and give people something to talk about to their friends.

**Separate coaster for the bottle and the glass**   Coasters or cocktail napkins keep the tabletop dry. Beer bottles sweat as much as glasses do. Your guests will appreciate your awareness that a wet table is an unpleasant experience.

**Chilled mugs and glasses**   Beverages stay colder in cold glasses. Although the practice of chilled mugs for beer is not particularly unique any more, those who like their beer cold always appreciate the service. Many establishments chill wine glasses for white wine sold in the bar. You have nothing to lose by making the gesture.

**Inventive garnishes**   There are some cocktails where guest expectations will dictate a particular garnish. In other cases, you have more options. Experiment a little and see if you can find a fresh way to present some of your old favorites.

**Exceptional snacks**   If your establishment only serves alcohol, guests will not expect much creativity. If you are a full service restaurant, though, you can use your bar snacks to display your culinary prowess and entice drinkers to stay for dinner. Go beyond what people expect. Paoli's in San Francisco built one of the strongest happy hours in the City by offering a free buffet that would put most hotel brunches to shame. They gave away a lot of food . . . and they sold a lot of cocktails! After all, how many cocktail franks and cheese cubes can people eat?

**Unusual glassware**   Visual appeal is an important part of beverage presentation. Unusual glassware is an easy way to create a point of difference for your bar operation. Pat O'Brien's, the legendary New Orleans bar, merchandises its world-famous Hurricane by using a distinctive glass that becomes a souvenir of the restaurant.

**Hors d'oeuvre with each drink**   A hot hors d'oeuvre with each drink is a very European touch. If it fits with your concept, the hors d'oeuvre approach can showcase your kitchen and increase your bar sales. If you use the hors d'oeuvres to allow guests to sample items from your menu, you also can build your dinner sales. At the least, you will create a point of difference and build your reputation.

**Logo on glassware**   Very few establishments are willing to spend the money for personalized glassware, creating an open field for those who see the power of it. Custom crested glassware makes a memorable impact on the public. It adds variety and distinction to your beverage service. It also can be an effective advertising vehicle if you use it as a giveaway. Since some guests are going to steal your glasses anyway, you might as well get the promotional value!

**Oversized wine glasses**   There is something elegant about a large wine glass that makes people feel more like ordering wine. When I had my restaurant in San Francisco in the late 1970s, white wine was the drink of choice. All my competitors were serving 9 ounces of wine in a 10-ounce glass. When we opened, we served 10 ounces of wine in a 17-ounce glass and promptly gained the patronage of most of the women in the Financial District! They loved the look and feel of the glass. We also found we were less likely to spill the glasses while carrying drinks to the table through a crowded bar. Better yet, we sold 10 ounces of wine for 25% more than our competitors were getting for 9 ounces . . . and had better word-of-mouth and happier guests in the process!

**Designated driver program**   An important part of the sale of alcohol these days is to promote sensible consumption. If the industry does not take the lead to promote responsible drinking voluntarily, you can be sure some bureaucrat will dictate how we have to run our businesses. Large groups of people create energy and excitement in the bar. If you can help them have a good time and get home safely, they will be alive to patronize you again. Support responsible drinking by providing an incentive for groups to have a designated driver. Call a cab for any guest who may not be in a condition to drive home safely. Have the house pick up the cost of the ride. Remember that one alcohol-related accident can put you out of business.

**Fresh-squeezed juices**   In an era of reconstituted juices, you can create another point of difference by using fresh juices at the bar. It takes more work to make a Screwdriver with fresh oranges, but imagine how distinctive the drink will be to the Screwdriver fan! It is not practical to do *all* your juices to order. For example, it is almost impossible to make an acceptable tomato juice on the premises. Still, the exceptional freshness and merchandising value of squeezing juices to order can put your bar on the map.

**Bottled mixers**  Bottled mixers have a sharper carbonation than post mix soft drinks from a gun. This is particularly true of tonic water. Since most of your competitors use guns, why not make another distinction for your bar by featuring bottled mixers? Train your staff to tell guests of this special touch and your patrons will have something to talk about to their friends.

**Individual coffee pots**  One way to be sure guests don't have to wait for coffee is to give them a personal coffee pot. There are attractive carafes of all sizes and styles on the market at very reasonable prices. If you present them properly, carafes are a welcome touch, particularly in the morning.

**Extensive alcohol-free selections**  People drink to be sociable, not to get drunk. If you can extend the length of the social period, your sales will benefit. With the growing awareness of drinking and driving, it only makes sense to get creative with alcohol-free options.

**Signature drinks**  Success in today's market takes more than just pouring a good drink. Every bar in town can put out Chivas Regal on the rocks. If you want to be a legend and draw business, be famous for something. Find an item you can do better than anyone else in town and push it. Better yet, invent a drink your staff can honestly recommend when talking to your guests. Pat O'Brien's success in New Orleans attests to the power of a signature drink.

**Extensive selection of wines by the glass**  As the public becomes more aware of the dangers of drinking and driving, they are consuming smaller amounts of higher-quality beverages. People who would have previously ordered a bottle of wine are showing particular interest in premium wines by the glass. You can easily take advantage of this trend. Some restaurants even offer individual glasses of most selections on their wine list. Wine lovers and would-be wine lovers will appreciate the opportunity to expand their wine experiences without having to buy a full bottle.

**Premium well**  Guests get nervous about brands of liquor they have never heard of. Why incur the expense of trying to have a bottle of every liquor in the world on hand, particularly when the majority hardly sell at all? A premium well may offer the solution to both problems. For example, instead of stocking seven medium-grade scotches, you might have Chivas Regal in the well with Glenlivet as a super premium upgrade. There are very few Dewar's drinkers who will refuse Chivas Regal. A premium well simplifies inventories and provides a point of difference for your establishment. In most markets, you can charge more for the premium pour.

# 12
# Cleaning Calamities

A consumer survey conducted by the National Restaurant Association voted cleanliness the most important consideration in choosing a restaurant. Guests ranked cleanliness ahead of price, food quality, location, speed of service, meal sizes, courtesy, and menu variety. If that is true, how much time and training do we give to cleaning compared with these other areas?

You clean your restaurant every day. Yet, how much thought have you given to it? Most people just assume they know how to clean. You may make the same assumption of your staff. Don't confuse *clean* with *sterile*. Sterile is a bacteria-free condition that not even hospitals can maintain consistently. Sterile has a harsh look to it and takes tremendous physical and mental energy to achieve. If your goal is to make your restaurant sterile, you will have a life of frustration. Clean, on the other hand, is more a state of mind. Clean is the absence of dirt and clutter. Clean is pleasing to the eye. If you have clean as a state of mind, anything that doesn't look clean jumps out at you and you just take care of it without a problem.

## Tableside Transgressions

A guest doesn't have to go looking for cleaning problems. Often they can just sit at the table and the problems will come to them.

**Dirty or spotted flatware**   Unclean flatware will bring the mood down quickly. Flatware must come to the table straight from the dish machine. Using a towel to polish off the spots is poor sanitation. Spotting is caused by a poorly adjusted machine or incorrect drying. Your detergent supplier can adjust your dish machine, but you have to train your staff in the proper way to clean flatware.

When used flatware comes back from the dining room, soak it until you are ready to wash it. This loosens food particles and makes cleaning easier. Spread the flatware on a flat dish rack and pass it through the dish machine. Then sort it into perforated silverware cylinders, *handle down,* and pass it through the dish machine a second time. Do not handle it again after the second washing.

Placing the handles down allows water to drain away from the eating surfaces. If there is a water spot, it will be on the tip of the handle, not the middle of the knife blade. This method will usually solve most of your soiled flatware problems. Carry eating utensils to the point of service in the cylinders and dump them directly into the silverware bins. If you dispense flatware directly from the cylinders, place a clean, empty cylinder over the full one and invert the pieces so they lie with the handles up.

159

**Streaked glasses**  Hard water or improper washing usually causes streaks and spots on glasses. Ask your detergent supplier for advice. Often a water softener or a rinse agent will solve the problem. If cost is a concern, bear in mind that you cannot use a streaked or spotted glass. Rewashing costs you time, supplies, and hot water. It is always less expensive to do it right the first time.

**Sugar bowls that are dirty inside**  When was the last time you emptied the sugar bowls and ran them through the dish machine? Make this a regular weekly duty.

**Salt and pepper shakers that are sticky, greasy, or half empty**  Make wiping the shakers a regular part of the table setup process. This is also the time to check to be sure the tops are on tight, particularly if you have playful younger guests! At least once a week, wash the shakers in the dish machine. Let them drain overnight before refilling.

**Stained coffee cups**  Tea and coffee will stain the inside of cups. It is particularly unpleasant if the cups are of a light-colored china. Train your dish crew to check for stains inside cups every time they handle them. Soak stained cups in a solution containing bleach or coffee pot destainer. Wash and recheck them before placing them back in service.

**Soiled china**  Nobody wants to eat off a dirty plate. It is critical that china come out of the dish machine clean and sanitary. Keep the dish machine clean. This means draining the tank, removing and cleaning the filter screens, and washing out the machine. Do this before every rush period and at the end of the day. Any food still on the plate when it enters the machine goes into the wash water.

Proper scraping and prerinsing will keep the water cleaner for a longer time. Scrape all excess food off the plates when they come into the dishroom. Either put them directly into the rack or stack them for later washing. Spraying the edge of a stack of plates will flood the surfaces and help loosen food particles. Load dish racks evenly, leaving space for water circulation between the plates. Rinse the plates with the prerinse hose before putting them in the dish machine.

**Glass coffee pot with stained bowl**  Coffee residue will build up inside glass coffee pots. This accumulation makes the pot look dirty when you pour coffee at the table. Guests will notice and become uncomfortable. To prevent buildup, wash the bowls every day using soap and a bottle brush. Once a week, soak them in coffee pot destainer.

# Dining Room Disasters

As your guests look around your dining room, what they see will either make them feel more comfortable or more nervous about their evening.

Cleaning problems are sanitation/safety worries and serious visual irritants. Chapter 5 discusses other unsightly scenes that can annoy your guests.

**Flies in the dining room**   Flies are a major annoyance. Flies have to come in from the outside, so if you can keep them out in the first place, your problems will be fewer. Install an air curtain over the outside kitchen door. Be sure there are screens on any open doors and windows. Check with your health department before using any insecticide sprays. Many are not approved for food preparation areas and can be toxic if they are misused. To reduce flies around the property, keep the back of the restaurant and the dumpster area clean. Wash dumpsters and trash cans regularly. Use your disposer to minimize wet garbage behind the building.

**Wiping tables with a greasy or dirty rag**   How can you make anything clean with a dirty rag? Pay particular attention to the cleanliness of your cleaning cloths. Keep them in sanitizing solution between uses. When they become visibly soiled, replace them. Overnight soaking in a mild bleach solution will usually restore the whiteness to cleaning cloths. Train your staff to measure the proper amount of bleach. Too much bleach in the soaking solution will destroy the fabric.

**Chairs or booths that are dirty, stained, or have crumbs**
Nobody wants to sit in a dirty seat. If all your seating is soiled, people won't want to sit in your restaurant at all! Train your staff to clean and wipe seats thoroughly when clearing the table. At the end of the day, spray plastic or vinyl upholstery with degreaser and wipe it clean. Vacuum fabric upholstery daily and schedule regular cleaning to avoid dirt buildup.

**Wiping seats and tabletops with the same cloth**   Almost every diner I talked with mentioned that this practice annoyed them. To be sure your guests know you are doing it right, just use two different color cleaning cloths. Clean the seats with the yellow cloth and the tabletops with the white cloth.

**Smudgy windows, doors, or display cases**   You have to stay ahead of fingerprints. The easiest way is to clean the glass thoroughly and apply a coat of silicone auto polish. That's right, auto polish! You can just wipe fingerprints off this surface for days before having to repeat the process. It is sure easier than cleaning the glass each time. Use a squeegee to clean windows and other large glass areas. It is faster than the spray bottle and towel method and less likely to leave streaks.

**"Fur" around the air supply outlets**   First, be sure your heating system has clean filters. Replace them every month. Vacuum the supply outlets at least once a week to stay ahead of dust and grease accumulations. Clean the air supply grills with degreaser every month. Clean or replace discolored ceiling tiles around the air vents. They only call attention to the problem.

**Dust or crumbs around the baseboards**   Upright vacuum clean-ers will not clean right up to the wall. Debris along the baseboards shows that cleaning efforts are only superficial. Use a straight broom to sweep these small pieces out where the vacuum cleaner can pick them up. Once a month, use a canister vacuum cleaner with a radiator nozzle (the long, thin attachment) to clean this area thoroughly.

**Dead bugs on the windowsills**   I suppose this is better than finding live bugs, but it is not an attractive sight for your guests. Vacuum or wipe windowsills every morning to remove any insects that may have perished during the night.

**Cobwebs in the corners**   It is almost impossible to keep spiders out of the building. You can spray around the foundation and try to seal every crack in the walls, but you will probably have the problem anyway. If you clean out cobwebs while they are still fresh, the job will be quick and easy. If you let them sit, they will collect grease and become obvious to your guests. Remove cobwebs with a lightly oiled dust mop or a damp towel on the end of a broom. A cobweb will stick to a damp surface and can be neatly removed. If you knock it loose with a dry broom, it will just float onto something else.

**Dirty carpets or floors**   You must vacuum carpets and mop hard floors at least once a day, more often when dining room use is heavy. You can count on gravity to pull every bit of dirt and debris onto the floor and your guests will notice a dirty floor every time. Many restaurants do their heavy cleaning at night. This idea makes sense but there is a danger. The typical dining room lighting level is too dim for proper cleaning. Your crew can do what appears to be a thorough cleaning job at midnight but the harsh light of day will show the cleaning missed many areas of the restaurant. If you are going to clean at night, install cleaning lights. These fixtures contain 300-watt bulbs that flood the room with brilliant light. It is far too intense for dining, but it will show every bit of dirt on the floor.

**Dirty table bases**   People often neglect table bases, probably because cleaning them requires that someone crawls under the table. Still, diners kick the table bases all day and you must clean them regularly. Check them at the end of each day. Clean them with all-purpose cleaner at least weekly, more often in inclement weather. While you are under the table, remove chewing gum and wipe the chair legs.

**Tarnished brass**   Brass provides sparkling highlights in the room. If you allow the brass to tarnish, you will instantly call attention to your lack of maintenance. If you are installing new brass railings, be sure to specify the type coated with an epoxy that prevents oxidation and keeps the brass from tarnishing. If you have uncoated brass, use a polish designed specifically for brass at least weekly. Keep brass looking sharp and your dining room will look the same.

**Cleaning or mopping next to guests' seats**   Excepting emergency cleanups, avoid routine maintenance activities near seated diners. Your activity will disturb and annoy your guests. You give the impression that your guests are not very important. Some may even think you are trying to rush them off the table.

**Scuffed baseboards**   Baseboards are the impact point for all the abuse in the building. Because they form a frame for your floor, their appearance can really undo an otherwise tidy dining room. Check your vacuum cleaner to be sure the bumper is clean and functional. Clean baseboards with all-purpose cleaner in a spray bottle and a white nylon-backed sponge. Avoid harsh chemicals that can damage the baseboard and stain the carpet. When you are recarpeting, you can save yourself a lot of baseboard maintenance if you install the carpet so it curves up the wall about 6 inches. This eliminates the need for conventional baseboards and gives the dining room a neat look.

**Careless spraying of cleaning solutions**   This is particularly disturbing when it happens on a table next to where guests are eating. People appreciate clean tables but they resent careless spraying of strong cleaning solutions. Train your staff to use spray bottles with restraint and respect.

**Too much ammonia in cleaning solutions**   There are few smells more overpowering than ammonia. The odor of ammonia will destroy a guest's dining experience. If you use an ammonia-based solution to clean floors, coach your staff carefully about the proper amount to use. Better yet, find another cleaner that is less aromatic.

**Hazy mirrors**   People always look in mirrors. Your guests will notice if your mirrors are not clean. Haze from smoke, dust, or grease in the air will destroy the brilliant sparkle that mirrors can bring to the dining environment. Clean your mirrors every day. Mirrors are not just another piece of glass. The silvering on the back is very vulnerable to liquid and will turn black if it is soaked with water or cleaning liquids. Clean mirrors with an alcohol-based glass cleaner in a spray bottle. Use a fine mist and wipe it dry immediately using long, full strokes. Never use ammonia or heavy-duty cleaners.

# Disturbing Details

Cleaning is a business of details. Trying to cover them all would be a complete volume, clearly beyond the scope of this book. For now, here are a few more points that can cause your guests to go away angry.

**Dirty or disorderly kitchens**   Yes, guests can see into the kitchen. If you don't have an exhibition cooking area, they will get a view through the pickup window. Even if you have an enclosed kitchen, guests will sneak a peek when the kitchen door opens. It is natural curiosity. Remember that clean is a state of mind. The condition of the kitchen will reflect the value you place on cleanliness.

**Dirty, smelly, or unstocked restrooms**   Most restaurant guests will visit your restrooms. If that experience is unnerving, it will color their impression of your operation. Train *all* staff in the proper techniques of restroom cleaning. This will help keep restroom cleaning from being "somebody else's job." In case you are wondering, all coaching staff ought to be qualified to clean restrooms and lend a hand when needed. If management avoids restroom care, what attitude do you think the rest of the staff will have? Restrooms are so important that I devote Chapter 13 entirely to the subject.

**Rancid smell from the back of the restaurant**   If you have any smell at all wafting over the parking lot, it should draw people in, not push them away. An unclean dumpster or an accumulation of grease behind the restaurant is most always the culprit. Local health codes usually require your waste service to remove, wash, and replace the container periodically. Demand that they do. Periodic application of a good degreaser around your back door and renewed emphasis on exterior cleanliness can keep this problem from affecting your business.

**Dirty door handles**   The dirtiest item in your restaurant may be your door handles. Everyone who enters or leaves puts their hands on the door hardware. Children with sticky fingers complicate the problem even more. Restroom doors are prime areas for spreading diseases. Train your staff to clean door handles and knobs several times a day. Spray them with a disinfectant cleaner and wipe dry with a clean cloth.

**Dirty telephones**   Doorknobs may be the dirtiest item in the restaurant, but the telephone has to be a close second. Who knows how many dirty ears, hands, and mouths have been in touch with your telephones? Guests put your phones to their faces. If the receiver is oily, they are not going to sing your praises. Wipe your telephones every day with a diluted disinfectant solution sprayed on a cloth. Your guests will appreciate your attention to detail.

**Back of the restaurant dirty or disorderly**   Your guests may have a good look at the area behind the restaurant from the parking lot. Some restaurant designs even require guests to drive past the back door to reach the parking lot. Train your staff that there is no place on the property that is out of sight of your patrons. The neatness of the outside area always reflects your attitude toward cleaning the inside.

**Pest strips or flypaper**   Check with your health department before using pest strips or flypaper for insect control. Some jurisdictions prohibit their use in food preparation areas. Even if they are permissible, their appearance will disturb your guests. Other methods of insect control are almost always preferable to hanging these eyesores in your dining room.

***Any* signs of insect or rodent infestation**   Diners are not encouraged by signs of infestation, especially if they see the pests in person. There is something about a cockroach crawling up the wall that ruins even the most brilliant dinner celebration. Every foodservice operation has a potential infestation problem. Contract with a reputable exterminator to spray your property regularly. If you wait until you notice a problem, it will be too late. Follow your exterminator's advice on steps you can take to reduce potential breeding areas and make your building less attractive to insects and rodents. A clean building is more enjoyable for your guests . . . and more enjoyable for your staff.

**Messy back bar**   Think of your bar as an exhibition kitchen for beverages and look at it with a fresh pair of eyes every month. Does it look inviting, professional, and businesslike? Is the appearance of the back bar pleasing to the eye? Is it cluttered with guest checks, snacks, menus, or personal items? Are the bottles clean? Do all the lights work? Is the mirror clean? The back bar is the focal point of your lounge. Be sure it reflects well on you.

**Dirt on the outside doors**   Wind, weather, and blowing dust continually ravage your building. It just gets dirty. The front doors are particularly important because your guests come so close to them. Clean your front doors at least once a week. If weather permits, scrub them with soapy water and hose them down. Clean the door hardware inside and out.

**Stained grout in tile walls or floors**   Ceramic tile is impervious to most common cleaning chemicals, but the cement in grout is more porous and fragile. Avoid harsh acids that can eat away the grout. Commercial grout cleaning compounds followed by a mild bleach solution will normally clean grout without much effort. Occasionally, you may need to scrub with a nylon brush.

# Bonus Point

Everybody likes pleasant surprises.

**Sparkling dining rooms and restrooms**    There are no clearly separate bonus points when it comes to cleaning. Your guests expect your restaurant to be clean. When you surpass *clean* and make your restaurant *sparkle,* you improve your score and put your guests in a better mood. Sparkling dining rooms and restrooms help make up for any lapses in the operation and give your establishment a reputation for spotlessness. All it takes is a passion for cleanliness and an unwillingness to accept anything as "clean enough" if it isn't immaculate.

# 13
# Restroom Repulsion

I include restrooms in this discussion for several reasons. First, most of your guests will use the restroom sometime during their visit to your restaurant. (Alert your staff that someone who asks the location of the restrooms is probably a first-time guest. Have them let management know at once.) Second, many people draw a conclusion about the cleanliness of the kitchen from the cleanliness of the restrooms. Finally, using a public restroom is a very personal experience. If this experience is not pleasant, it can create an uncomfortable memory of your restaurant and cause guests not to return.

Conduct a periodic checkup on your restrooms. Have different staff members repeatedly visit each restroom during the rush. Note if the facilities are adequate and where the congestion occurs. See what maintenance problems come up. If you have problems, fix them.

# Design Deficiencies

Many restroom irritations are created by the design of the room. The fortunate part of this unfortunate situation is that once the deficiency is corrected, you don't need to be concerned by it any longer. Don't you wish all your problems were that easy to solve?

**Poor lighting** Illumination in the restrooms needs to be bright enough for comfort and not so bright that it is blinding, particularly in more dimly lit restaurants. Think about installing makeup-style lighting around the mirrors in the ladies room.

**No place to put down a purse and apply makeup** A woman must be able to properly adjust her makeup in the ladies room. Be sure your design makes the necessary allowances for this. Free-standing sinks with no landing space just won't do the job.

**Spring-loaded faucets** This is one of those annoying items installed for the convenience of the operator and not for the convenience of the guest. If you install spring-loaded faucets, they must allow the water to run long enough to wash your hands. Your restroom surveys can tell if your faucets are an irritant—just glance at people's faces while they are washing their hands.

**Electric hand dryers** Hand drying methods are purely a question of preference. I understand the arguments of cleanliness and reduced maintenance made for electric dryers. My unofficial surveys have yet to come up with anyone who prefers hot air to paper towels. If you have electric hand dryers installed, you might want to put in paper towels as an alternative.

**Restrooms that provide a view to the fixtures**  This means that when the door is opened, people in the hallway have a view of the urinals or stall doors. Most codes don't allow this condition in new construction, but you may have an older operation where the problem exists. Often, changing the direction of the door swing can help. In other situations, you may have to make a single occupancy restroom with a locked door. Whatever the case, the privacy and security of your guests is important enough to fix the problem without delay. Embarrassment brings a person's mood down quickly.

**Poor ventilation**  Make sure there are enough air changes to keep the room fresh. You can't count on windows to make up for the lack of proper mechanical ventilation.

**No mirror**  Strange as it sounds, not long ago I was in a hotel men's room that had no mirror! The women I know would shoot the restaurant owner if this happened in the ladies room!

**No place to hang a coat or bag**  Bear in mind that the floor of a public restroom is not an inviting place to place anything. If the stalls don't have hooks, install them.

**Tiny restrooms**  If you can, make an extra effort in the ladies room. Women will appreciate the extra space. Remember there is also a certain social dimension to the ladies room that men will never understand. Get the suggestions and reaction of several women before finalizing any plans for the ladies room.

**Splashback urinals**  Extensive discussion of this topic is neither appropriate nor necessary. Perhaps it is enough to note that the design of some fixtures creates a cleaning problem for you and a major annoyance for your guests.

# Quarterly Questions

Every so often, take a fresh look at the physical condition of the restrooms. The room deteriorates so gradually that you are unlikely to notice the small points. Your guests notice, though, and it affects the way they feel about your restaurant.

**Chipped paint on the stall enclosures**  Using an electrostatic paint process, you can easily rehabilitate your stall dividers. Because the process pulls the paint onto the metal by magnetism, you can paint the dividers without removing them. No paint will adhere to anything else in the room. Repainting is an easy way to change the look and feel of the restroom for a small cost.

**Soiled or faded paint on the walls**  When the walls start to look less than sparkling, it's time to act. The first solution is to give the walls a good washing. If that doesn't give the freshness you want, several coats of a gloss enamel will brighten the room.

**Torn, spotted, or faded wallcoverings**  If they are easily clean-able, wallcoverings can give a classy look to the restroom. They are more vulnerable than tile or paint, though, and you must watch carefully for damage.

# Daily Duties

At least once a day, check the integrity of the restrooms. The problems noted cannot remain uncorrected or you risk offending your guests.

**Leaking soap dispensers**  Perhaps it's just a question of tightening a connection. Maybe there is a crack somewhere. Whatever the reason, correct it at once. It is an irritant for your guests and creates a cleaning problem.

**Cracked, chipped, or desilvered mirrors**  It is a bad look and does not reflect well on your concern for details (pun intended!). The problem with an imperfect mirror is that it is the one place you can count on people to look! Fix it.

**Sinks or fixtures falling off the wall**  Loose soap and towel dis-pensers are the most common problem, although your porcelain fixtures also can loosen up over time. Check the solidness of fixtures and dispensers as part of your regular daily inspections. If there is a problem, repair it at once before it becomes dangerous.

**Sink drains that don't**  It doesn't take much to clog a drain and it will be a real irritant to your guests. Check the flow at least once a day. Be sure your maintenance closet stock includes a plunger, drain opener, and the tools you will need to remove the sink trap. Clear any blockages at once or accept a parade of angry guests and an extensive cleanup problem.

**Broken tiles on the floors or walls**  Broken tiles are unsightly and pose a cleaning problem. Examine the physical integrity of the tiles at least once a day. Repair cracked tiles promptly. If you retile, keep some extra tiles as replacements.

**Graffiti**   Unless you have a clientele that creates classy graffiti, it is better to clean off these scribblings at once. In the graffiti mentality, one good word deserves another. Once it starts, graffiti can rapidly get out of control. If you attract people who write on the walls, consider renovating the restrooms with materials that do not provide a writing surface.

**Stall doors that do not latch**   Privacy and security are big issues for your guests. Wrestling with a stall door is embarrassing. Embarrassment is not the memory you want someone to have after an evening in your restaurant.

**Cracked toilet seats**   The health department doesn't allow it. Your guests hate it. The company that sells you the replacement seat will love it. Make someone happy.

**Broken or missing lights**   Check the restrooms every day for burned out lights or missing light covers. The physical integrity of the facilities creates an impression on your guests. Make sure that impression is positive.

# Hourly Imperatives

The condition of your restrooms can change rapidly. At least every hour (more frequently during peak times), inspect the restrooms and correct any of the following situations.

**Dripping bars of soap**   If you don't have wall-mounted soap dispensers, consider a pump container of liquid soap. Avoid bar soap at all costs. I have yet to see anyone truly excited about picking up a drippy bar of soap! Bar soap is only acceptable in an emergency.

**Dispensers crusted with dried soap**   Crusted soap shows that the dispenser has not been cleaned or wiped off for days! Some dispensers are easier to clean than others. When making your choices, pay attention to how easy they will be to keep clean.

**Stale smell**   Lack of cleaning or improper air circulation will cause a stale smell in the air. Whatever the reason, you don't want guests equating your restrooms with those in most gas stations. Find the cause of the odor and correct it.

**Overflowing trash containers**   You have to stay on top of this. The quick fix is always just to push the paper down in the container. Be cautious about using your hand to compress a bin of used paper towels. There has been more than one report of someone puncturing their hand with a discarded needle. I won't elaborate on the potential dangers of that. Line all trash containers and keep a supply of replacement liners readily available.

**Dripping faucets**  Washers wear out. Once the drip starts, it only gets worse. If you delay the simple repair, dripping water can permanently discolor the sink.

**Damp or soiled cotton roll towels**  If you wait until a roll is gone before you replace it, you will continually be facing the problem of towels too damp or dirty to dry guests' hands. Check the rolls regularly and make sure you have enough capacity to get you through the rush.

**Overpowering perfume or antiseptic smell**  The restroom ought to smell clean, not like a hospital or a bordello! Some scent is desirable, but check it out first. Make sure the dispenser emits the proper amount for the size of the room.

**Countertops dripping with water**  You have to stay on top of this situation because you can't stop people from splashing. When you renovate your restrooms, keep the water problem in mind when you design the sinks. Some faucets splash less than others. A deep sink will create less splash than a shallow one. One-piece counters and sinks allow water to drain more easily.

**Stopped-up fixtures**  Take care of stoppages immediately. So what if nobody likes to do it? How do you think your guests feel having to work around this problem? Besides, you know it always happens in the middle of the rush! A blocked fixture won't fix itself. Have a plunger and a bowl snake readily available. Take care of stoppages immediately.

**No toilet tissue or paper towels**  The only good answer is to replace or refill before the rush and periodically throughout the day. You can also install oversized rolls of toilet tissue that hold the equivalent of 10 to 12 regular rolls. They are worth considering in a high-volume operation.

**No hand soap**  People who notice are the ones most likely to make a fuss. Plan for peak periods and stay on top of soap supplies. It is a good idea to keep an emergency stock of pump dispensers on hand just in case.

**Cigarette butts in the urinals**  Because restrooms are available to the public, many local ordinances require they be nonsmoking. Even if you are not under a requirement to do so, it is a courtesy to your nonsmoking patrons to make this designation. Smoking in a confined space like a restroom renders the room inhabitable for nonsmokers. If you do not make this restriction, you must clean out smoking debris at least every hour. Ashes on the sinks or fixtures are irritating to all patrons. Cigarette butts on the floors or in the urinals make the room look and feel dirty. Your best defense is a good offense (no smoking in the restrooms). Eliminating the mess before it starts is easier than cleaning it up!

**No toilet seat protectors**   Personal protection in public restrooms is important, especially for women. Paper toilet seat protectors are a small touch that can make your guests feel more confident when they use your facilities. The investment is small. If you do not have seat protectors, get them. If they are out, replenish them.

## Truth Is Stranger Than Fiction

It is hard to know *where* this incident belongs, but it belongs somewhere. A friend reports being in a ladies room when a cocktail waitress came in carrying a service tray with several cocktails on it. The waitress entered a stall and placed the tray on the floor while she used the toilet! I suppose she toddled off afterward and served the drinks. I hope she at least washed her hands!

## Bonus Points

Everybody likes pleasant surprises. These little unexpected touches are opportunities to improve your score and put your guests in a better mood. They help make up for any lapses in the operation and give people reasons to recommend your restaurant to their friends.

**Facial tissue**   What if a guest needs to blow their nose, wipe off some makeup, or do other little odd jobs? In most places, the choice is only paper towels or toilet paper—not really much of a choice! Follow the example of most hotels and install a dispenser of tissues. Facial tissue is an inexpensive small touch that creates another point of difference from your competition.

**Panic Button**   A restroom "panic button" is simply a switch that turns on a flashing light somewhere else in the restaurant. A small sign asks guests to flick the switch if they see that the restroom needs attention. Make sure someone responds at once when the light comes on.

**Amenities**   Although amenities probably have more relevance in upscale operations, anyone can add a few pleasant surprises. Unexpected touches like hand lotion, dispensed paper cups, and complimentary packets of pain reliever will reflect your concern. Consider a selection of aftershave lotions in the men's room. Amenities like a magnifying makeup mirror, a couch, or flowers in the ladies room can make a big impression. A little effort in this direction and you will pick up the points even with people who don't take advantage of the amenities.

**Telephones**   People appreciate a private place to make a telephone call, particularly single adults. The restrooms are a perfect place to use the telephone without a date (or a would-be date) being aware of the call. Besides, restrooms are usually quieter than public hallways.

**Separate table for diaper changing**  If a parent has to change a child's diaper, the counter at the sink is *not* an appropriate location. A changing table can be easily wall-mounted to save space. Those who use it (and those who don't) will appreciate and remember your thoughtfulness. If you install a changing table, remember to put one in the men's room as well. Include a separate, covered waste container for the soiled diapers. For a real point bonus, have some spare disposable diapers in different sizes on hand.

**Full-length mirrors**  If you have the wall space, place a full-length mirror in each restroom. Most people check their appearance before returning to the dining room or lounge. If they can see themselves fully, there is less chance they might be embarrassed by a detail they couldn't see in the mirror over the sink.

**Style**  People expect restrooms to be utilitarian. Style is an unexpected surprise! Give the same attention to decorating your restrooms as you do to decorating your restaurant and watch the compliments you get! Fresh flowers in the ladies room might not be appropriate in a coffee shop. Still, a small vase of dried flowers on the counter could work. Interesting pictures on the walls or interesting light fixtures help avoid the institutional feel. If it makes your guests feel more comfortable it is worth considering.

Restrooms also can make a statement. Consider the Madonna Inn in San Luis Obispo, California, where they give tours of the men's room! Could it be something about having a 9-foot waterfall over natural rocks instead of more traditional urinals? P.J. Clarke's, a 100+-year-old New York saloon, used to place 300-pound blocks of ice in their oversized antique urinals. The practice is an early form of bacteria control and it made their men's room a must-see experience. Sadly, they have discontinued the practice in recent years but the idea still has value for many operations. If you fill your urinals with ice cubes every hour or so, you will eliminate odor without the need for chemicals . . . and guarantee that everyone will ask you about the ice!

# 14
# Family Fiascos

Families with children can be a profitable source of business for many restaurants, not just those that focus on the family. The trick in developing this market segment lies with understanding what families want and taking care of the details.

When dealing with families, it helps to understand that adults and children view dining in two different ways. For adults, meals are a social experience. Adults come to restaurants for conversation and to enjoy the company of their companions. Children's lives revolve around play and meals are mostly a biological function ("I'm hungry, feed me." "I'm full, now what?"). Serving the family effectively means addressing both needs. Let the children be children while their parents enjoy their meals more leisurely.

Remember, too, that taking several children out to eat can be like trying to nail jello to a wall! Anything you can do to make it more painless for the adults, especially a single parent, the more you will endear yourself to them. Even if you do not actively market to families with children, families will come to your establishment. To serve them well, there are some basic problems to avoid.

## Seating Shortcomings

Service to families starts the minute they walk in the door. Give the children something to do while you get the table ready—something to play with or even a packet of crackers. If you cannot seat children immediately, they will find something else to do. This will most likely be exploring your playground (restaurant)! Seat the family as soon as you can.

**No high chairs or booster seats**  Even a restaurant that doesn't encourage children needs some provision to handle them. High chairs and booster seats are the minimum requirement. It is difficult to improvise children's seating safely. Make the investment.

**Not positioning children's seating before bringing the family to the table**  Give the parents a break. Don't make them have to ride herd on their young ones at the table while the busser prowls around in the back looking for the booster seats! If you must delay the family anywhere, delay them in the lobby, not in the middle of the dining room.

**Dirty high chairs or booster seats**  People are more sensitive to cleanliness when it affects their children. They know children will put their hands (and mouths) anywhere. Be sure you do not give them any reason to worry.

**Broken or rickety high chairs**  Unstable seating is extremely dangerous for children. Even if *you* know the high chair won't collapse, the parents will ruin their whole meal waiting nervously for their heir to hit the floor!

**Waiting in line**  Many "family restaurants" have a service system where guests wait in line for their food before going to the table. On one hand, this may help keep the check average within the family budget. On the other, a single mother with three young children in tow will have her hands full trying to keep control of her brood during the wait. Find a way to keep the wait in line from being a struggle for families or risk losing them to a more compassionate competitor.

**No place to leave a stroller while the family is dining**  Create a "parking lot" for strollers and be sure everyone on the staff knows where it is. Families will appreciate a less-crowded table. Your other guests will appreciate your maintaining the general order and neatness of the dining room.

**Unsafe placement of high chair**  Give some thought to where you place a high chair or booster seat. If possible, avoid seating children adjacent to traffic lanes where a careless diner might bump them.

**Seating families at a table with a tip on it**  This is bad form under any circumstances but far more critical with children. Little ones will put the money in their mouths! Make sure the table is completely cleared and properly set before you seat the family.

# Tableside Turmoil

What happens when the family is finally seated sets the tone for the rest of their meal. How you relate to the children and how well you understand their needs will determine whether the family starts to relax or prepares for the worst. Here are some details that can tip the scales.

**Not anticipating the needs of families**  Bring extra napkins right away. Be ready with an extra spoon. Leave a clean, damp cloth when there is a child in a high chair. Consider Wet-Naps for afterdinner cleanup of sticky faces. What are you pretending not to know about taking children out to eat?

**No children's menus**  Children appreciate having something that is just for them because they are always having to work with other people's standards. Adults appreciate the simplicity of knowing what you have in children's portions. Children's menus can be as simple or elaborate as you choose. Keep them consistent with the theme and look of your restaurant.

**No provisions to keep the children amused** Coloring books are inexpensive and easy to get from specialty/novelty houses. Even a blank piece of paper and a pencil will work. There is no end to the possible ways to amuse children. Children run rampant in the dining room because there are no other acceptable (to them) play options!

**Leaving the place setting in front of small children** Defer to the parents—they know their children's capacity for handling utensils. Often youngsters can make do with just a spoon. Never leave a two-year-old alone with a steak knife! Even if the children can handle a full set of silverware, let the parents decide. They will appreciate your awareness and concern for the safety of their children.

**Using tall glasses for children's beverages** Unless you want to spend half the meal cleaning up spills, choose a low, broadbased glass with a short straw. Give children something they aren't as likely to turn over! Always serve flexible straws with children's beverages.

**Not giving young children something to do immediately** Children are either eating, sleeping, or playing. Since they won't go to sleep when you seat them, at least give children some crackers to occupy them until their meal arrives.

**Not listening to parents** People know what their children like and don't like. They will tell you if you ask them and pay attention to their answers. They will appreciate your concern and you can gain some free market research.

**No bibs available** Although many families will bring their youngster's favorite bib with them, be sure to have a few bibs readily available if needed. Also be sure that all your staff know where to find them.

**Taking a long time to settle the check** By the end of the meal, some children can become restless and hard to control. Take care of the check quickly. The parents will thank you.

# Service Slipups

Serving a family has a different pace and different requirements than a party of adults. How well you handle these small points will determine the success of your efforts.

**Disrespect or lack of concern for the well-being of the children**  Parents appreciate people who appreciate their children. Children like places that like them. Since the children often decide where the family dines, treat them with the same respect you give your adult guests. Parents often judge their own dining experience by how sensitively you handle the needs of their family.

**Not properly taking care of the adults**  Parents do not lose their appreciation of a good time just because they have their children with them. The youngsters may influence where the family eats, but the adults drive the car and pay the check! Parents still judge their dining experience by adult standards.

**Not bringing side bowls or plates for sharing**  The children will want some of whatever their parents are having. Provide a convenient way to give the children a taste. A side plate with the parents' meal shows your awareness of what it's like to take the family out to dinner.

**Inability to heat baby food or a baby's bottle**  This is not an uncommon request if you cater to families, so work it out with the kitchen. All you need is a microwave and a few minutes. Knowing what to do will keep you from flinching when asked for this service. If you want to pick up a few points, make the offer before the guest even asks.

**Expecting adult behavior from children**  Count on children to behave like children! Don't pretend they can be otherwise. If you find yourself losing your composure just step back, take a deep breath, and count to ten. Relax. Let their innocence and energy touch you. If you can't shake your irritation, have someone else serve the table. Children are very sensitive and will pick up on your upset. They won't know why, but they'll remember they didn't have a good time at your restaurant. When their parents suggest dining in your establishment, the children will not want to come back and the family can become regulars at your competition.

**Not cleaning under the table when the family leaves**  When the children leave, count on a floor full of french fries, cracker wrappers, and other assorted debris. The next guest at the table won't appreciate slipping in someone else's trash. A carpet sweeper or cordless "dust buster" will make this task easier and faster.

**Not serving children first**  Be sure the youngsters get their food before the adults. It will keep their fingers out of the parent's meals!

# Poor Practices

To be truly responsive to the needs of families you must allow for some special requirements. If your policies and practices are too rigid to accommodate these needs, you will not become the restaurant of choice for the family. If you can avoid the problems here, you are on your way toward developing a strong source of business.

**No provisions for diaper changing**   Each restroom needs a shelf wide enough for this purpose. Using the countertop by the sink is irritating to your other guests. A separate covered trash for dirty diapers is also worth considering.

**No plan to handle breast feeding**   It will come up and your staff must know how you want to handle it. Remember a nursing baby does not have any other meal options! Knowing how to handle the request will save embarrassment for the mother and your other guests as well.

**Pricing yourself out of the market**   For perspective, calculate your average check per family instead of just your average check per person. Your prices may be reasonable, but if it costs $50 for a family of four to eat, you will not serve many families!

**Not allowing for food preferences of children**   Most young-sters are not very trendy. If you don't have white bread for their sandwiches, many will make a fuss. Be sure to use unseeded rolls. There are some menu choices you almost *have* to offer, but give your children's menu some thought. You can have signature items for children as easily as you can have signature items for adults.

**No healthy menu options for children**   Go the extra step beyond simply "junk food" or fried choices when designing a menu for children. Parents will appreciate your thoughtfulness.

# Bonus Points

Everybody likes pleasant surprises. These little unexpected touches are opportunities to improve your score and put your guests in a better mood. They help make up for any lapses in the operation and give people something to talk about to their friends.

**Wet towels**   Children's hands are always dirty. If you provide a way to clean sticky hands at the table, you will win the undying appreciation of the parents. It's hard enough to take a group of children out to eat without having to shuttle them to the restrooms for a cleanup. The solution can be as easy as packaged Wet-Naps or as classic as warm damp washcloths.

**Stock of disposable diapers**   Most parents come prepared, but if an emergency arises, it's hard to improvise. Have an assortment of dispos-ables in different sizes and let the parents know with a sign in the restrooms.

You will gain a few points for attention to detail even if they never take advantage of the offer.

**Diaper changing tables**   If a parent has to change their child's diaper, the counter at the sink is *not* an appropriate location. A changing table can be easily wall-mounted to save space. Those who use it (and those who don't) will appreciate and remember your thoughtfulness. If you install a changing table, remember to put one in the men's room as well. Include a separate, covered waste container for the soiled diapers.

**Separate area for nursing**   Knowing how you will handle this question when it comes up is important. Having a comfortable area set aside for nursing mothers is even better. Nursing babies in public is more common than it used to be. Still, it can be a delicate situation for both for the mother and your other guests. It does not bother the baby, I suspect! If possible, a separate room with a comfortable armchair will resolve the situation to everyone's delight.

**Routinely (and quickly) checking for forgotten articles**
It is not that the family will never recover the lost items. It is more a recognition that families don't need the inconvenience of having to return for forgotten items. They will appreciate and remember that you found that favorite toy that rolled behind the plant before their youngster threw a tantrum about it!

**High chairs on wheels**   Particularly in restaurants where the parents have to wait in line for their food, rolling high chairs by the front door are a definite plus. Parents can place their small children in the chair and keep them under control while waiting and all the way to the table.

**Stands for infant carriers**   Molded infant carriers are becoming more common. Unfortunately, they don't usually fit on chairs. They are dangerous to put on the floor and awkward on top of the table. You can buy stands that attach to a high chair and hold infant carriers securely. They are worth a look.

**Special treats**   Children love gifts. A memento of their meal (and of your restaurant) can do wonders for developing loyalty in the younger set. Call it bribery if you like, but it works!

# 15

# Disabled Disasters

Legendary operators have always offered the same level of excellent service to all their guests. If you have been providing different service to the disabled, it is time to change your style. The provisions of the Americans with Disabilities Act (ADA) will require all restaurateurs to better accommodate disabled guests. Why not make changes sooner, from choice, than later, from necessity?

Remember that disabled diners are people, too. They have some extra challenges in their lives and are among the most courageous people on the planet. All they ask is the same respect and opportunities for life that able-bodied people enjoy. Since dining out is one of life's pleasures, making the restaurant experience part of their lives is a special service you can provide. If you give them the service they want, they can be extremely loyal and enthusiastic guests. Your other diners will notice the compassion with which you treat the disabled and think of you more favorably.

## Universal Irritants

Despite their particular disabilities, all handicapped people I spoke with mentioned the following irritations in restaurants.

**Condescending tone from staff**   Disabled persons are not second-class citizens. Do not treat them that way. They are just people with a few more obstacles than the rest of us. Treat them with respect and courtesy. Remember, your message is always carried by your tone of voice, never in your words.

**Lack of awareness of special needs**   Although disabled diners are people like anyone else, they have different needs than able-bodied patrons. Equal treatment does not mean treating them just like every other guest. Giving equal treatment to disabled patrons means providing them with a dining experience of equal quality. To do this, you have to be aware of their special needs.

**Taking a roundabout route to the table**   Understand that most disabled persons have a more difficult time moving around. It is inconsiderate and embarrassing to make them run through an obstacle course to get to a table in the back of the dining room. Whenever possible, seat disabled parties close to the door.

**Impatience**   Disabled diners do not enjoy many advantages that able-bodied people take for granted. Communicating with the disabled is often more difficult. The pace of service for a disabled diner takes different timing than for most of your parties. When serving a disabled diner, just relax and let your heart go out to them. Remember that good service is defined from *their* perspective, not from yours. If you become impatient, it only shows your lack of understanding and lack of professionalism.

**Talking in a loud voice**   Many people have an annoying tendency to increase the volume of their voices when talking to the disabled. Keep your voice modulated. Blind guests or patrons in wheelchairs are not hard of hearing. Guests who are deaf can't hear you anyway! Raising your voice only calls attention to the diner and makes them more uncomfortable.

**Seating other parties ahead of disabled parties**   Treating everybody equally well means that all guests receive the same level of attention. There is never a good reason for making a disabled party wait while you seat diners who arrived after them.

# Wheelchair Wickedness

Most local codes require that newly remodeled facilities be accessible to persons in wheelchairs. Besides physical access, there are a few other facts about dining in a wheelchair that you should know.

**No access ramps**   You don't make able-bodied guests climb over a wall to get in. Why would you make it impossible for a chair-bound diner to enter your establishment? Adding an access ramp also will make it easier for elderly diners and children. If you receive deliveries through the front door, you will appreciate how easy it is to bring a hand truck up a ramp instead of the stairs.

**Undersized restrooms**   Disabled diners are as likely to use your restrooms as anyone else. Compact restrooms can be difficult for wheelchairs to maneuver in. Put yourself in their position. How welcome would you feel in a place where you couldn't use the restroom? If your public restrooms are too small to accommodate a wheelchair easily, look for options. Perhaps there is another toilet in the building you could use for a single occupant in a wheelchair.

**Inaccessible tables**   Have some tables in your restaurant that can accommodate a wheelchair, preferably tables near the door. Booths are more efficient seating for most people, but they are extremely awkward for a diner in a wheelchair. A chair-bound guest cannot slide into the booth. Don't even suggest it. Sitting on the end of the table usually puts the chair in the middle of a traffic lane. Only tables where you can remove a conventional chair will give wheelchair diners the feeling of receiving equal treatment.

**Pushing the chair without permission** Just because someone is in a wheelchair does not mean they are incompetent. Most disabled individuals are proud of their independence. Most will resent it if you try to help them, no matter how well-intentioned your motives. Escort guests in wheelchairs to the table as you would accompany any other guest.

**Seating in the back of the dining room** Seat wheelchair diners close to the door. It is difficult to maneuver a chair through most restaurant traffic lanes. Trying to seat a wheelchair diner in the back of the dining room can inconvenience every guest seated along the aisle and embarrass the disabled person. Make it as easy as possible for a guest in a wheelchair and shorten the distance they have to travel to reach their table.

**Insufficient space for chairs** Narrow traffic lanes and small lobbies are difficult to negotiate in a wheelchair. Look at your layout to see if a simple rearrangement would make it easier for a wheelchair diner to get around.

# Sightless Oversights

Blind guests (or those with reduced vision) are loyal patrons of those restaurants that understand and respond to their needs. Here are a few common errors to avoid if you want to attract these steady guests.

**Petting the guide dog** Never pet the guide dog. Guide dogs for the blind are highly trained, hard-working animals who are on the job when they are in your restaurant. Train your staff not to treat a guide dog like a pet or another friendly puppy. Be friendly to the blind guest, not the dog.

**Unwillingness to read menu and prices** Not all restaurants have braille menus, but every restaurant has someone who can read. Without one or the other, how is a blind patron supposed to know what to order? Table service restaurants generally do a better job of this than quick service operations or cafeterias. Be sensitive to the problem and have enough compassion to read your menu board and prices.

**Talking to the sighted companion instead of the blind person** Don't treat the blind guest like a nonperson. Nobody likes to be ignored. Respectful service, for anyone, requires that you talk to them directly and courteously. It does not matter if the guest can't see your face. They will know when you are focused on them and they will know when your attention is elsewhere. Give all your guests your undistracted attention.

**Refusing to admit guide dogs** Most local ordinances require you to admit guide dogs for the blind. Even health department regulations, which normally prohibit animals in foodservice establishments, make an exception for guide dogs. Use your head and don't give anyone a hard time. Remember you are not talking about an ordinary animal, you are talking about someone's eyes. Besides, guide dogs require less attention than children!

**Seating at a table with dim lighting**   Many visually impaired people are not completely blind. With a reasonable amount of light, they can function in a fairly normal fashion. When seating a blind patron, choose a well-lighted table close to the door. They will appreciate your understanding.

**Giving blind patrons the wrong change**   It is a sad commentary, but there are people in the world who will take advantage of another's lack of sight. When settling the check, ask the blind guests if they would prefer their change all in one-dollar bills. Many would ask you to do it anyway. By bringing up the subject first, you will show your awareness of their needs.

# Deaf Displeasures

Guests with impaired hearing do not appear much different from other guests. It is easy to forget that they need special consideration. To avoid offending deaf diners, be aware of the following details.

**Refusing to admit hearing dog**   Some deaf persons have specially trained dogs who help them live more productive lives. If they bring the dog into the restaurant, give the animal the same respect you would a guide dog for the blind. The same laws and exceptions apply to hearing dogs.

**Not facing a deaf person when talking to them**   Many deaf persons are very skilled lip-readers and you will find you can readily communicate with them. When talking to a deaf diner, face them squarely and speak in a normal voice. Talk a little slower than your normal pace. After all, how is a deaf diner going to read your lips if they can't see your face? They will respond either by pointing to items or with a note.

# Bonus Points

Everybody likes pleasant surprises and the disabled are no different. These little unexpected touches are opportunities to improve your score and put your guests in a better mood. Because they usually receive such indifferent treatment, disabled diners will be enthusiastic about even the most basic respect and understanding.

**Seating close to door**   Disabled guests want to live their lives as normally as any of us. Since most have some trouble navigating, it is difficult for them to walk to a remote seat in the dining room. It also draws attention to them, something anyone would find uncomfortable. Seats by the door, which some diners find less desirable, are ideal for disabled diners.

**Braille menus**   If a guest spoke another language, you would try to get someone who could translate, wouldn't you? Why not extend the same courtesy to deaf or blind guests? Most towns have a local agency who provides services for the blind. Ask them to translate your menu to braille.

**Staff member who can sign**   If you have someone on your staff who can speak sign language, you will open an entire new dining experience for deaf guests. There are many people who have learned to sign to communicate with hearing-impaired friends or family. Ask your staff if anyone has this skill.

**TDD/TTY Telephone**   This device is essentially a teletype machine that will allow hearing-impaired guests to communicate with anyone. Talk with your local agencies for the deaf about how to get one installed in your restaurant.

# 16

# Teenage
# Turnoffs

Y ou can love them or you can hate them, but you cannot deny that teenagers are your future consumers. They may even be a big part of your business already. Teens are at the age when they develop the habits that will carry them into adulthood. If you understand their needs and treat them well, dining in your restaurant could be a habit that stays with them for years.

If you need a more immediate incentive, here are a few more points to ponder. In many families, the teenagers are the ones who decide where the family goes out to dinner. Parents often make calculating the tip an exercise in practical mathematics, so teens often decide how much of a tip the family will leave. Teenagers will patronize your restaurant with their parents, in groups with their peers, or on dinner dates. Each situation has slightly different challenges and opportunities.

Don't make the mistake of treating teenagers like children. They are as aware and observant as any adult diners. Forget the idea that all they know about is fast food and pizza. Today's teenagers have extensive dining-out experience in a wide range of restaurants. Never think that teens don't have their own opinions about things. You may be surprised at what they like and dislike about restaurants.

# Attitude Annoyances

As you might expect, a major adolescent complaint about restaurants has to do with the attitude of restaurant staff toward teens.

### Obvious sense of displeasure when a teen party arrives
Teenagers are very sensitive. They can always tell what you are thinking. If you see teens as pests, they will react to you with annoyance. On the other hand, if you welcome teen parties and make the dining experience pleasant for them, you help instill the habit of dining out as a satisfying activity.

### Seating adult parties ahead of teens
Escort guests to the table in the order of their arrival. Period. Many restaurants discriminate against teenage parties. Maybe they think the teens don't care. Perhaps they feel adults are more important patrons. Maybe they think they will insult the adults if they seat the younger group first. These notions are wrong. Good service is equal service, regardless of age.

### Different treatment for adults and teens
There are no second-class citizens in a great restaurant. Often teens receive incomplete service.

Perhaps servers don't think teenagers will know the difference. Believe me, they know. Unless there are other mitigating factors (like you have the best enchiladas in town), teens will not patronize your restaurant if you treat them poorly. When it's time for the family to go out, your establishment will not be in the running, either.

**Impatience with limited funds**   It's amazing how quickly some people can forget. Do you remember how it was when you were a teenager and low on money? More than once, I recall taking up a collection at a gas station to put 73 cents' worth into the tank! Teenagers still find themselves short on cash. If a teenager chooses to spend their last dollars in your restaurant, don't lose patience if you need to adjust the order to meet the funds available. The situation is touching proof of the loyalty of your young diners.

**Assigning inexperienced staff to teen tables**   Often a restaurant will assign its least experienced staff to serve parties of teenagers. The rationale, I suppose, is that the teens won't know the difference. They not only notice, but they resent the inference that they are not worth your best efforts. Teens do not come to your restaurant to provide training to your new servers. Don't reassign stations for groups of teen diners.

**Asking the parents for the teen's order**   You are being rude any time you do not speak directly to a guest. Age, sex, or physical condition has nothing to do with good service. Teens are particularly sensitive to poor treatment. They are not children and will resent your treating them that way. They know what they want. Always address them directly and with the same respect you give their parents.

**No substitutions**   Younger diners' tastes are different from those of your adult patrons. Teens will often request substitutions from your standard fare. Give them the same consideration you would offer to an adult diner. After all, if you won't give them what they want, they'll find another restaurant that will!

**No attempt to make suggestions or explanations**   Many items on your menu may be unfamiliar to your teenaged patrons. They also may be uncertain about which foods go well together. Teens appreciate helpful suggestions and recommendations as much as any of your patrons. Don't talk down to them or become annoyed if they ask endless questions about your menu. Remember, you are helping educate them about the joys of dining out.

**Not showing any personal interest**   Teens are still learning social skills and may be a little nervous when they go out. Staff who are abrupt and uninterested in providing good service offend teen diners. Take a personal interest in helping teenagers have a pleasant and comfortable experience. They will appreciate your caring and will become enthusiastic regulars.

**Failure to bring food to the table quickly**    Teenagers are active and eat a lot. As you would with younger children, get some food in front of them quickly. If you have a basket of an item (like tortilla chips) on the table, keep it resupplied throughout the meal. If teens don't have something to do, they will *find* something to do!

**Not listening when addressed by teens**    Talking to someone who is not listening will create rage in even the most reasonable person. Anytime a guest talks to you, drop all other thoughts from your mind. Hear what they are saying, but pay particular attention to what they mean. Teenagers are very sensitive to your lack of presence. You cannot fool them and they will not appreciate your attitude.

**Shortchanging teens**    Some people try to take advantage of teens' inexperience. For example, I have seen adults take a $20 bill from a teenaged patron and only return change for $10. They insisted the youngster was lying about giving them a larger bill. Teens are still learning how to stand up for their rights and a belligerent adult can often intimidate them. Before you try to make a quick profit this way, remember that teenagers talk to each other . . . a lot. The word will travel quickly and cost you more than just the business of the high school crowd. Once you get the reputation of being a ripoff, it is hard to recover. What goes around, comes around.

**No sense of humor**    There are many unexpected events in the restaurant business, more when you are serving a party of teens. A sense of humor will help you provide more memorable service to younger diners. They appreciate people who are comfortable enough to joke with them. A little levity can make the dining experience more enjoyable for everyone.

# Menu Mistakes

Teenagers know what they like and what they don't. Here are a few menu errors that irritate younger patrons.

**Limited menu choices**    Teens are not particularly adventurous diners. Still, they like to have choices. They will experiment with new items. You can help expand their culinary horizons with helpful suggestions. Yet, if you only have three items on the menu, there is not much you can do to help. To attract more teen business, give them a variety of interesting dishes from which to choose.

**Self-serve food bars**    Teens are sensitive to the sanitation problems of food bars. The teenagers I spoke with do not like salad bars because they see too many people mishandling food. If you have a salad or food bar, be sure someone continually supervises its operation. Clean up spills promptly. Do not pour new product on top of old product. Change serving utensils when you change food containers. *All* your guests will appreciate your concern.

**Boring beverage and dessert choices**   The adolescent years are a time to experiment and discover. Do not assume that all a teenager wants to drink is a cola. If there is something worth trying, you can count on teens for a dessert order every time. Give as much thought to offering interesting beverage and dessert choices as you do to writing your entrée menu. With a little bit of thought, you can increase your sales from the teen market and give them a more enjoyable experience in your restaurant.

# Atmosphere Aggravations

Teenagers are sensitive to what is going on around them in a restaurant. There are several details they find particularly irritating.

**Inappropriate background music**   Many teens do not like restaurants that use a radio for background music. They hear radio all day and think restaurants should offer something unique. Most do not find heavy metal or rap music an appealing choice. If you draw (or want to draw) a teen market, consider classic rock.

**Noisy video games**   Contrary to what you might think, an incessant din from video games annoys teenage diners. They like having video games in the restaurant, but they don't like the noise intruding on their meal. If you offer video games, soundproof the game room. All your patrons will appreciate the gesture.

**Dim lights**   Perhaps because they live active lives, dimly lit dining rooms do not appeal to teens. They prefer brighter lighting, perhaps so they can see what is happening around them. A higher level of illumination also shifts the focus from the table, where there may be some social awkwardness. To make dining attractive for younger diners, keep the lights up or seat them at tables that have brighter lighting levels.

**Dirty restaurant**   Teens are very sensitive to cleanliness and sanitation. They notice the clutter, dirt, and stains. Dirty restrooms offend them. They see the soiled seating and poor sanitation habits of your staff. In short, they are just like any of your other guests. Do not think you can get away with anything. Teens will not patronize restaurants they do not trust to be safe.

**No uniforms**   You will not make adolescent diners more comfortable by allowing your young staff to wear their regular clothes to work. Teenagers think that a uniformed staff is a mark of professionalism. They feel better being served by someone in a clean uniform than by a worker in a T-shirt and jeans. Workers in uniform, particularly younger ones, show more pride in their behavior and their work.

**No nonsmoking area**  Some teenagers smoke, but most think the habit is disgusting. If you cannot seat them away from the smell of smoke, they will not patronize your restaurant. Unless they request it, never seat teen parties next to smokers. Those tables are undesirable for *any* non-smoker. Teens may think you are just taking advantage of their youth by giving them poor seats. If your goal is to create happy guests, find a way to avoid the irritation.

# Bonus Points

Everybody likes pleasant surprises, especially teens who rarely see people truly concerned with their needs. These little unexpected touches will endear your restaurant to teenage diners. They will give a reason to recommend you when the family is dining out and provide something to talk about to their friends.

**Free gum after the meal**  You give mints to the adults after the meal, why not give gum to teenagers? If you really want to make some points, make it bubble gum!

**Bottled sodas**  As you might expect, teens are connoisseurs of soft drinks. They appreciate the sharper carbonation of bottled sodas over the post mix product.

**Something to look at**  Teens thrive on visual activity and enjoy having something to look at. They like restaurants that have "a lot of junk" on the walls, television sets, windows on the street—anything that is highly visual.

**Souvenirs**  Teens will prize keepsake glasses with your restaurant's logo. They are collectors and look for places where they can add to their accumulation of memorabilia. Tie the glass in with a signature drink that enhances your establishment's image (and profitability).

**Free beverage refills**  Adolescents have a continual thirst. They appreciate restaurants that recognize this need with prompt (free) beverage refills. The initial price of the drink is only a partial consideration. You will gain points by charging a little more for a drink and giving free refills. You can do even better by making the cup a souvenir of your restaurant.

**Unusual desserts**  Teenage guests love anything sweet. They are enthusiastic to find a restaurant with many different desserts from which to choose. Offer interesting desserts with clever names and you will increase your teen patronage as you build your dessert sales.

**Cool T-shirts**   The Hard Rock Cafe is a definite stop for teenagers because it has a distinctive T-shirt that everybody wants. There are many other examples of restaurants that have built their fame with a distinctive logo and a well-merchandised line of clothing. Eskimo Joe's in Stillwater, Oklahoma, even has a four-color, 16-page clothing catalog published twice a year. If you want teenagers to think about your restaurant, get a great T-shirt.

**Mocktails**   Don't automatically assume that teens only want soft drinks. They love the idea of having a range of beverage choices as diverse as that available to your adult diners. The same alcohol-free signature items that appeal to adults can give teenage diners a new range of beverage choices.

**Sensitivity to conversational stalemates**   When teenage couples go out for dinner, they often find themselves caught in a socially awkward situation when nobody at the table can think of anything to say. I'm sure you can remember these uncomfortable social deadlocks when you were growing up. Be sensitive to this situation and stop by the table to make a comment or suggestion when you sense an impasse. Your presence will loosen up the situation and make all your young guests more comfortable.

**Exhibition cooking**   Young diners are very sensitive to how you prepare their food. They are also curious about what the process looks like. Exhibition kitchens are a real attraction. If you sense that your teenage diners are restless (and if your layout permits), offer them a quick tour of the restaurant. They soak up new experiences like a sponge. You can use the excursion to point out what makes your restaurant different from your competition. Educate them about what they should be looking for when they go to restaurants. Teens love to have something to tell their friends about. It can't hurt to have them talking about what a great restaurant you have.

**Attentive, respectful service**   Teenagers just want the same responsive service that any other guest expects. They don't want to be treated like children or second-class citizens. They appreciate friendly staff who show a genuine concern for their well-being and enjoyment.

# 17

# Elderly Irritations

Socially and personally, dining is as much part of a satisfying life for seniors as for any of your other guests. Older diners grew up when standards of service were higher than those typically found today and they expect more. They know what they want and they know when they don't get it. Seniors are more vocal than younger diners. They are more likely to complain, not because they are more critical but because they are not afraid to ask for what they want. They will not tip for service they did not receive. They are "tough customers" who will demand nothing less than your best efforts. Your ability to meet the expectations of senior diners is a good measure of your professional skill.

Seniors' expectations are not unreasonable. They want the same friendly, efficient service as other diners. They appreciate restaurants that understand and satisfy their particular needs. You don't get many second chances with older diners. They figure you should know what you are doing. If you don't, they will find another establishment that does. With good reason, older diners have more concern for their personal safety and are sensitive to potential risks. Many are less likely to dine in the evenings, since physiological changes to their eyes make driving after dark more difficult.

Still, senior diners can be a valuable source of business for your restaurant. Their funds often are limited, but they are not afraid to spend their money with people who earn it. They can fill your restaurant when it would otherwise sit empty. They are intensely loyal to establishments that treat them well. They thrive on respectful service and gratitude for their patronage.

To serve this growing market properly, you must be aware that senior diners are not older versions of your younger patrons. There are some basic changes, both in physiology and motive, that make senior diners unique. Since the graying of the baby-boomers is imminent, you may want to consider some adjustments in your operation to be more responsive to the needs of older guests. Often what is good for the older diner turns out to be a service to younger diners as well. Here are some details you should know to be more responsive to seniors.

## Terrible Treatment

Older diners have a wealth of experience and know good service when they get it. They also know when you are treating them poorly, and they are not afraid to tell you about it.

**Waiting in line**  Seniors hate to wait in a line. Some do not have the physical stamina to stand for long periods. If you must ask older diners to wait, find them seats and make them comfortable. Offer to get them something to drink. Keep them informed of the status of their wait. If your service system requires guests to bring their food to the table, offer to carry the tray for older guests.

**Calling seniors by their first names**  Your mom knew what she was saying when she told you to respect your elders. Seniors deserve respectful treatment, including addressing them as "Mr., Mrs., Ms., or Miss." Never address elder patrons by their first name unless they ask you to do so. Remember that seniors grant the first-name permission on a person-by-person basis. Just because a senior has given one server the privilege does not mean that everyone on the staff has permission. When in doubt, err on the side of formality.

**Uncertainty where to go or what to do**  Seniors do not like to feel incompetent or out of control. For maximum peace of mind, they want to know where to go and what to do. Should they wait for a greeter or seat themselves? Which way is the nonsmoking section? Ideally, the greeter will be at the door when guests arrive, but display clear directional signs for the times when the staff is elsewhere.

**Seating other parties before older diners**  Some greeters ignore seniors and give preferential treatment to other parties. Nobody likes to be treated like a second-class citizen, particularly older diners who deserve more deference. Remember that some elders find it physically difficult to stand around waiting for seating. Do not make them wait any longer than necessary.

**Seating seniors beside loud groups**  Families with children and groups of teenagers usually create more noise than other diners, which can be disorienting and stressful to elders. A sensitive greeter will make it a point to seat seniors away from loud groups at well-lighted tables.

**Staff apparently making fun of elder diners**  Seniors face a variety of problems that younger people can only imagine. Older people are doing the best they can and are very sensitive to what they perceive as ridicule. It is inexcusable to appear to joke about the infirmities or limitations of any guest. Do not permit any member of your staff to engage in this thoughtless behavior.

**Talking down to older guests**  Just because someone is old doesn't mean they are stupid. Quite the opposite is usually true. Always treat older diners with respect and courtesy. Remember that your tone of voice carries the message, not your words. Avoid sarcasm and innuendo in your choice of words and inflection.

**Talking more loudly to seniors**   Many people have an annoying tendency to increase the volume of their voices when talking to elderly people. Keep your voice at a reasonable level. If a senior diner has a hearing problem, they will tell you. Raising your voice only calls attention to the diner and makes them self-conscious.

**Impatience**   Many older people live their lives at a slower pace. Thought processes may slow down for some and many tasks simply take longer for some senior citizens. Your skill as a foodservice professional is measured by your ability to delight *all* your guests, not just diners of your age group. If you become impatient, you only show your immaturity.

# Atmosphere Irritations

Because of natural changes in the body, elderly diners sometimes are more sensitive to extremes of sight, sound, and touch than your average patron. Recognition of these sensitivities helps provide seniors with a more pleasant meal.

**Seating seniors in drafts**   Drafts are uncomfortable for any guest but can be particularly bothersome to seniors. Older diners tolerate extremes of temperature less well than younger people due to changes in the tactile responses of the skin. Pay particular attention to the temperature and humidity conditions in your dining room when selecting seats for older guests.

**Not enough light to read the menu**   Your guests cannot order what they cannot read. Vision changes as people get older, and compassionate operators make allowances for the limitations of their elder patrons. To make it easier, you can raise the lighting level or use larger type on the menu. Matte finish papers are easier to read than glossy stock. Paper or ink color combinations also affect the readability of your menu. If the menu you use for the public is difficult for senior diners to read, it may be worth making a special menu for them.

**Noisy dining rooms**   Hearing loss inevitably occurs with age. Many people experience a loss of tone sensitivity in higher ranges, causing sounds to converge. Poor acoustics in the restaurant only increase the stress on seniors. In the extreme, harsh acoustics will cause elderly diners never to return.

# Menu Missteps

Your menu is the operating plan for your restaurant. If you want your establishment to attract older diners, be sure your menu provides the items they want in the way they want them.

**Menu items unavailable in smaller portions**   Older diners just do not eat as much food as they once did. Huge portions and doggie bags are not attractive to most seniors. Price is always a consideration for people on a fixed income, but the waste of food is equally unnerving. Offer several of your entrées in half portions. You will be doing a favor for all your guests.

**No familiar foods on the menu**   Many seniors like the comfort of familiar foods. They will try new items but are not attracted by trendy menus offering entrée combinations that are strange to them.

**Items covered with sauce, gravy, or dressing**   This is an example of something that is good for older people being a service to younger people as well. Older digestive systems do not handle fat as easily as younger ones. Food with excessive sauce is difficult for some seniors to digest. Offering more low-fat entrées on your menu and offering sauces on the side will meet the needs of seniors. It also will respond to the growing health-consciousness of the public.

**Highly seasoned food**   Most elder diners do not like foods that are extremely spicy because their digestive systems can be easily upset. If you have spicy items on your menu, be sure to warn seniors what to expect when they order. Bear in mind that what may not seem spicy to you may still irritate a senior guest.

**Lack of menu variety**   Seniors like to have a choice of entrées, though they may choose to order the same item most times they dine. As their options for activity decrease, the lives of elders can take on a certain sameness. Seniors enjoy the ability to choose their meal from a range of interesting selections.

**Uncut sandwiches**   Seniors sometimes have trouble cutting and eating food. Even sandwiches that are cut in half can occasionally be a problem. If you notice your older guests are cutting your sandwiches into smaller pieces before eating, that should be a clue. If possible, cut sandwiches into four to six pieces for older guests. This presentation can be attractive and your guests will have a more enjoyable time. Parents also might appreciate this gesture for their small children.

**Prices too high for the diner's limited budget**   Many seniors live on a fixed budget and simply cannot afford the prices at many establishments. Still, they enjoy dining out as a social and personal experience. Many prefer eating in restaurants to cooking at home. To make your restaurant more attractive and accessible to older diners, offer a senior menu or discount program. This is as much an acknowledgment of the older diner's importance to your business as it is a cost savings. Seniors appreciate both motives. There is no reason you can't offer the discounted price to everyone at certain times of the day.

**Menu items in large pieces**   A menu composed only of soft foods will not interest most seniors. Still, cutting, chewing, and swallowing can be more difficult for elderly people. Entrées with smaller pieces of meat are more appropriate choices. If you do not offer such items, offer to have the kitchen cut the food to a more manageable size. It will show your awareness and concern.

# Bonus Points

Everybody likes pleasant surprises. These little unexpected touches are opportunities to improve your score and put your guests in a better mood. They help make up for any lapses in the operation and give people something to talk about to their friends.

**Manager contact**   Older people always like to know who is in charge and love attention from "the boss." They favor restaurants where the owner or manager actively works the floor.

**Escort to the car**   Seniors, especially women, have concern for their personal safety. They appreciate an escort to their cars in the evening. If you choose to provide this service, give seniors official notice of your offer. They are suspicious of strangers who offer to help. If possible, have your escorts wear your restaurant's uniform. It will help put elderly guests at ease.

**Benefit of a doubt stance**   A wonderful woman in her 70s told me of going to a restaurant near her home for lunch. When the check arrived, she realized she had left her wallet at home. She told the manager of her plight and was delighted when he trusted her to come back later to settle the bill. The point is that you can usually trust seniors. Give them the benefit of the doubt and you can make a friend for life.

**Take-home menu**   Many seniors do not cook but still like to eat at home. Going to the market is often inconvenient for elderly people, so they appreciate the ability to get restaurant meals to go. An extensive menu of items available for take-home service can be very attractive to seniors. If you really want to serve the older market, consider a delivery service.

**Prompt resolution of complaints**   Never negotiate a senior's complaint. The only approach that will work is to apologize for the situation and fix it immediately. Do not ask the guest what they want you to do—it puts the guest on the spot and makes them uncomfortable. When you understand the nature and source of the problem, propose a generous solution that will make the guest happy. Remember that you are not just solving a problem, you are making an investment in securing a regular patron.

**Location within walking distance**   Many elderly people do not drive and prefer to patronize restaurants within walking distance of their home. You cannot move your business, but you *can* actively market your operation to seniors living in the neighborhood.

**Single-priced buffet**   Because of their fixed incomes, seniors like to know what their meal is going to cost. If your operation lends itself to this format, offering a fixed-price buffet will make you very popular with older diners. Make the fixed-price meal available during your slower hours when you have excess capacity. Since seniors eat less and go out as much for the social contact as for the meal, you are not taking much of a risk.

**Respectful service**   Unfortunately, our society often ignores senior citizens. This creates the opportunity for your restaurant to give seniors the recognition and respect denied to them elsewhere. Although they have some special needs, older diners want the same enjoyable dining experience as any other guest in your restaurant. If you are compassionate enough to serve seniors with courtesy and respect, they will be your most loyal guests.

# 18

# Management
# Mistakes

In the words of Walt Kelly's swamp philosopher, Pogo, "We have met the enemy and he is us!" The sad truth is that most the problems that occupy our time are problems of our own creation. We are not trying to make our jobs more difficult. We have just lost some perspective on what is really important to the success of our operations.

The problem is not really our fault. We learned "how to do it" from those who preceded us who learned the business from *their* predecessors. This long line passed down some wonderful skills and traditions. It also passed along a way of doing business derived in response to needs and conditions far removed from those of today. We do it the way we do it because we have always done it that way.

The industry operates with the mentality of a policeman. We are always watching for people we think are trying to get away with something. We create a web of rules and policies to maintain order. We find more ways to say "no" than to say "yes." We find ways to do things that are efficient for the restaurant but are often frustrating for our guests.

It's time to wake up and get serious. If what we have been doing doesn't work for our guests, more of the same activities will not solve the problems. Take a hard look at your operation and see if you have created any of these problems for yourself.

## Dense Decisions

Many restaurant policies are well intentioned but ill-advised. Anytime your priority is to make the experience easier for the restaurant or the staff instead of easier for the guest, you are asking for problems.

**No substitutions**  Service guru Peter Glen suggests that the way to make guests happy is to find out what they want, find out how they want it, and give it to them just that way. If you refuse to make reasonable substitutions, the requirements of the restaurant are obviously more important than the desires of your guests. Does your staff think substitutions are an imposition? If they do, you are asking for unhappy guests. Not all substitutions are possible, of course. If you cannot do what the guest asks, tell them what you *can* to and then do it with a smile.

**Not reimbursing vending machine losses**  It does not matter who owns a vending machine. If it is on your premises, it is part of your restaurant in the eyes of your guest. Reach an agreement with the vending company on reimbursement for guest losses. Remember that no matter who is responsible for the machine, *you* are responsible for your guest's experience in your restaurant.

**Not accepting credit cards**   Many restaurants have a policy against accepting credit cards in general or a specific credit card in particular. Management has the right to make this decision. Many diners use different credit cards for business occasions than they do for personal ones. Some guests will not patronize your restaurant if they cannot use the credit card of their choice.

**No separate checks**   If you want delighted guests, make it as easy as possible for them. A party might want separate checks for many reasons. Just because it requires additional time for your staff is not a valid reason to refuse. Fortunately, electronic point-of-sale systems make separate checks easier to do. Unfortunately, relatively few restaurants have the electronic systems. Train your sales staff to ask large parties if they prefer separate checks. Ask at the beginning of the meal and there will be less work to do later. Work with the kitchen staff to develop a system where the entrées all can be ready simultaneously. If guests change their minds, take it in stride. They will remember and appreciate your patience. Besides, in my experience, the tips were always better with separate checks!

**Charging more for the same portion at dinner**   People usually expect to pay more for their evening meal. However, when the same size portion has a higher price in the evening than in the afternoon, guests feel cheated. If you have similar items available at lunch and dinner, offer them in a different presentation or portion size. Avoid the impression of exploiting your guests.

**An automatic service charge and indifferent service**   The debate over service charges versus tipping probably will always be with us. If your guests feel forced to pay for service they did not receive, they will not be anxious to return.

**Not allowing transfer of a bar check to the dining room**
It's a busy Saturday night and your restaurant is jammed. People are waiting in every available corner. The dining room is mobbed. A couple has been sitting in the bar for well over an hour, sipping wine and waiting for their table. Suddenly the greeter appears to tell them their table is ready. She is in a rush because there are many other guests waiting. The couple is anxious to eat. They start toward the dining room and ask the greeter to just transfer their bar tab into the dining room. The greeter says they can't do it. Now what?

The couple can't leave the bar until they find the server, get the check, give them the credit card, wait for it to be processed, and sign the charge form. This is going to take a little time. What does the greeter do meanwhile?

Does she seat one person alone and make the other guest try to find their table somewhere in the dining room later? Does one guest stand around while the other closes out the bar check? Meanwhile, the table is sitting empty in the dining room and other guests are waiting to be seated. Do you see the problem? Do everybody a favor. Change your system to allow guests to transfer bar checks into the dining room.

**Minimum charges**   Many diners object to minimum charges, especially when you impose them on families with children. Most minimums are for the benefit of the house instead of for the benefit of the guest. Policies of this sort are dangerous. If you have a minimum charge policy, be sure your staff understands *why*. Reach a consensus with your staff about when they should impose the minimum charge.

**Unexpected charges**   Be aware of the customs in your area and don't surprise your guests with charges they do not expect. For example, let's say you operate a Chinese restaurant. If all other Chinese restaurants in your area include rice in the price of their meals, do not charge for rice without letting your guests know in advance.

**Not allowing guests to take home items from the table**
People are becoming more aware of waste. As prices rise, many diners are doing all they can to get the most value for their dollar. I hope your guests are enthusiastic about your food. Any of these motives may cause guests to ask for the leftovers. You will create suspicion if you do not allow them to take home items from the table. For example, most guests know you should not reuse rolls. If you refuse to let them take the extra rolls home, it is logical to wonder what you plan to do with the rolls! You do not need rumors like this in the community. Do all you can to minimize leftovers at the table . . . and cooperate with guests' requests.

# Control Collapses

The management of a restaurant is responsible for the efficient operation of the business. When you do not maintain a sense of order in your restaurant, guests do not feel comfortable.

**"Who's in charge here?"**   Nobody likes to walk into a restaurant that is operating in chaos. If your guests experience confusion in your dining room, you will start losing points at once. When your staff is "in the weeds," you must be on the floor keeping the panic away from your guests.

**Crimes against guests**   You have a responsibility to protect your guests' safety while they are on your premises. Whether this is a legal requirement or just part of good hospitality depends on the circumstances. Still, if someone is assaulted in your restaurant, they will not be back. If people are worried that they *might* be assaulted in your restaurant, they will not be back. Talk with other operators in your area. Find out what crime-related problems they have been having and what they are doing about it. Make sure you are doing at least as much as they are.

**Any sort of bother for the guest**   Nobody wants a hassle when they go out to eat. There is no way to win a dispute with a guest. Give your staff the authority to do whatever they feel is necessary to correct irritations on the spot. If they spill food on a guest, they should be able to pay for the cleaning without having to make the guest wait for management approval. If your staff thinks that protecting the house is more important than helping the guest, the diner might not be paid for the cleaning bill at all!

**Failure to resolve a complaint promptly**   Always resolve complaints in the guest's favor. There is no negotiation when it comes to correcting a guest annoyance. The only approach that will work is to apologize for the situation and fix it immediately. Do not ask the guest what they want you to do—it puts the guest on the spot and makes them uncomfortable. When you understand the nature and source of the problem, propose a generous solution that will make the guest happy. Remember that you are not just solving a problem, you are making an investment in securing a regular patron.

**Failure to respond to written complaints or compliments**
Of all the guests who have a problem, only one in ten will care enough to tell you about it. When you get a written complaint (or compliment), it is a rare gesture of caring. Always respond promptly, appropriately, and personally to written complaints or compliments. Guests will appreciate your acknowledging their messages.

**Making the guest feel wrong, stupid, or clumsy**   This is a most uncomfortable feeling for people. It happens when your staff gets into their notions of what is right and what is wrong. Right and wrong are concepts, not absolutes. What is right for you may not seem right to someone else. In the restaurant business, the only values that matter are those of the guest. Never do anything that would cause a guest to feel wrong, stupid, or clumsy. Watch your tone of voice when a guest does or says something you think is inane. Your patrons do not know your rules and customs, nor should they have to. There are lots of places people can go to for abuse. Make your restaurant an oasis of understanding in an otherwise hostile world. You will pull in business like a magnet!

**Failure to apologize for an error**   If you don't apologize immediately for every error, oversight, or difficulty experienced by the guest, they will think you don't care. You do not have to admit guilt to apologize—even acknowledging that you are sorry a situation was an upset will help.

**Disturbances in the dining room or bar**   You cannot always prevent disturbances from happening, but you always have control of how you handle them when they arise. When you have a disruption in your restaurant, management or staff must resolve it immediately and discretely.

# Jaundiced Judgment

Even with an enlightened perspective and proper priorities, judgment is still a factor in guest gratification. Here are some examples.

**Not having enough staff to provide good service**   If guest gratification is your most important job, you must have enough staff to do the job. I have been in many restaurants that could not provide responsive service because they were one person short. They ruined the evening for most of their guests just to save two bucks an hour! Wake up to reality. Labor is a profit center, not an operating cost.

**Serving minors or intoxicated persons**   Serving drunks puts your liquor license in danger. It also encourages inebriates to stay in your restaurant. Guests are uncomfortable in the presence of intoxicated persons. People go out for a drink to be sociable, not to get drunk. Serving minors is making a bet you can't afford to lose. It will only give you an unprofessional reputation and discourage the business of your responsible guests.

**Conducting business in the dining room**   I was in a coffee shop recently where an Avon representative had set up her office at a table in the middle of the dining room. For almost an hour, there was a steady stream of people in and out of the dining room to drop off orders. It was obvious they were not there to dine and I found the experience extremely distracting. Our guests must be able to meet at the restaurant to talk business, but it is also reasonable to expect they will do it over a meal!

**Sudden changes in operating style**   Unless your restaurant is in serious trouble and needs a complete change of concept, don't do anything rash. Evolution will keep you prosperous, revolution will confuse your market. Remember that the marketing battle is fought between the ears of the public. To be successful, you must have a memorable place in their minds. Sudden, severe changes will most likely cause them to forget you.

**Uncorrected complaints**   If someone cares enough to complain, care enough to listen. If you care enough to listen, care enough to do something about it. If you cannot solve the problem, tell them what you *can* do to make their experience more pleasant. You will only hurt your reputation if you let a guest detail a complaint without really listening. Guests will always know when you are not paying attention and it will enrage them even more. They will interpret your lack of interest as meaning that you don't care (and they probably will be right!). On the other hand, if people sense that you are really listening and sincerely want to solve any problems in the restaurant, they will give you all kinds of helpful hints. Your openness will dissolve their frustration and they will leave your establishment feeling well cared for. It is a lot easier to discover problems this way than to hunt them all down by yourself.

**Smoking in the nonsmoking section**   I had the experience of having dinner in the nonsmoking section of a restaurant where my family knew the owner. After dinner, the owner visited with us at the table for a few minutes. She lit a cigarette and puffed away throughout the conversation. She never asked our permission. Since she had bought us after dinner drinks, it was awkward to ask her to put out the cigarette. Everyone at the table was uncomfortable as were diners at adjoining seats.

# Diabolical Details

This may be redundant, since *all* details are diabolical. Still, there are a few important points that don't fit neatly anywhere else.

**Empty dining rooms or lounges**   People want to be where the action is. They can be self-conscious when they feel they may be the only people in the restaurant. Since you can't always have a full house, the most effective defense is a good design. Break the dining room into smaller seating areas with half walls and dividers. Your design might create platforms or level changes. If possible, create some private dining rooms that open into the main seating area. Design the room so it will always feel full, despite the number of guests.

**Driving company vehicles inconsiderately**   When your trucks are on the road and your name is on the side, your reputation is riding right with them. If your staff drives considerately, it will reflect positively on your restaurant. If the truck is spreading terror on the road, expect other drivers to draw a conclusion about how you run your business. Carefully coach your drivers on the importance of highway etiquette. Be sure they fully understand their responsibility as ambassadors for your operation. It may be helpful to paint your telephone number on the vehicle and ask for comments on how your drivers are doing.

**Not receiving value**   When your guests pay top dollar for quality food and beverage and don't get it, they go away angry. This is a question of value and it is very simple—if you do not provide value, your guests will not return. Remember that value is determined by the guest's perceptions and standards, not yours! To assure guests receive value, find out what they want and how they want it. Give it to them just that way . . . with a little something extra. Always give your guests *more* than they expected.

**Suspicion of drug activity**  Just the rumor of drug activity in your restaurant can damage your business. It does not have to be proven. The best defense is a good offense. Take a pro-active stance against drugs in the workplace. Screen all job applicants thoroughly. Conduct random drug tests if your state law permits it. Treat all members of your staff the same, managers and staff alike. Support local anti-drug efforts in your community. Don't give rumors a reason to start.

**Company vehicles in poor condition or spewing smoke**  Just as people draw conclusions about the cleanliness of your kitchen from the cleanliness of your restrooms, they reach similar opinions from the condition of your trucks. Everything the public sees with your name on it represents your restaurant and makes a statement about how you run your business. This detail is particularly applicable to caterers. If potential guests would feel embarrassed to have your trucks seen in front of their house, they will call someone else.

**Store labels or price stickers**  Once something gets into your restaurant, it is part of your operation. There are many sources for the myriad of items we use in the industry every day. You may bring items onto the premises that have labels or stickers from another enterprise. No matter how urgently you need to put something into service, take the time to remove the labels and price tags. They will only remind your guests of another place when you want them focused on yours.

**Leaky take-out containers**  It takes more than price to make a take-out container work. Before you commit to buy a large quantity of a container, test samples of it on all items you plan to offer for take-out. Make sure you are not risking irate guests by having your famous Fettucine alla Puttanesca dripping all over the back seat of their Volvo!

**No working audio-visual equipment for meetings**  Having a TV, VCR, and so on can help you attract meeting business. However, if the equipment doesn't work, the meeting doesn't work. Be sure to test out all equipment and connections well before the start of the meeting. Give yourself enough time to solve any problems before your guests arrive.

**Handling lost and found articles inconsiderately**  Leaving personal property in a restaurant is bad enough. Having that property abused or mishandled is worse. When you find lost articles, remember you are dealing with someone's personal property. Treat it with respect until they pick it up. If you can locate them, call to let them know you have found their item. If you really want to pick up points, give them a coupon for a free dessert to make up for their inconvenience.

**Tip jar in a self-service restaurant**  How rude! Why not just put out a begging bowl? The staff of a restaurant where food is ordered and picked up at the counter has not done anything to earn a tip. Your guests will resent the staff's asking for (or expecting) gratuities.

**Excessively high prices**    This does not mean you are trying to gouge your guests. If your prices are not reasonable for the items offered, that is another issue. Perhaps your guests just cannot afford the expense of dining in your restaurant. The economy changes and people's habits change with it. If you find your patronage declining, do something about it. Adjust your menu to offer more reasonably priced entrées. Offer a smaller portion at a lower price. Stay in touch with what your market wants . . . and give it to them.

**System breakdowns**    Your guests get annoyed when you have no one who knows how to change the printer paper, cash register tape, or reboot the computer. Count on this problem to come up in the midst of the rush! Include these items in every staff member's basic training to be sure the operation doesn't grind to a halt at a critical time.

The same problem comes up if you have no manual backup systems when the computer goes down. There is no question that electronic point-of-sale systems offer advantages to most restaurants; however, everything mechanical or electrical is vulnerable to power surges and unexplained crashes. To avoid lapses in guest service when the inevitable happens, be sure to have a solid manual system ready to go. Train your staff in how it works so they won't panic when they have to use it. Be sure they know how to manage the transition from and to your computerized system.

## Truth Is Stranger Than Fiction

I was having a late lunch in a midscale table service restaurant. As I waited for my broiled fish, I watched the managers bring in bags of food from Pizza Hut. They sat happily in the back of the dining room and ate lunch! It made me wonder what they knew about their kitchen that I didn't! I don't know if there is any connection, but the restaurant is no longer in business.

## Bonus Points

Everybody likes pleasant surprises. These little unexpected touches are opportunities to improve your score and put your guests in a better mood. They help make up for any lapses in the operation and give people something to talk about to their friends.

**"The answer is yes. What's the question?"**    If you want to eliminate most guest relations problems before they start, adopt this simple management policy. It is a simple way to say that guests are always right, even when they are wrong. It acknowledges that you can never win an argument with a guest. It keeps the emphasis on assuring that guests have an enjoyable experience in your restaurant. What have you got to lose but unhappy patrons?

**Service guarantee**   Service guarantees are the natural result of a guest-oriented business posture. When you offer an unconditional service guarantee, you pledge to do whatever is necessary to assure that your guests have a wonderful experience in your restaurant. It is going to cost you some money to carry out an effective service guarantee, but the idea may not be as radical as it sounds.

If your guests are not having a good time, it is already costing you money. You just don't know how much. Paying off on the guarantee will quickly point out the breakdowns in your system so that you can correct them. Be careful that you don't let paying off on the guarantee become a substitute for providing good service in the first place. There are many elements of guest satisfaction that are beyond your control. If people go to your restaurant and don't enjoy themselves, you are going to have a bad memory of the experience. Since you are going to take the hit anyway, what have you got to lose by taking responsibility?

**Social consciousness**   Concern for the environment is increasing and restaurants are the targets of criticism from many consumer groups. If you are not part of the solution, you are part of the problem. Recycle whatever you can and reduce your use of chemicals. Get your staff involved in finding ways to be more responsive to environmental concerns. Let your guests know that you care and are doing something to help. It can't hurt.

**Conspicuous support of local charities**   Be a good citizen. Your success comes from the support of your local community. If you only *take* from the people and never give anything back, you will look like an opportunist. Share your success and you will attract more of it. What goes around, comes around.

**Free local phone calls**   Guests appreciate making local calls without having to part with a pocketful of change, particularly as phone rates rise. Although pay phones may provide a small source of revenue, you will make more money by giving people a reason to patronize your restaurant more often. Free local phones can be a point of difference in the market. The gesture is even more appreciated if the phones are on the tables.

**Making a big deal of special occasions**   When people go to restaurants to celebrate special occasions, they want a festive time. If you are going to help them celebrate, do it right! Be consistent with the theme and tone of your restaurant so that you do not disturb your other diners. Find out what your competition is doing and be sure to do something different. It might be sparklers on the cake, a special song, or a gift from the restaurant. Talk it over with your staff and see what you can do to make your place the restaurant of choice for special occasions.

**Frequent diner plan**   A simple fact of human nature is that people will do what you reward them for. If you make it worthwhile for them to return to your restaurant, guests will return. A frequent diner plan has several advantages. Repeated visits help develop the habit of dining in your restaurant. You can often use the plan as a way to direct business into periods when you have excess capacity. The most effective plans are the ones that create an incentive to return. Instead of a straight discount, offer a percentage of tonight's meal as a credit against their next meal.

**Owner or manager on the floor**   Train your staff and let them be stars. Even with a room full of stars, be sure to spend more time on the floor talking with your guests than in your office pushing paper. There is no substitute for personal presence and proprietary interest. Everybody enjoys knowing "the boss."

**Something for nothing**   Everybody loves something for nothing. Upscale restaurants do not have an exclusive hold on this touch. I remember having breakfast at Lou Mitchell's in Chicago. Halfway through the meal they brought a little frozen yogurt strawberry sundae as a palate cleanser— at breakfast! I was impressed. Mike Hurst, owner of 15th Street Fisheries restaurant in Fort Lauderdale regularly gives out free samples of potential new menu items. His guests are delighted. Giving something for nothing is a wonderful gesture of hospitality. It helps your patrons try something new and gives them something to talk about.

**Selection of reading glasses**   For your guests who need a little optical help and have forgotten their reading glasses, have a selection on hand to help them out. Reading glasses in standard prescriptions are readily available in most pharmacies. Present the selection in a good-looking lined wooden box. Your guests will appreciate and remember this unexpected amenity.

**Free coffee for breakfast guests who have to wait**   If you can get someone's day off to a good start, you have done them a real favor. Timing is critical during the breakfast period, so anything you can do to make a delay less painful is a good move. Offering free coffee to a guest that has to wait is a small gesture that will yield big returns in guest satisfaction.

**Thank you notes**   If you have a guest's telephone number, you can get their address from a reverse directory. Imagine the impact of a polite note thanking them for dining with you! People never receive the thanks they feel they deserve. Show them you appreciate their patronage and you will stay in their minds.

**Striking logo used tastefully**   Image is everything. Look at the impact the Hard Rock Cafe has received from the widespread use of its logo! Create a distinctive logo. The more times you can put it in front of your guests, the more they will associate the image with the quality of their experience. This can work to your benefit if guests are enjoying themselves.

**Singing a song other than "Happy Birthday to You"**   Show a little originality! The traditional birthday song is what your competitors sing and your guests are immune to it. Get their attention with something short and personalized to your restaurant. Make it a song that your staff enjoys singing. It is unsettling to see people singing if their hearts aren't in it. If you do it well, diners will think of your restaurant for their next special occasion.

**Pictures or sketches of guests on the walls**   The theme from the television show "Cheers" talks about a place "where everybody knows your name." People love to feel like they belong and nothing makes that statement like posting their picture in the restaurant. It is a memorable gesture to acknowledge your regular guests in this way. It has more impact than displaying the owner's ego in pictures taken with celebrity guests (unless this is part of the concept). Then, invite the honoree to a special ceremony where their picture is unveiled! It is always prudent to get the person's permission before you put their picture on your wall. However, most people never get the recognition and appreciation they deserve and will be honored by your recognition of their loyalty and patronage.

**Special events and promotions**   It doesn't matter what the events are or even if they are profitable. The goal is to break the routine for both your guests and your staff. Special events and promotions create a sense that something is happening at your restaurant and people like to be where things are happening. If you tie these events to a charitable cause, you can do some good for others simultaneously while you gain valuable free publicity for your restaurant.

**Classic take-out packaging**   If you enjoy a significant take-out business (or would like to), spend some money on customized packaging. Your containers can be an effective image-building tool, particularly in an office environment. Making this investment can change packaging from a cost item to a profit center.

**Unexpected touches**   Find a way to do a better job with something ordinary. For example, when you order coffee at Hudson's Bar & Grill in San Luis Obispo, California, it comes with a cinnamon stick, chocolate chips, and fresh cream . . . and priced like regular coffee! Lambert's Cafe in Sikeston, Missouri, has a reputation for "throwed rolls," a unique way of passing out the bread! The advantage of making a point of difference out of a common item is that your guests will think of you every time they dine at another restaurant.

**Finger bowls or hot towels**   There is nothing like beginning and ending a meal feeling clean and content. Japanese restaurants have traditionally offered hot towels at the beginning of the meal. Consider the gesture at the end of the meal as well. You could be as formal as finger bowls with fresh towels or as informal as packaged Wet-Naps. The Japanese approach of providing a hot washcloth is easy to do and makes a wonderful impression on your guests. Your guests will appreciate your caring, particularly if your menu includes finger foods like ribs, fried chicken, or corn on the cob.

**Reading material for single diners**   Solo diners do not have the conversation of dining companions to occupy their time during lulls in the meal. Often they will bring a newspaper, book, or office work with them. If you attract (or want to attract) single diners, have reading material available and train your staff to offer it politely.

**Calculator with the check**   Parties of singles with a common check especially appreciate this touch. Even if there is no entree cost to divide, many people appreciate a little help with calculating a tip. Credit card-sized calculators are inexpensive and easy to attach to a tray or check folder. It creates another point of difference and is worth considering.

**Cheerful handling of special requests**   This is where stories of legendary service come from. If a guest wants something you don't normally offer and you go to the grocery store to get it for them, you will make a friend for life. Let's say a guest at the bar in Minneapolis wants a margarita the way they make it at the Macayo in Phoenix. If your bartender makes a long-distance call to get the recipe, what do you think the impact will be? The possibilities are endless once you decide that your only real job is to make sure your guests are delighted! You can't buy the kind of publicity and word-of-mouth you earn just by going out of your way for a guest. After all, this *is* the hospitality industry!

# Closing Comments

## Put This Material to Work

Use this book to raise your awareness and perspective. For example, you may not have known that bright red nail polish on the hands of a waitress bothers some people. Knowing that, it might be prudent to have your waitresses avoid bright red nail polish. On the other hand, you might feel bright red nail polish is an important part of your image and choose to do nothing. If so, at least you would be aware of the potential reactions to your decision.

Often you have a dilemma. For example, it will bother some people if you don't take reservations; it will bother others if you do. Making your entire restaurant nonsmoking will attract a particular segment of the market and drive away some of your regular patrons. In each solution may lie the seeds of another potential problem.

Life is like that. This book is not a blueprint on what you *should* do, it only suggests what you *could* do. It offers an insight into why your guests have enjoyable experiences or miserable ones. It can help you understand why you have been popular and give you ideas on how you could be even more successful.

## Get the Message to Your Staff

Correcting and eliminating guest distractions is a five-step process. You do not have to approach it this rigidly, but you need to be sure that all the steps are covered.

**Raise Awareness** Be sure your staff understands *what* the points of guest irritation are. As a simple solution, consider posting ten of these points on your staff bulletin board each week. They may not be anything you haven't told your crew before. Still, hearing it from another source shows that you are not the only one who thinks details are important.

220

The list of points appears to provide the most impact. If you present everything in terms of what people *should* do, it sounds like a sermon. I found that just giving my staff the list without the lecture was an effective and painless way to raise their awareness. With a sharp crew in a positive working climate, you may have to do no more than this. Some problems are more elusive and I suggest you bring up these points for discussion at your staff meetings.

**Establish Perspective**   Find out to what extent your staff agrees or disagrees with the particular point. To what extent does the problem exist in your restaurant now? It is important they understand *why* the point can be a distraction to your guests and *how* distractions affect the experience your guests have in the restaurant. Be sure they also understand why it is important that your guests enjoy themselves. Let your crew know what is in it for them.

**Identify Causes**   The next point is to determine *why* the problem exists in the first place. It is also appropriate to establish *what* results you hope to achieve. Get your staff involved. Focus on breakdowns in your system and not on problems with individuals. For example, delays at a particular station in the kitchen may be due to an unbalanced menu, inadequate equipment, or incomplete training at that position. Search for the why, not the *who*. If you attempt to assign blame to an individual, you will not be addressing the real cause of the problem and you will never get another suggestion from your staff!

**Take Action**   Once you know the cause of the problem, ask your staff what they suggest could be done to correct the situation. Listen respectfully to what they have to say. The ingenuity of your crew may surprise you. Better yet, you will not have to solve the problem by yourself. You also will not have to force your solution on anyone. When a plan of action is determined, assign responsibility for its implementation. Be clear about *who* is going to do it, *when* it needs to happen, and *where* the action will be taken. The plan must address *what* equipment or training will be required and *how* you will be able to tell when the problem is effectively under control. A word of caution: If you attempt to specify in advance just *how* the results have to be achieved, you will kill the creativity and enthusiasm of your staff.

**Coach Consistently**   Coaching is the place to deal with *how* the results are being achieved. Coaching is more powerful than management because it requires a presumption that the worker is capable. Coaching includes regular inspection as well as recognizing and rewarding successful efforts. Approaching your staff as a coach rather than as a cop is more enjoyable for everyone. You also will achieve better results with less effort and stress. Think about it.

As your staff becomes more involved in the problem-solving process, their personal levels of well-being rise and they find it easy to take better care of your guests. The better treatment your guests receive, the more they will return. The more they return, the more profit you make. In short, everybody wins!

# Create Points of Difference

Every time one of these irritations arises in your competitor's operation and does not happen in yours, you create a point of difference in the market. Coach your staff on how to tell your guests about the exceptional job you are doing for them. This is what creates word-of-mouth advertising.

Here is an example of how you can use trivia to your advantage. When I opened my first restaurant in 1976, plate garnishing was still an afterthought in most restaurants. By contrast, we were dressing our plates with the colorful arrangements of fruit more common today. When we presented a plate to the guest, we usually received a spontaneous positive reaction. At that point, the waiter might chuckle and say, "Isn't it refreshing to see a plate that's not covered with parsley?" When that same guest next dined with my competitors, their plate would invariably arrive covered with parsley. Do you think they noticed? Who do you think they thought of? What do you think they said to their dining companions? How do you think my restaurant looked by comparison? I have many more examples but I think you get the point.

Sales that first year were more than 60% higher than comparable operations in our market! We were the topic of enthusiastic conversation among our guests because we created and exploited small points of difference. We educated our guests about why they dined with us and gave them something to talk about! A 60% increase may not seem feasible to you, but what if you could increase your volume even 10% at almost no cost? Think about it. There are a wealth of profit-making opportunities in this book.

# Practice What You Preach

Your staff will treat your guests the same way they are treated. We have discussed the idea that state of mind determines the experience guests will have in your restaurant. It is no different for your staff. If you maintain a positive atmosphere free from distractions, your staff will be more productive, service will improve and most problems will seem to solve themselves. They way to create this environment is simply to serve your staff as totally as you want them to serve your guests. It is another facet of the coaching mentality.

In my experience working with consulting clients, it is not uncommon to see a 20% increase in volume simply by raising the level of well-being in the organization. Remember that the choice of a restaurant is just a decision your guests make. The better the atmosphere in your restaurant, the more often they are likely to choose to dine with you instead of going elsewhere. If someone who used to come in once a month decides to patronize you twice, you have doubled your sales!

# Make a Statement

My last suggestion is that you put your money where your mouth is. Your staff will believe what you *do* more than they will believe what you *say.* If you are truly serious about developing legendary guest service, I urge you to get enough copies of this book for all your management and staff. The nature of details is that they are insidious—always lurking in the shadows to trip you up. Staying on top of them is an ongoing process, not the subject of a one-hour staff meeting. If you issue the book like you issue uniforms, you will assure that your staff will always have access to these reminders. Start an ongoing education program with regular homework assignments from the book. Over time, I guarantee the continual exposure to these trivialities will increase your staff's awareness of the fine points of guest gratification.

The books will cost far less than sending a few of your staff to even a single training seminar and will gain more long-term benefits. Assigning each member of your crew his or her own copy of this material delivers a powerful message. Your staff will understand that they are important to your operation and that handling these details is vital to you. With this material readily at hand, your staff can become more involved in improving your level of guest gratification. Better yet, they will have reference information that will help them make you money every day you are in business.

The implications of this gesture are wide-ranging. For example, dish-washers and bussers are typically our highest turnover positions. In my experience, the key to retaining entry-level staff is to increase their under-standing of how the restaurant works and how they fit into its success. If you include dishwashers and bussers in all aspects of training, you will show them they are important to your operation. The more important they realize they are, the more dedicated they become. The more dedicated they become, the longer they will stay. Take a chance and issue them a book. By their questions and comments, you can quickly tell if you have a future star on your hands. No pressure, but think about it. After all, you have nothing to lose but your turnover.

# Helpful
# Homework

There is never enough time or space to treat every topic in the depth it deserves. I recommend the following books for those readers who wish to examine some of the ideas more deeply. If you have trouble finding any of them, please give me a call.

Aslett, Don. *Is There Life After Housework?* Writer's Digest Books, 9933 Alliance Road, Cincinnati, OH 45242, 1981.

Aslett, Don. *Do I Dust or Vacuum First?* Writer's Digest Books, 9933 Alliance Road, Cincinnati, OH 45242, 1982.

Aslett, Don. *How Do I Clean the Moosehead?* New American Library, 1633 Broadway, New York, NY 10019, 1989.

Bradley, Marcia. *The Professional Server's Guide to Excellence.* Hospitality Systems International, 20 North Main Street, Pittsford, NY 14534, 1990.

Dass, Ram, and Gorman, Paul. *How Can I Help?* Alfred A. Knopf, New York, NY, 1985.

Glen, Peter. *It's Not My Department.* William Morrow and Company, Inc., 105 Madison Avenue, New York, NY 10016, 1990.

Heskett, James L., Sasser, W. Earl, Jr., and Hart, Christopher W. L. *Service Breakthroughs.* The Free Press, A Division of Macmillan, Inc., 866 Third Avenue, New York, NY 10022, 1990.

Kausen, Robert. *Customer Satisfaction Guaranteed.* Life Education, Inc., Star Route 2-3969G, Trinity Center, CA 96091, 1988.

Martin, William B. *Quality Service: The Restaurant Manager's Bible.* Cornell University School of Hotel Administration, Ithaca, NY 14853, 1986.

Marvin, Bill, and Aslett, Don. *How to Clean Your Restaurant . . . and Most Everything in It.* Van Nostrand Reinhold, 115 Fifth Avenue, New York, NY 10003 (scheduled for publication in early 1992).

Sullivan, Jim, and Roberts, Phil. *Service that Sells.* Pencom Press, 511 Sixteenth Street, Suite 630, Denver, CO 80202, 1990.

Wolfe, David B. *Serving the Ageless Market: Strategies for Selling to the Fifty-Plus Market.* McGraw-Hill, Inc., New York, NY, 1990.

I have also found some excellent training videos you may want to add to your library.

*Customer Satisfaction Guaranteed.* Life Education, Inc., Star Route 2-3969G, Trinity Center, CA 96091.

*The Art of Waiting Tables.* Professional Waiters School, 17924 Tarzana Street, Encino, CA 91316.

*More Cash in Your Pocket.* Pencom, Inc., 511 Sixteenth Street, Suite 630, Denver, CO 80202.

*National Restaurant Association Video Training Series.* The Educational Foundation, 250 South Wacker Drive, Suite 1400, Chicago, IL 60606.

*The Professional Server's Course in Excellence.* Hospitality Systems International, 20 North Main Street, Pittsford, NY, 14534.

# About the Author

Wmilliam R. Marvin, "The Restaurant Doctor™," is an advisor to restaurateurs across the country. Bill is the founder of PROTOTYPE RESTAURANTS, a restaurant consulting, development, and management company based in Colorado Springs, Colorado. He started in the industry at the age of 14, washing dishes (by hand!) in a small restaurant on Cape Cod. He went on to earn a degree in Hotel Administration from Cornell University in 1966. His operational experience includes hotels, clubs, restaurants, and institutions. Bill moved to Colorado in 1984 to design the foodservice system for the U.S. Olympic Training Centers.

Before joining the Olympic Committee, Bill spent twelve years in San Francisco. He developed and operated two restaurants of his own. He was also an independent restaurant consultant specializing in marketing, new concept development, and Chapter 11 reorganizations.

Bill is a member of the Foodservice Consultants Society International (FCSI) and the Council of Hotel and Restaurant Trainers (CHART). He is one of the first to earn certification as a Foodservice Management Professional from the National Restaurant Association. He has been a Director of the Colorado Restaurant Association since 1986. He teaches a regular foodservice class for the City of Colorado Springs. His second book, *How to Clean Your Restaurant . . . and Most Everything in It*, is scheduled for publication in early 1992. Bill is a frequent contributor to Restaurants & Institutions Magazine.

In addition to his private consulting practice, he operates restaurants in Colorado Springs and conducts management seminars across the country. You can contact Bill at:

PROTOTYPE RESTAURANTS
332 West Bijou, Suite 107
Colorado Springs, CO 80905

Toll Free: (800) 767-1055
FAX: (719) 635-4594

## SHARE YOUR OWN MONUMENTAL DETAILS

Bill Marvin's list of the little annoyances that can ruin a diner's experience — turning a good time into a tooth grind — is growing. Your pet peeves and "war stories," from the guest's point of view, are welcomed and could enhance future editions of this book. By sharing them, you may help restaurateurs to get a handle on how to assure all their guests a pleasant meal, with many repeat visits and many generations of word-of-mouth referrals.

_____

_____

_____

_____

_____

_____

_____

**TELL US ABOUT YOURSELF:**

Name _____

Title _____

Company _____

Address _____

City/State/Zip _____

1. What is your company's primary business? (Please check one.)
   ___Full-service Restaurant
   ___Fast Food
   ___Hotel/Motel Foodservice
   ___Health Care Foodservice
   ___School/College Foodservice
   ___Business/Industry Foodservice
   ___Other (Specify) _____

2. Where/how do you usually purchase books related to the foodservice industry? _____
   _____

3. For which purposes do you purchase books?
   ___Reference
   ___Instructional material
   ___Product ideas
   ___Recipes
   ___Latest technology
   ___Industry trends
   ___Consumer information
   ___Government regulations
   ___Increasing profitability
   ___Employee training
   ___Other _____

4. Do you use books as gifts or premiums? _____

   Would you like information on special quantity discounts for this book? _____

---

## SHARE YOUR OWN MONUMENTAL DETAILS

Bill Marvin's list of the little annoyances that can ruin a diner's experience — turning a good time into a tooth grind — is growing. Your pet peeves and "war stories," from the guest's point of view, are welcomed and could enhance future editions of this book. By sharing them, you may help restaurateurs to get a handle on how to assure all their guests a pleasant meal, with many repeat visits and many generations of word-of-mouth referrals.

_____

_____

_____

_____

_____

_____

_____

**TELL US ABOUT YOURSELF:**

Name _____

Title _____

Company _____

Address _____

City/State/Zip _____

1. What is your company's primary business? (Please check one.)
   ___Full-service Restaurant
   ___Fast Food
   ___Hotel/Motel Foodservice
   ___Health Care Foodservice
   ___School/College Foodservice
   ___Business/Industry Foodservice
   ___Other (Specify) _____

2. Where/how do you usually purchase books related to the foodservice industry? _____
   _____

3. For which purposes do you purchase books?
   ___Reference
   ___Instructional material
   ___Product ideas
   ___Recipes
   ___Latest technology
   ___Industry trends
   ___Consumer information
   ___Government regulations
   ___Increasing profitability
   ___Employee training
   ___Other _____

4. Do you use books as gifts or premiums? _____

   Would you like information on special quantity discounts for this book? _____

# BUSINESS REPLY MAIL

**FIRST CLASS    PERMIT NO. 2277    NEW YORK, N.Y.**


POSTAGE WILL BE PAID BY ADDRESSEE

NO POSTAGE
NECESSARY
IF MAILED
IN THE
UNITED STATES

John Wiley & Sons, Inc.
Attn: Stacy Prassas
605 Third Avenue
New York, NY 10158-0012

# BUSINESS REPLY MAIL

**FIRST CLASS    PERMIT NO. 2277    NEW YORK, N.Y.**

POSTAGE WILL BE PAID BY ADDRESSEE

NO POSTAGE
NECESSARY
IF MAILED
IN THE
UNITED STATES

John Wiley & Sons, Inc.
Attn: Stacy Prassas
605 Third Avenue
New York, NY 10158-0012